logolounge 2

2,000 International Identities by Leading Designers

Bill Gardner and Catharine Fishel

GLOUCESTER MASSACHUSETTS

ROCKPORT PUBLISHERS

First published in the United States of America by

Rockport Publishers, Inc.
33 Commercial Street
Gloucester, Massachusetts 01930-5089

Telephone: (978) 282-9590
Fax: (978) 283-2742
www.rockpub.com

Library of Congress Cataloging-in-Publication Data

Gardner, Bill.
LogoLounge 2 : 2,000 international identities by leading designers /
Bill Gardner and Catharine Fishel.
p. cm.
Includes index.
ISBN 1-59253-112-1 (hardcover)
1. Logography—Design Catalogs. 2. Corporate image—Catalogs.
3. Designers—Directories. I. Title: LogoLounge Two. II. Title: 2,000 international identities by leading designers. III. Fishel, Catharine M. IV. Title.
NC1002.L63G372 2004 2004013439
025.06'7416—dc22 CIP

ISBN 1-59253-112-1

10 9 8 7 6 5 4

Design: Gardner Design
Layout & Production: *tabula rasa* graphic design
Cover Image: Gardner Design
LogoLounge Font: Baseline Fonts, Nathan Williams

Printed in China

This book is dedicated to my parents who instilled in me the value of books and the importance of discovery. To my partners in LogoLounge.com who make great ideas happen: Cathy, Troy, Brian, and Gail. To my wife, Andrea, and our daughter, Molly, for letting me steal their time and share it with you.

–Bill Gardner

Many thanks to the entire LogoLounge team; to the many wonderful designers I have the privilege to serve; to my three sons, who are endlessly patient; to Kristin and Cora, who are infinitely patient; and especially to Bill and several other saints who truly have been lifesavers.

–Catharine Fishel

contents

Portraits

Sketches

Collections

introduction

As LogoLounge.com was established in 2001, one of our first challenges was to describe this unique site to the design industry in less than a handful of words. The phrase that kept floating to the top was "a searchable, real-time compendium of logo design." We knew this described our intent but the enormity of making this description a reality suddenly appeared much more daunting. That was until we started to share our plans with other designers and friends around the world.

In a gesture that felt much like a firestorm, word of LogoLounge.com spread almost faster than the site could manage it. Six degrees of separation must be for the rest of the world because all designers seem to be connected by no fewer than three degrees. And the democracy of the site became evident. Our membership was at once a mix of both "who's who?" and "who's that?" Now numbering in the thousands, our users represent one of the most internationally diverse assemblies of designers imaginable.

The juxtaposition of logos submitted by our members is a daily surprise: a new design for an international cruise line followed by a brilliant solution for a local marina; an identity for a winery in Napa Valley next to a logo for a vineyard in Tuscany. It quickly becomes evident that great logo ideas are not limited to any one firm or any one country.

At this writing, there are more than 18,000 searchable logos on LogoLounge.com. It is from this foundation that the works in this book have been selected. Our esteemed panel of eight international judges reviewed the more than 11,000 logos submitted since the judging of the first edition of *LogoLounge.*

Continuing with the theme of the best-selling *LogoLounge*, we have selected specific contributions to showcase the behind-the-scene challenges that lead to eventual solutions. Learn what did and didn't fly for clients as diverse as Cingular, the Islands of the Bahamas, Intel, Target, Total Petroleum, and more.

This book allows you to review 2,000 exceptional logos, categorized for easy reference. Or, with this book, log onto www.logolounge.com/book2, and you will be able to swiftly navigate through the logos in this book by searching by designer, client, industry, type of logo, or keyword.

Our goal is to inspire and educate you without exhausting you (or your supply of sticky notes) in the process. LogoLounge.com and this series are truly hybrids of print and the Web: You may read at your leisure, or do a quick, intuitive search. Our sincere hope is that *LogoLounge 2* will open up more time for you to do what you like best: design.

Bill Gardner and Catharine Fishel

jurors

Dana Lytle
Planet Propaganda, Madison, WI

Paradox Media logo, by Alterpop
"There's abstract, there's representational, and there's So-Representational-It-Whacks-You-Upside-the-Head. The Paradox logo is definitely SRIWYUTH, but with a pleasing twist: It represents an abstract concept, relying on a nearly universal cultural reference to bridge the gap between image and idea."

Dana Lytle is creative director and cofounder of Planet Propaganda, a creative communications firm in Madison, Wisconsin. He holds a degree in graphic design from Montana State University. When not designing, he spends his time rearranging his basement to make room for his collection of vintage letterpress equipment. Though his heart belongs to print, Lytle also professes to love the smell of a freshly launched website.

PARADOX

Joe Duffy
Duffy & Partners, Minneapolis, MN

Natasha Doll logo, by CDI Studios
"In a seemingly effortless and loopy stylized series of calligraphic strokes, the designer has managed to evoke the notions of doll, music, fun, and femininity. It's all contained within a very bold, distinctive, and artistic mark. I love that the logotype works as a symbol and vice versa. It's typically more difficult, and in this case, more direct."

Joe Duffy is chairman of Duffy Worldwide, which he started in 1984 and has transformed into an organization with offices in Minneapolis, New York, London, Singapore, and Hong Kong. His understanding of how design affects consumer attitudes has led to many big ideas executed in advertising as well as in design. He has guided the design component of significant integrated programs for EDS, Qualcomm, Ameritech, FAO Schwarz, Minute Maid, Nuveen Investments, International Truck and Engine Corporation, and Nikon.

doll

Ken Shadbolt
FutureBrand, Australia

Elvis: 30 #1 Hits logo, by Thomas Vasquez

"This stood out to me for all the right reasons. Great idea, great execution (I wish I had done it). I really admire the way the design hints at all the emotion and excitement of an epic Las Vegas show of the late 1960s. It is not hard to imagine those letterforms 20 feet [6 m] high, ablaze in animating light. For the designer to be able to capture all the romance of that era and distill it into a simple, timeless design that will also appeal to a new Elvis audience is exceptional. I also enjoyed the combination of letterforms cleverly punctuated by the numeral, allowing for multiple wordplays. A big design for a big brand."

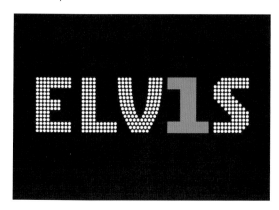

ELV1S

Ken Shadbolt is creative director of FutureBrand, Australia. He and his team are responsible for many of the most significant brand identity projects in the region across a diverse range of industry sectors, including the Sydney 2000 Olympic Games, Telstra, ANZ, Crown Entertainment Complex, Royal Australian Navy, Cricket Australia, Melbourne 2006 Commonwealth Games, and most recently, the brand identity for Australia. At the heart of FutureBrand's philosophy is a strong focus on the future and the belief that the boundaries of brand strategy and creativity are best blurred to allow for a potent combination of logic and magic.

Marcus Greinke
Enterprise IG, New York, NY

PocketCard logo, by Segura Inc.

"Smart and impactful: That's what I would call the identity for PocketCard. Simple, straightforward wordmark, in line with the overall appearance of the symbol—one could argue that it is too simple and could benefit from some differentiating touches, but would anybody see them? Nah, so it's perfect as is! The symbol doesn't really need any words: in-your-face communication that is smart, simple, nicely executed, and very differentiating—what else is there to say? Color? Fine. If there is anything to comment on, it would be the lock-up of the symbol and the type—a little standard and pedestrian, and we've seen that a million times. I just hope that this is an actual brand and not just a pretty logo. Of those, we've got too many already."

PocketCard®

Marcus Greinke is managing director, U.S. Consumer Branding, for Enterprise IG. He has extensive experience in the fields of corporate and consumer branding. He is responsible for the New York and San Francisco offices, focusing on developing and translating compelling consumer brands from brand strategy to all areas of brand experience. His competence is based on more than fifteen years of experience working on domestic and international strategic design projects and design management. Greinke has led branding programs in the United States, Europe, and Asia for clients such as Masterfoods, The Coca-Cola Company, and the Wm. Wrigley Jr. Company. He studied at the Art Center College of Design in Los Angeles and was awarded a bachelor's of fine arts with honors. He has received numerous national and international design awards and is often invited as a guest speaker on topics pertaining to design and design management. He speaks fluent German, English, and French.

Rian Hughes
Device, London, UK

Paul Wu & Associates, Chartered Accountants logo, by Nancy Wu

"I liked the accounting logo for Paul Wu & Associates, Ltd., because it contains a simple idea, elegantly executed, that humanizes a somewhat dull and staid business. I just wonder what percentage the company charges!"

Rian Hughes studied at the LCP in London before working for an advertising agency, *i-D* magazine, and a series of record-sleeve design companies. Under the name Device, he now provides design and illustration for advertising campaigns, record sleeves, book jackets, graphic novels, and television. For Belgium's Magic trip, he cowrote and drew a graphic novel titled *The Science Service,* published in five languages. This book was followed by *Dare,* an iconoclastic revamp of the 1950s comic hero Dan Dare. Since setting up his studio, he has worked extensively for the British and American comic industries as a designer, typographer, and illustrator. Moving away from comics, his recent work includes title sequences for *The Box,* poster designs for Tokyo fashion company Jun Co.'s Yellow Boots chain, a collection of Hawaiian shirts, a range of products for Swatch, and both a BDA International Gold Award- and Creative Use of Print Award-winning brochure for MTV European Music Awards. He has contributed to numerous international exhibitions, lectured widely in the United Kingdom and internationally, and has an extensive collection of Thunderbirds memorabilia, a fridge full of vodka, and a stack of easy-listening albums, which he plays very quietly.

Rüdiger Goetz
Simon & Goetz, Frankfurt, Germany

BP logo, by Landor Associates

"It is a remarkable brand evolution—from a traditional oil and gas company to a contemporary energy business. A conservative traffic heraldic turns into the positive symbol of a flower. It is communicating convincingly the challenging and ambitious repositioning of the brand. The redesign is an impressive example of a perfect combination of formal design quality, creativity, and strategy. The logo is very noticeable, congenial, internationally understandable, and highly differentiating. Most likely I will come across this logo several times each day over the next years; therefore, as a designer, I am happy that this major brand took a good step toward reducing visual pollution."

After working as a designer for design agencies in San Francisco and Minneapolis, Rüdiger Goetz joined the design agency Factor Design in Hamburg in 1992, as a managing partner and managing creative director. In 1995, he switched to Simon & Goetz in Frankfurt as acting partner. The agency currently has thirty employees. His professional focus is corporate and brand identity. Goetz has been awarded several international design prizes and has taught corporate design and typography for six years at institutions such as the Free University of Berlin and the University of Applied Arts of Wiesbaden. At the start of the 2003 summer semester, he was appointed to a professorship in the field of corporate identity and corporate design.

Tony Spaeth
www.identityworks.com, Rye, NY

Williams Landscaping logo, by The Bradford Lawton Design Group
"What a joy! For sheer efficiency, a wordmark that can (with a twist) express the spirit of a brand beats a symbol most every day. This Williams mark does it with style and humor. As for legibility, by resisting the temptation to dot the i's, both client and designer have shown their trust in people's willingness to work with them."

As a corporate identity consultant, Tony Spaeth is a professional champion (as well as client, critic, partner, and friend) of great logo design. After serving as account manager, strategist, and namer with both Lippincott & Margulies and Anspach Grossman Portugal during some of their most classic years, he launched his independent consulting practice in 1990, specifically to help great designers provide better-planned and more fully rounded identity solutions. At www.identityworks.com, Spaeth provides candid reviews of noteworthy new logos and freely offers professional tools and insights to identity enthusiasts and students worldwide.

Tom Nynas
RBMM, Dallas, TX

Sea World logo, by Landor Associates
"I chose this logo because of its simplicity, timelessness, elegance, and appropriateness. The shapes are beautifully crafted and give enough of a message about the nature of the business to intrigue the viewer. Together with the accompanying type, the whole thing works extremely well as a visual bull's-eye that is extremely legible in any range of applications, from the smallest electronic version to full outdoor signage."

Tom Nynas holds a bachelor's degree in visual communications from the University of Minnesota and is a graduate of the Creative Circus. He is principal of RBMM and is also a guest speaker at the Portfolio Center, AIGA Dallas, and the Art Institute, Dallas. Currently, he is an adjunct instructor at Texas A&M-Commerce and is on the board of advisors of the Art Institute of Dallas. Nynas is married to the lovely and wonderful Nichole and daddy to Stewie Nynas, who Nynas says is the coolest kid he has ever met.

portraits

Design Firm	**VSA Partners**
Client	**BellSouth and SBC Communications**
Project	**Corporate Identity and Naming**

cingular℠

For buyers in the wireless-communications market, purchasing decisions typically come down to phone features, calling plans, and price—end of story. But when BellSouth and SBC Communications merged their eleven existing wireless properties in 2000, they sought out VSA Partners to write a different story. What they got was something more offbeat than they expected—and something even more relevant.

Instead of establishing the new company as another price-and-service-based competitor, VSA established a brand that communicated the human value of wireless communications, including a name that stood alone in the industry: Cingular. Although with twenty-one million customers, Cingular became the nation's second-largest wireless company upon its creation, it was a late entry into an already crowded wireless-communications field. Because of its belated arrival, Cingular (at the time unnamed) had to create a strong and immediate presence. And if it was going to compete successfully, it was going to have to win customers who were being wooed by commodity-based companies whose brands promised cheap plans, sound clarity, and up-to-the-minute technology.

> "The assignment had so much potential on many levels. But I was concerned about the timing, the approval process, and if we'd be allowed to do something great."

From assignment to launch, the new brand would have to be developed in eight weeks at VSA. Facing this unprecedented schedule and the number of leaders involved among the partner companies, VSA partner Jamie Koval was at first a little reluctant to get involved with the project. "The assignment had so much potential on many levels," he recalls. "But I was concerned about the timing, the approval process, and if we'd be allowed to do something great." But after meeting client representatives, Koval was convinced that the potential could be realized.

To begin, VSA conducted market research to uncover what the competition was doing in terms of positioning, message, and image. The VSA team saw that competitors in the wireless market essentially stressed the same thing the same way—all had fairly similar identities—and they understood that the client was looking for something unprecedented in the marketplace.

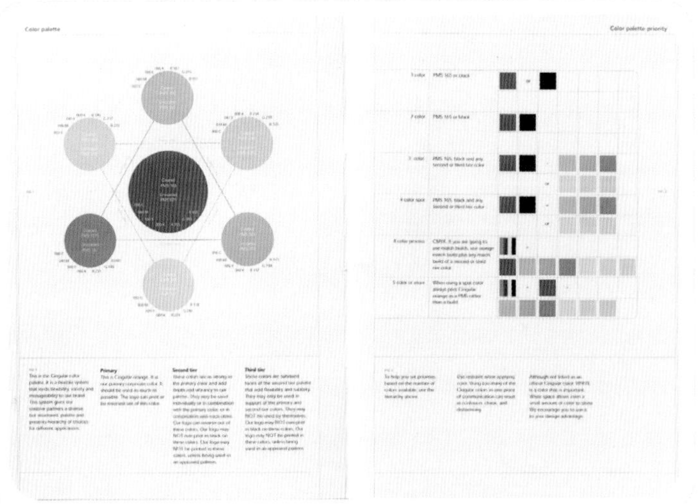

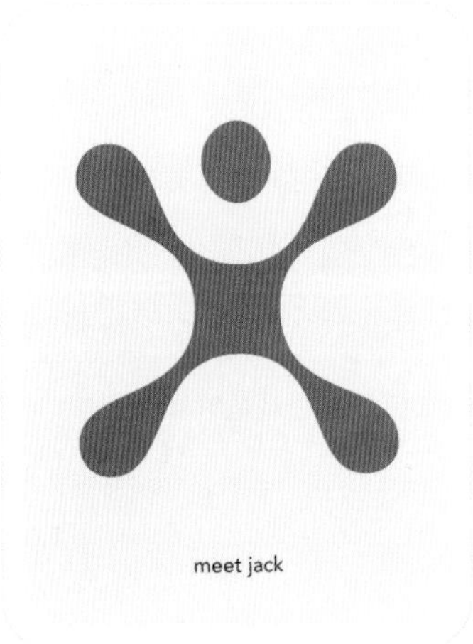

(Top and Bottom) Jack, Cingular's spirited logo, was not a conventional, safe solution, says Jamie Koval of VSA Partners, the firm that brought him to life. But the little character has charmed consumers and the telecommunications market.

(Middle) The logo's impact is undeniable. Maintaining its sense of celebration and singularity is achieved through guidelines offered in the Cingular style guide, also created by VSA.

Part of the beauty of the Cingular logo is that it can be used both as a part of one design or as an inspiration for another. In addition to being used alone, it can easily be used to create patterns or to provide a visual cue to photography, which can either follow its shape or its mood. The bright orange reinforces the good cheer and energy of the brand.

USA presented some 4,000 names for client evaluation—a remarkable quantity given the constraints.

Working within the tight timeframe, VSA strategists, writers, and designers were captivated by the idea of redefining the category by creating a positioning that was warm and human, not just about selling minutes. "No one was talking about people's need to communicate or the idea of human connection," notes Koval. "The position was wide open."

One of the immediate hurdles was the new company's name. It had to be self-positioning; be intuitive to the wireless/cellular category; be markedly different from the competition; be based on a real word, with a real meaning; and be reflective of the client's goal to become the single source for all wireless needs. It also needed to be appropriate not only to cellular technology but to any future technologies or endeavors the client might undertake.

> "We wanted the mark to be a strong graphic symbol, but it also had to be soft and playful."

VSA presented some 4,000 names for client evaluation—a remarkable quantity given the constraints. In addition to the strategic considerations mentioned previously, the new name had to be available as a brand name and as a domain name worldwide, and it could not start with v, s, a, or n, the first initials of its competitors. It had to be appropriate in meaning in any one of twelve languages. Another challenge was, because of the nature of the client's business, the new name could not conflict with that of any other technology-based or communication-based company.

In an exhaustive culling process, the list was pared down to three names, including Cingular, which had the right associations: the name communicated that fourteen independent companies were combined into one, and it was a real word, with an unconventional spelling, whose C suggested cellular. Despite the name's advantages, client decision-makers weren't sold on the Cingular name, and neither BellSouth's nor SBC's chief executive were enthusiastic about any of the three names. So, as time ticked away, VSA began creating more names. "But we felt strongly about Cingular from the beginning and kept pushing it—mostly politely—in every conversation," recalls Koval. "We had to convince them that it's unusual for anyone to fall in love with any name when it's just a word on a piece of paper."

Soon they brought back Cingular, with two new names. But this time, the designers presented all the names in context, developing a visual language to support the positioning and bring the names to life. "Going that extra step dramatically helped everyone better understand the potential of the Cingular name," Koval says. The name was approved. Now Cingular needed a full visual identity to infuse the name with meaning.

With only three weeks left, VSA began building on the conceptual presentation to develop the final look and feel for the program. The design team explored hundreds of different directions (from individual symbols to logotypes and everything in between). There was a conscious effort to keep the program simple and appear effortless. "We tried to stay away from all the corporate identity clichés already in use—like italic type or logos suggesting reach or movement—anything that felt big, cold, and heartless."

Although the VSA team never made a conscious effort to confine their design explorations to the human form, the team's design certainly communicates human expression. This message is very different from those being issued by other telecommunication companies, who speak mostly of technology. The freshness of the brand is especially evident in the urban environment.

Koval says, "Instead, we focused on ideas that felt approachable, human, and easy, and communicated a timeless idea."

And so Jack—the nickname of the Cingular Wireless's sprightly logo—was born. With his jaunty X shape and spirit, Jack embodied the idea of human expression and the goal of helping users "make their mark." His uplifted arms and outspread legs are a clear signal of personal celebration. In application, his basic, rounded forms, all-lowercase typography, and bright orange color brought energy and freshness to signage, point-of-sale materials, and retail operations.

"We wanted the mark to be a strong graphic symbol, but it also had to be soft and playful," Koval says, adding that the VSA team never made a conscious effort to confine their explorations to the shape of a human form. "It was one of many directions we needed to explore. But to communicate self-expression, the human form felt the most logical and powerful."

Koval says he's been surprised and delighted at how the new mark has been embraced by the public. Four years later, he's seen the incarnation of Jack everywhere—imprinted on an NFL coach's headphones, as a prominent product placement in the movie *Spiderman,* and animated in TV commercials. Even his seven-year-old daughter brags to her friends that she knows the story behind Jack. "He made an immediate impression and was an instantly recognized brand. Jack has a universal appeal that you hope for in every large identity project."

But Koval takes the greatest satisfaction in knowing that the marketplace risk he encouraged his client to take has paid off. "This is not your standard solution," he says. "Jack was not the conventional, safe way to go. But he is clearly enjoying the long and productive life we imagined for him."

cingularexpression

In 2000, it was the perfect match: the merger between a back-office software and systems integrations firm named Whittman-Hart, the management consultancy Mitchell Madison Group, and the interactive creative firm US Web/CKS. At the height of the Internet boom, the three groups joined forces to create a business hybrid that no one had previously attempted—technology, strategy, and brand-building, blended into a single consulting firm with deep roots in the Web.

As complementary as the three organizations were, offering a unified set of services was uncharted territory. “It was a very ambitious stance—establishing a business model in which they could really excel at all of those things,” recalls Jamie Koval, a principal with VSA Partners, Chicago, the design office that was tapped to create the name and identity for the new company, which became marchFIRST. “The name grew out of the date of the company’s founding,” Koval adds, “but it came to mean more.” In developing the marchFIRST brand, VSA expanded the definition of the name to suggest forward movement and the business imperative of competitive leadership.

“From an identity standpoint, I believed the new company needed to create a signature that was the anti-identity of what had been going on during the go-go 1990s,” he says. “We wanted to create something that was timeless and grounded with classic sensibilities so the company would look current both then and twenty years later.”

Because the company was so unusual for its time, Koval and his team wanted to create an identity that had clarity and a universal appeal—one that would be a business asset rather than a creative sideshow. Externally, the identity had to appear strong, stable, and established; it had to appeal to corporate leadership and decision-makers worldwide. Internally, the identity needed to appeal to and represent all the different disciplines within the organization, including organizations whose own disciplines included design and branding. This was no small order.

The identity VSA ultimately created was extremely restrained in its execution, yet fresh and consciously international in its feel. The logo itself is a simple lowercase m, its first stroke forming the numeral 1.

“If you are visual, you’ll pick up quickly on the detail of this symbol,” Koval says of the design. In the full visualization of the wordmark, the typography expands from lower- to uppercase to create a subtle sense of movement or expansion. “It visually illustrates a step up. Anytime the name would appear—internal communications, in press releases, in the media—it would be typeset that way.” By dictating that others be case sensitive with the use of the company name, the designers ensured that every time the name was printed, the design of the identity and distinctiveness of the company would be reinforced.

The visibility of the identity really began, however, with the launch

trading on NASDAQ. "It's one thing to design a great symbol, but it is another thing to create a context for that symbol that makes people understand and believe in what you offer," Koval explains. "Because the identity itself appears so simple, the execution of the program is where the logo shined."

Launch elements included aluminum-bound media kits; a multipage, business card–size company manifesto; a multimedia presentation broadcast on the NASDAQ MarketSite; and a multicolor stationery system that included business cards with individual messages on the back sides. "We went to great lengths to consider form, materials, and messaging to give the identity life," Koval recalls. "When marchFIRST launched, it was an instantly recognized company that was seen as a leader, and people were understandably intrigued."

Ultimately, marchFIRST the brand lasted longer than marchFIRST the business. A year into its young life, the company was engulfed by the dot-com bust and went out of business before its integrated business model was fully realized. Yet there's still some life in the marchFIRST brand. "To this day, people share stories about marchFIRST and tell me how much they loved the identity program and the ideals of the company," Koval states. "Many employees and clients still have their materials from the program, and we get requests for samples all the time."

Design Firm | **Segura, Inc.**

Client | **Corbis**

Project | **Corporate Identity Redesign**

A terrible logo can stand for something very good. Look at Apple's very first logo, says Carlos Segura of Segura, Inc., Chicago. Or consider the marks of Yahoo, MTV, Google, or even eBay: None are especially well-regarded design-wise, but they have become an accepted part of the consumer landscape.

Corbis, however, faced a more honed, critical audience—designers. It had limped along for almost two decades with a dated logo and marketing that suffered from poor design, production, and distribution. Sales figures were concrete evidence of impending disaster.

"They have all these wonderful photos and collections," offers Segura of client Corbis, which supplies photography, art, and footage to creatives around the world. "But they weren't offering it in an intelligent, mature, relevant way to one of the most intelligent audiences there could be. Designers are into fashion, architecture, art, everything. It is a big task to talk to us."

> "He let us do what we were hired to do. The number one error that clients make is to not allow firms to do what they are hired to do."

Great logos—for any audience—can be filed in one of two categories, Segura says. In the first, the logo does not stand for an obvious idea. For instance, BMW's blue and white checkerboard in a circle represents blue sky as seen through spinning propellers because BMW began its life making aircraft. Today, the mark represents fine engineering.

The second type of effective mark stands for something very concrete. Witness again Apple, with its now remade and greatly simplified mark. In the end, the new Corbis mark as designed by Segura, Inc., would carry traits from both categories.

"Corbis had such an uphill climb to recover that it was almost scary to get involved with the project. In fact, when we first started meeting with the client, we stated clearly that we couldn't promise anything, and that Corbis would have to be willing to stick with us for the long haul," Segura recalls.

The design team began the new brand development by reinventing the way Corbis spoke to designers. First, they addressed the logo, which Segura calls decorative and dated, right down to the typography. The

(Top) The revamped Corbis logo has a pure, transparent nature that clearly identifies the company while allowing the impact of the company's visual products to show through.

(Middle) The old Corbis logo had exactly the opposite effect of the new one: It was overly loud in color and design.

(Opposite, Bottom; Top) On the cover and inside pages of *Crop,* the visuals are the hero. Segura designers select photos that are similar in shape or nature to their content but are extremely diverse in actual meaning. Note how minimal the Corbis logo is on the pages.

Segura says that their goal was to create a custom typography treatment that was clean and simple—an unobtrusive signature that would define Corbis without distracting from the collection's images.

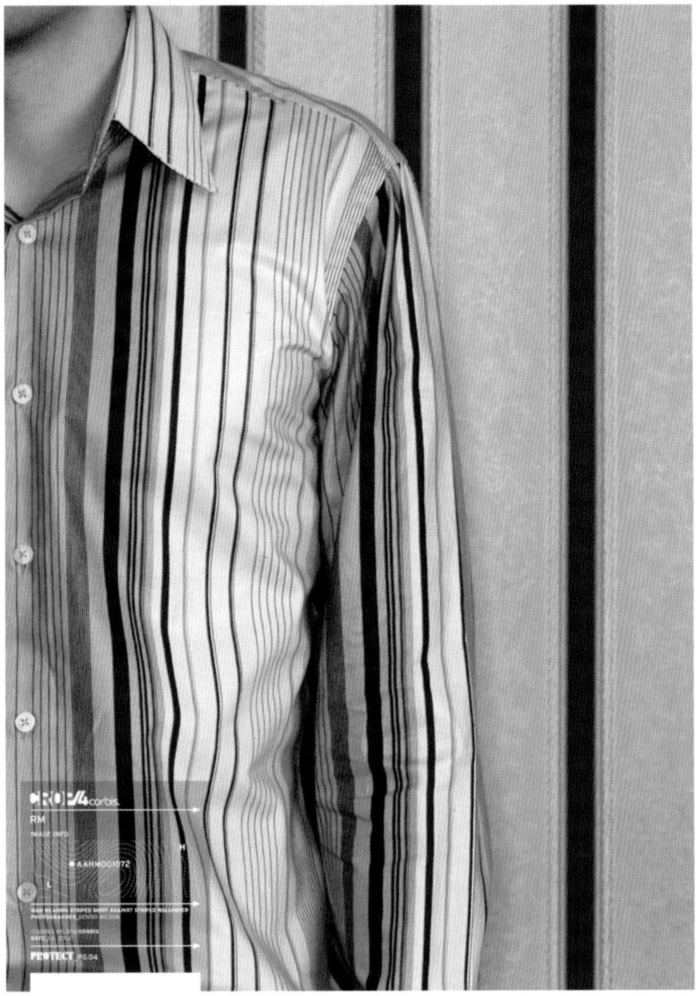

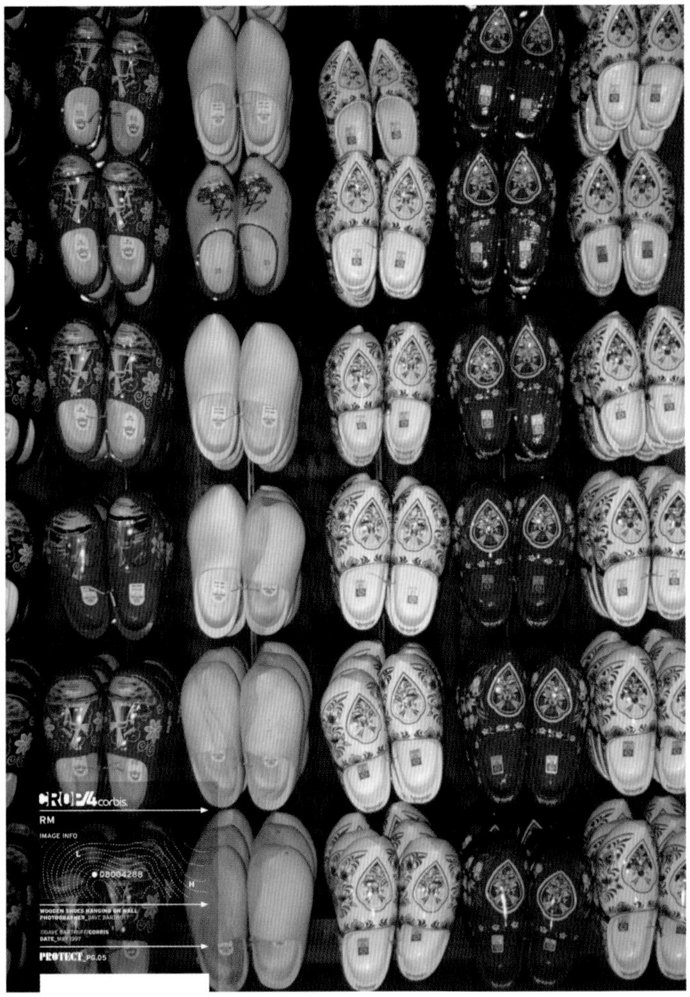

(Top and Opposite) Issues of *Crop* are themed, making them more like magazines than catalogs. In this issue, which supports the theme of "protect," all the photos revolve around the subject but from different angles—here, camouflage, unique culture, Samurai soldier, and the poisonous spines of a sea creature. Note, too, the thought-provoking match of visual shapes between facing pairs of photos.

mark's type used a serif face that was kerned to capture a very concrete time period in design. It was combined with a logomark that contained an organic swirl of colors that fought any image it sat on or near.

Segura says that their goal was to create a custom typography treatment that was clean and simple—an unobtrusive signature that would define Corbis without distracting from the collection's images. In fact, in the end, an all-type solution made more sense than a logotype.

To get to that solution, Segura's team created nearly forty different explorations. The ideas ranged from extraordinary printed collateral to three-dimensional, multiple-structured pieces that fit together, constructed in diverse materials, from aluminum and plastics to rubber.

In Segura's office, everyone—from interns to Segura himself—works on a single project. This process, Segura believes, empowers every member of the staff and creates a family feeling. But it also gives the client greater depth and breadth in possible solutions. From the dozens of marks the team created, about twelve were selected for presentation to the client—among them a very simple, flowing typographic solution that was a clear in-office favorite. To the team's delight, that was also the mark the client preferred.

"We only show the client what we like, whether it is one or twenty pieces," Segura says.

The selected solution is almost like an artist's signature that would be found at the bottom of a painting. A custom face, clean and simple, embraces every letter in the client's name and balances them in an elegant manner. An accompanying logomark would not be needed.

"It's important that the hero is Corbis' photography, not our graphic design. We cannot introduce elements that fight with the client's product. And an all-type solution is able to unify all the disciplines [Corbis] deals with," Segura explains, noting that his office does embrace solutions with what he refers to as "the realities of our craft" in mind. In this case, the solution

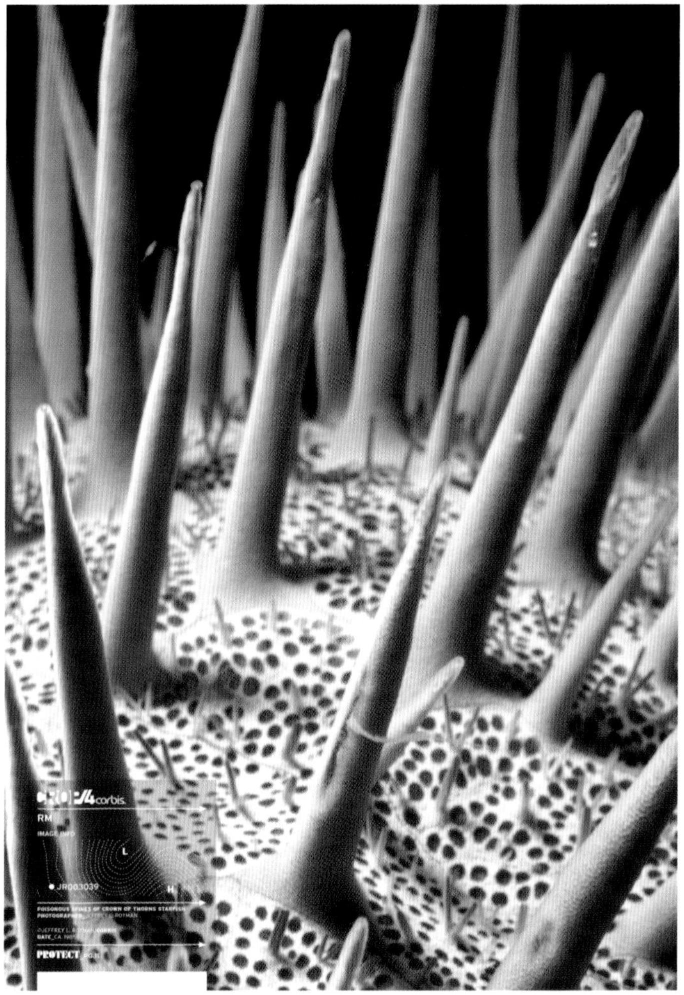

should not only focus on photography but should also work well in design, typography, illustration, texture, papers, packaging, special inks, and unique printing techniques.

The flavor of the design was based on a belief in the purest simplicity, such as might be seen in beautifully designed European furniture or on an Apple laptop. "How simple could we possibly make it?" Segura recalls.

The new logo is so simple that it can be viewed as a form and not just as a word because of the shapes found inside of the design. Consider how a famous artist's signature is recognized as a shape and not read as individual words, Segura says. He credits Corbis marketing director Joe Barrett for trusting Segura, Inc., to do its best.

"He let us do what we were hired to do. The number one error that clients make is not allowing firms to do what they are hired to do," Segura says.

Because designers at Segura are a perfect fit for Corbis's target audience and because they have worked with other stock companies in the past, they became quite emotionally attached to this project.

"Clients often want logos to do what they cannot do; they think that a new logo will give them a new history. But the logo is nothing more than what you are. With Corbis, a bad logo stood for something potentially very good but that at the time was bad," Segura says. His team's design righted the equation with a logo that appropriately and adeptly represented the concept of the client as well as its products.

"It's important that the hero is Corbis' photography, not our graphic design. We cannot introduce elements that fight with the client's product."

Yosho
Identity Design

Segura, Inc., Chicago, Illinois

Yosho is a Japanese war cry, uttered to inspire confidence and success. It is also the new name for a company previously called Graphica Multimedia, which used to provide programming for clients who were producing CD-ROMs. When the Web came along, the company had to reinvent itself and now writes code for clients' online products.

Although its name was thought provoking, Yosho's product was intangible and decidedly difficult to represent visually, says Carlos Segura, principal of Segura, Inc., the firm that created Yosho's new identity.

The client had initially asked the Segura design team for a logo flavored by Japanese anime—robotic and cartoony—because of its Japanese-inspired name. Such a direction, says Segura, might be interesting to look at for a while, but it would get boring quickly.

Even so, his designers did provide the client with several anime-based trials. In addition, they presented a clean and futuristic logo that had concept embedded in it. "The logo needed to be modern in a clean way—almost classical but fresh," Segura says.

In the process of studying the assignment, the designers noted that programming is essentially writing long strings of numbers and that code is a different language altogether. To create the logo, they snipped numbers into the shape of the letters to form the word Yosho. In effect, the designers created a new language that operated in the same way as actual programming code.

The logo is especially engaging because it forces the viewer to work to interpret it. In fact, the viewer must fight his or her brain's own natural inclination to complete the familiar shapes of numbers—the trimmed numbers are a signal that can't be ignored.

The logo, designed by Segura designer Tnop, is a perfect example of how to inject not only a concept but a representation of the client's product offering into a mark, Segura says. This feat is difficult to accomplish in a small space. Logos have a tremendous task and to do it with intelligence is significant.

"When we are involved in branding, our task does not end with the mark, as seen in this example. Our thoughts expand to color schemes, patterns, applications, location of applications, interior design, decorations, and more. An example of that is when we created wallpaper from the pattern on the back of a client's letterhead. The wallpaper was then applied to one of the four walls in selected rooms in the client's office," Segura says.

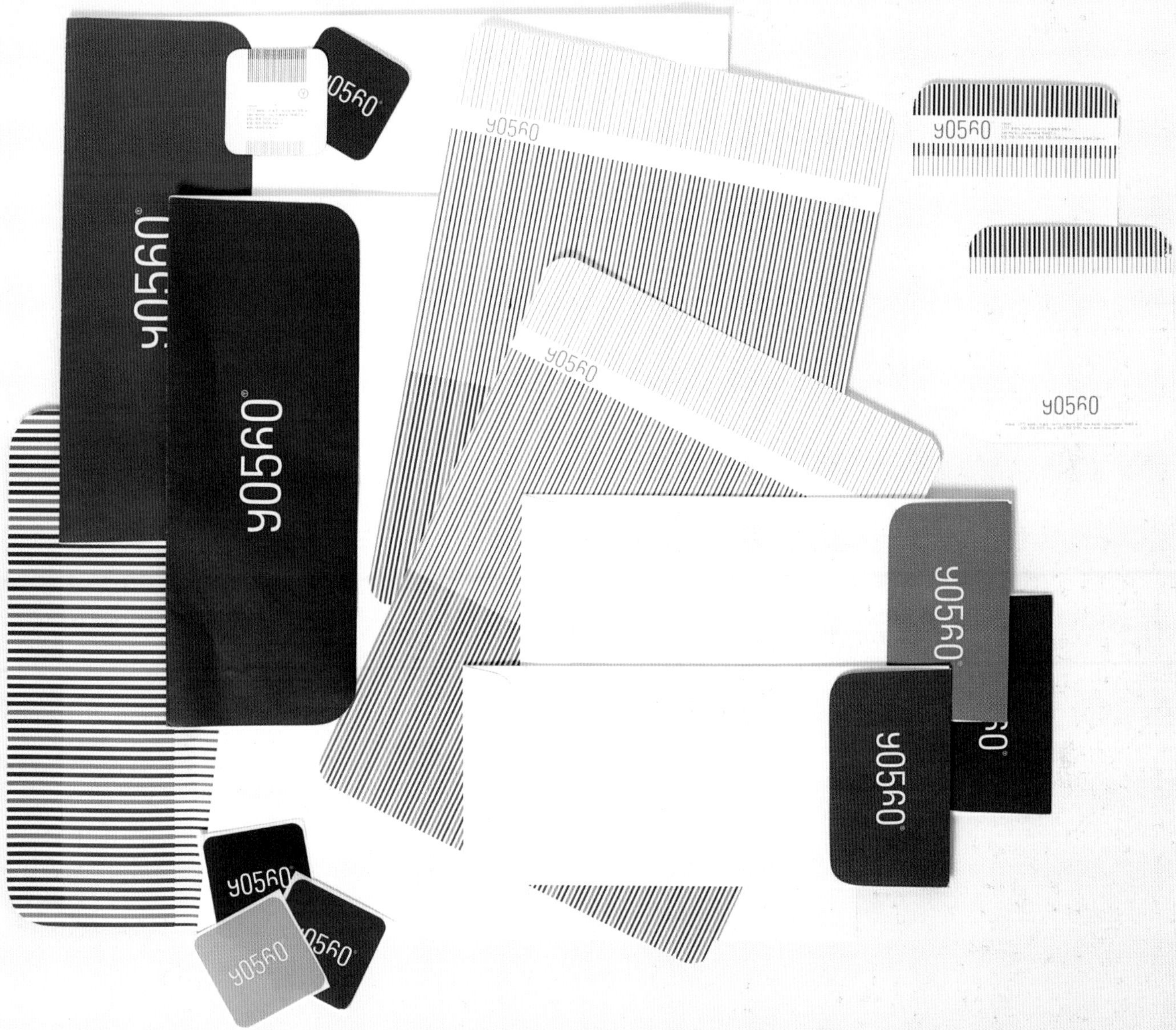
y0560

Design Firm	**Duffy & Partners**
Client	**Bahamas Ministry of Tourism**
Project	**Identity Design**

In many crowded product categories, strong branding is the differentiator, leading consumers to prefer one product over another—especially when so many of the product attributes and claims are perceived to be identical. This belief is well understood in commodity categories such as beverages, cereal, or other common household goods, but could it also be true with such a considered, emotional, and expensive consumer choice as the destination for a tropical vacation?

That was precisely the case when Duffy & Partners began to work with the Bahamas Ministry of Tourism. The island nation was competing for tourism dollars with branding and communication that was virtually identical in imagery and messages as its competitors. As a result, consumers concluded the Bahamas were interchangeable with other warm-weather destinations such as Jamaica, Mexico, or many other Caribbean islands. And although the Bahamas does offer the tantalizing promise of a sensory, emotional, and physical vacation, they are perceived to be a "stereotypical paradise." The challenge for the ministry: How could they differentiate the islands as the preferred vacation destination?

THE ISLANDS OF THE bahamas

The new logo and brand identity for the islands of the Bahamas—a clever maplike representation of the arrangement of main destination islands, and a pattern that can be repurposed on everything from T-shirts to websites—is fresh and bright, like the place itself. The mark distinguishes the Bahamas as not a single destination but many.

> "It quickly became clear that everyone from the tourism office to souvenir manufacturers would have to be able to work with the new design."

"As you can imagine, in this category, there is a sea of sameness among all sand and sea destinations—tropical colors, water, sun, palm trees," says Joe Duffy, chairman of Duffy & Partners. "With our client's previous approach, you could have pulled out the name 'Bahamas' and substituted 'Jamaica' or 'Barbados,' and the identity would have worked just as well. It was not unique or grounded in any differentiated truth that makes the Bahamas a unique destination."

Contributing to the ministry's challenge was that although the Bahamas had an existing identity, it had never been used consistently. Essentially, the previous brand identity was just a tagline, "The Islands of the Bahamas: It Just Keeps Getting Better"—undistinguished at best. And it was applied in hundreds of different ways, with different typefaces and colors, driven by different constituencies with different needs.

THE ISLANDS OF THE BAHAMAS

It Just Keeps Getting Better

Less than inspiring, the Bahamas' old logo didn't say "tropical," much less "unique" or even "fun."

They determined the best solution was to create not just a logo but a more fluid brand expression of the actual geographic positioning of the islands of the Bahamas on a map.

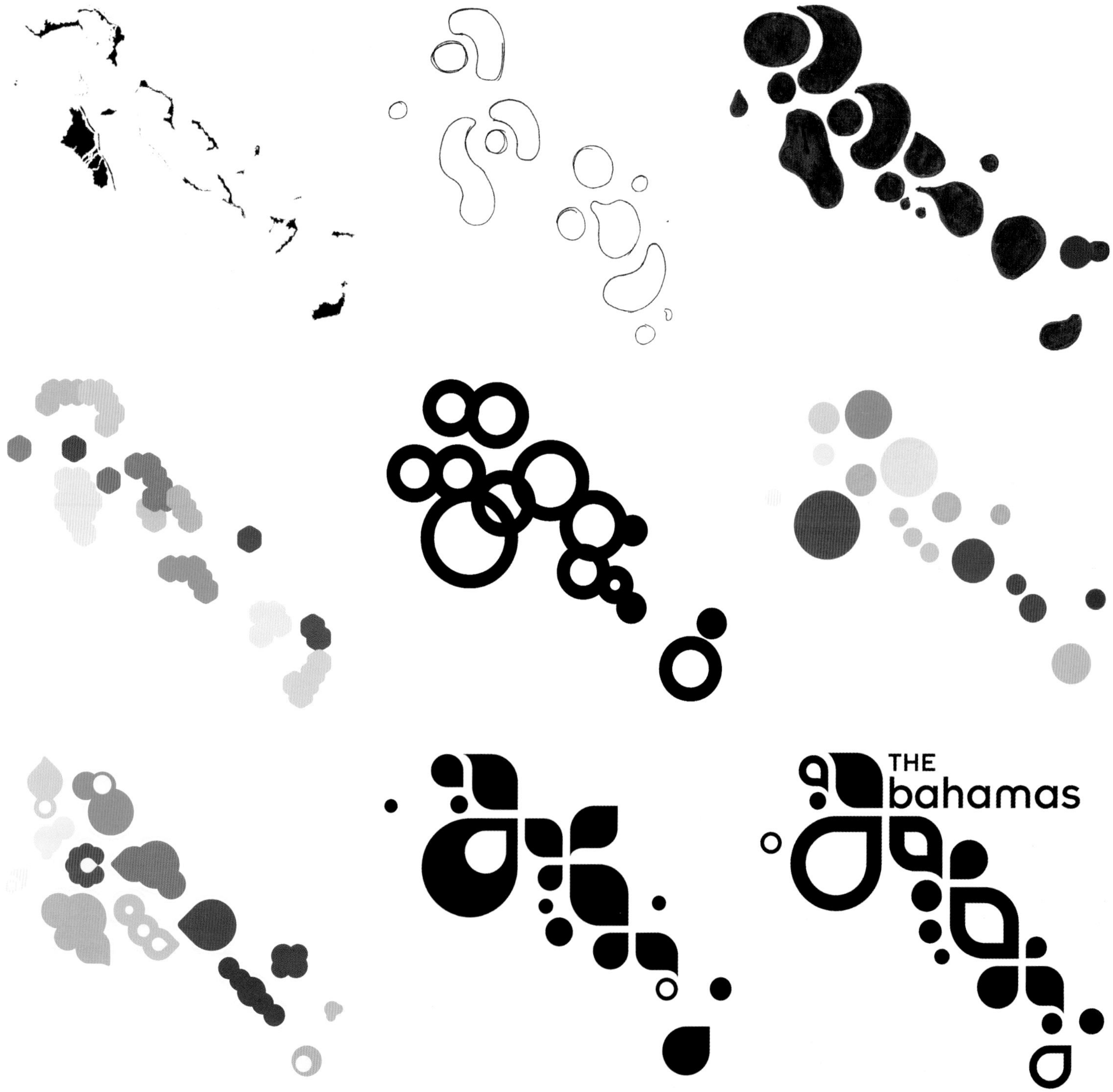

Building off flower shapes and other organic forms, the Duffy design team began to experiment with different ways to express that the Bahamas was not one destination, but many. The concept of using geography as a design element emerged here, through different shapes.

The individual islands can be completely split out when necessary—say, for a Web page that gives information about just one island—or they can be distinguished from the grouping of other islands solely through the use of color.

Duffy concluded that the Bahamas needed an entirely new brand identity, one that not only made the country stand out from other equally pleasant vacation spots but that was also practical for many different constituencies to use. The Duffy team began with a complete visual audit of all former uses of the identity. "It quickly became clear that everyone from the tourism office to souvenir manufacturers would have to be able to work with the new design. Making it appealing and flexible for all was critical to get the consistency that was missed in the past. That was central to our thinking and constituted the creative challenge," remembers Duffy.

Duffy determined the Bahamas did have one distinguishing factor, one that no other vacation destination offers: It is not one place but many places. A map of the country reveals that it is made up of 700 islands, with seventeen major tourist destinations, each with its own special attractions—scuba diving, fishing, sunning, historical sites, luxury accommodations, or nightlife. Each destination also has its own unique flora and fauna. Expressing the breadth of the offerings of the Bahamas quickly became the most promising and distinctive design direction.

A team traveled from Duffy's Minneapolis office to the island nation to begin developing a differentiated brand visual language that challenged consumer expectations as well as their own. Creating this brand experience presented a contradiction to the designers.

"One of the things you want to do is distill an identity down to its core essence and root it in a brand truth," explains Duffy. "The obvious here is the blue water and palm trees and sand—that is what you are initially impressed with when you visit. But it is really important to dig past this common surface to find what can be really unique and special about the brand."

The team took in the turquoise blue waters. They studied pink flamingoes and the pastel sands. They took hundreds of pictures of flowers and other details and of people from all walks of life, and they enjoyed the sunshine and the hospitality.

Back in chilly Minneapolis, the team had many positive memories, images, and impressions of shapes and colors from their visit. But one thing stood out: the forms that made up the constellation of islands themselves. They determined that the best solution was to create not just a logo but a more fluid brand expression of the actual geographic positioning of the islands of the Bahamas on a map.

"When you compare that map to other island destinations, we win," Duffy says.

The solution they created is a stylized map using the manner and flavor of the shapes and colors the designers observed in the Bahamas. The collection of islands pulls on visual cues that are already in the consumer's mind—organic, rounded forms shown in a sophisticated, tropical palette. However, in sum, it is a collection of shapes that is anything but predictable.

Duffy explains, "An actual map of the islands does not look like this. The stylization comes from what we saw—the birds and shells and flowers. Here, we present each of the main island destinations but in an abstract way. It is a relatively simple solution, but you can feel the flamingoes, the turquoise water, and the pink sand represented in the colors and forms," he says. "This approach challenges perceptions and creates a new language for the brand."

The beauty of the identity is that it sets in motion an entire brand language that is endlessly adaptable—in signage, in patterning for clothing and interiors, in iconography. Especially promising are product applications—swimwear, T-shirts, fabrics, Web wallpaper, towels, and more. Each application will further the brand.

"We branded the country, and people will actually end up wearing the brand. Every single element working together will contribute to differentiation and a stronger brand," Duffy notes. Another practical aspect of the new identity is that it can be used to point to specific destinations within the Bahamas. For example, in an ad or on a webpage where Bimini is discussed, the rest of the logo is muted in gray while the shape representing that island and its name are printed in color (green, for this island). So, various destinations can be graphically pinpointed, from north to south, with their own unique stories. The cumulative effect underlines the many different experiences the Bahamas has to offer.

Television ads, some of the first communication to be created with the new brand identity, take the notion of island-hopping literally—again, stressing the many destinations. A happy visitor is shown jumping from one island and experience to another.

"The spots reveal the secret of all there is to do in the Bahamas. They make you think differently," Duffy says.

Print advertising highlights various shapes from the identity and uses them as frames for photos of wonderful experiences from the islands. The color palette feels natural for a tropical destination, but its complexity makes it special to the diverse nature of the Bahamas.

The program was unveiled on the Bahamas' official website (www.thebahamas.com) in December 2003, and as of this writing, reactions are just beginning to come in to Duffy. However, reception in the Bahamas itself and with the Ministry of Tourism is enthusiastic.

"Strong branding elegantly and simply captures what is unique, special, and enduring about the product," said Duffy. "We're extraordinarily proud of this approach because we believe it represents the true character and diversity of the Bahamas and that will encourage visitors to return again and again. Also, it is presented with the flexibility that will stand the test of time."

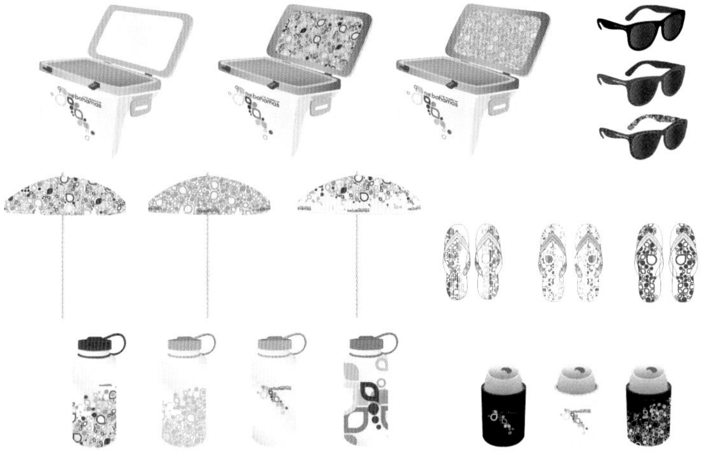

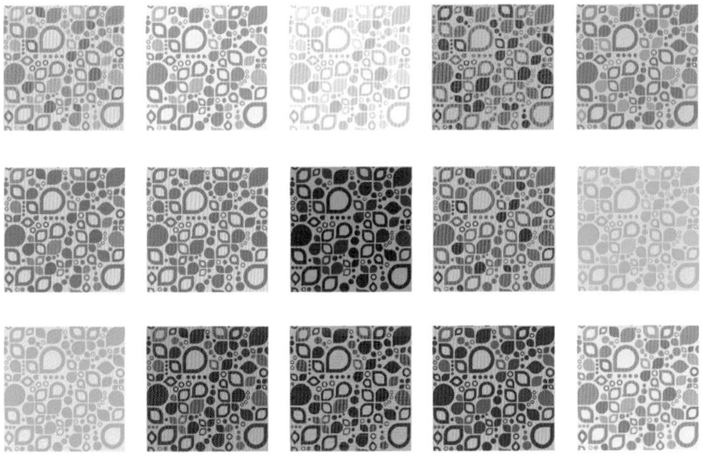

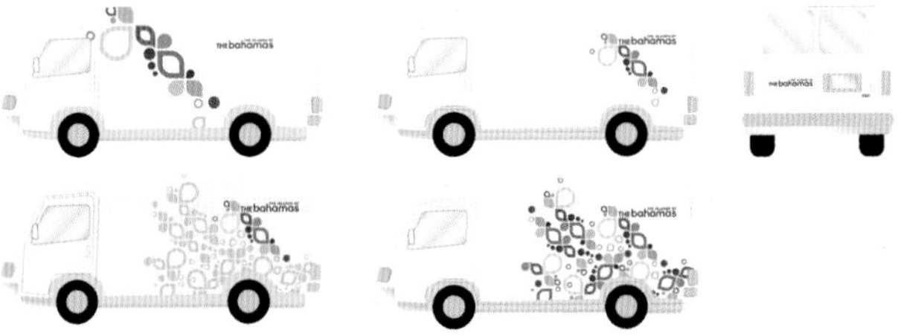

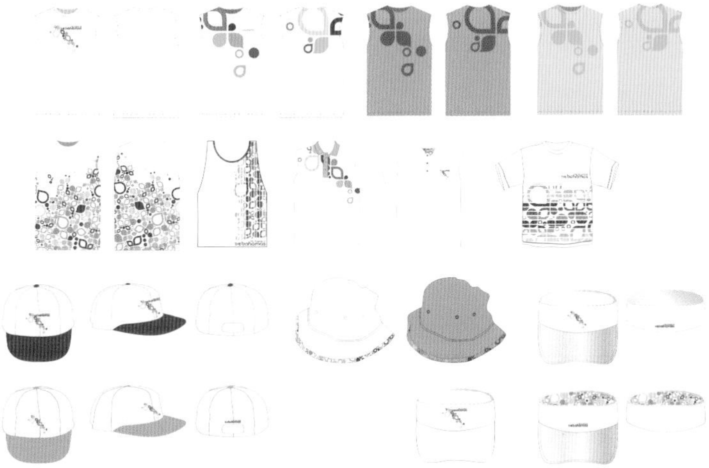

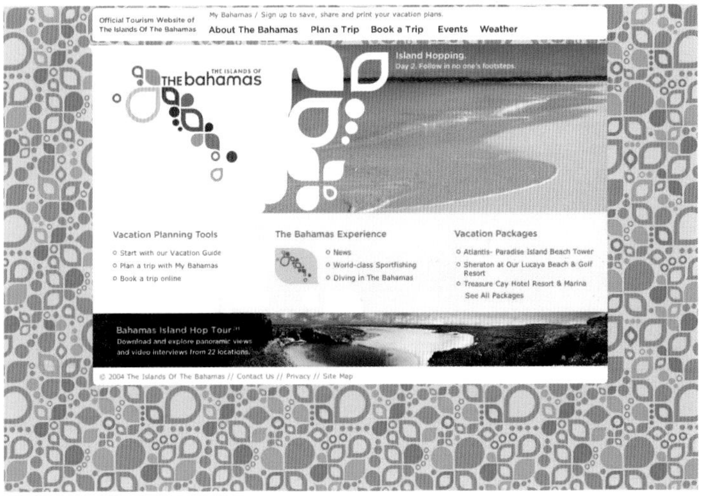

The shapes formed by the new logo have been worked into many different patterns and applications, all of which further the brand identity and effortlessly promote the client.

International
Identity Design Update

Duffy & Partners, Minneapolis, Minnesota

Navistar may be a familiar name in stock trading circles, but it doesn't exactly evoke pictures of its core products—trucks and buses. Sometime in the 1970s, consultants had convinced International Harvester to change the name of its bus and truck division—then called International—to Navistar: the IH name smacked of farm implements, the experts insisted.

But the International name also had many positives: a tradition of dependability and ruggedness; a heritage that predated many of its better-known competitors such as Peterbilt and Mac Truck; and a logo that was very recognizable within the trucking market.

Joe Duffy and his team at Duffy & Partners suggested it was high time to change the name back to International; surround it with a compelling, updated identity system; and return the company to its roots and core values.

"There was a tremendous amount of equity in the International name—a hard-working, Midwestern ethic. When we did a visual audit, we discovered the strong, distinctive color of orange and the diamond-shaped road logo were the things that people thought of when they heard the name 'International,'" says Duffy. "We suggested that they build on what people already admired. We created an entire brand language from that familiar mark."

Competitors in this market were all trying to promote similar product traits: quality, endurance, and toughness. Everyone was marketing to large-fleet operators who buy several trucks at a time. These people didn't want to have to worry about how the vehicles would perform in tough conditions or the expense of frequent servicing.

The Duffy team rebuilt the brand around four main visual and emotional aspects, creating a palette of materials, colors, photography, and typefaces that could be extended across all aspects of the brand presentation, in advertising, on vehicles, on signage, and more.

- All the materials used in the design have a heavy-duty quality. For instance, in a trade show display, the concrete, bolts, wire mesh, black-and-white photography, and even the typefaces chosen have a powerful and bold industrial feel.
- The diamond-shaped road logo was resurrected from one of the old International logos. A rich industrial orange was selected for the mark because of its breakthrough quality, its historical association with the brand, and its connection to road signs.
- The typeface created for the new mark was drawn from type that was widely used in International identities in the 1930s. This aspect of the new branding subtly referenced the company's history and stability.
- Because the company produces a rugged and durable product, the designers decided to give the new logo a sense of dimension, projecting it in the form of a 3-D metal truck badge.

Another consideration for the designers was that International already had many vehicles on the road, and these could not be retrofitted with the new logo. Therefore, the new creation had to live in a transitional way with the old marks.

Duffy says the new design has received a tremendous reception. "International chairman John Horne understood the new identity was a rallying cry for the rejuvenation not of only the brand but of the entire company. It helped employees, dealers, customers, and other key audiences reconsider International in an entirely new light."

Today, although Navistar is still the company's corporate name, International and the revamped brand image is proudly put forth in every aspect of marketing. It's an all-American identity, even without red, white, and blue.

"International was a sleeping giant," Duffy explains. "Few companies have been around as long as it in the American industrial landscape. International needed to leverage its heritage but also be seen as an innovator for the future. We believe their new identity and brand language perfectly capture that critical balance."

The triple diamond design of the original International logo, created in the early 1980s, contained a name that was familiar to customers in the trucking industry, but it had strayed from valuable brand identity cues—mainly, the color orange and a split diamond shape.

(Above) The diamond-shaped logo with a road bisecting it, created some years ago, was the mark that most quickly came to mind when customers were presented with the International name. Duffy designers decided that it needed to be reintroduced to the new identity.

(Left) The final International mark builds on plenty of historical equity: the diamond-shaped road mark; the color orange; a rugged, three-dimensional look; and a typeface drawn from a font first used by International in the 1930s.

Design Firm **Addis**

Client **Intel Centrino**

Project **Corporate Identity**

The Intel Centrino logo is one of those marks you might never notice—until someone points it out. Then you'll see it everywhere you look. Centrino is the brand name for the Intel processor that gives computer users a truly mobile lifestyle.

The creation of the technology's logo posed special problems. Because Centrino mobile technology is built into different varieties of software and hardware, its logo would need to be a perennial and polite guest on other vendors' packaging. Also, it was likely to be reproduced at a small size, so the logo would need to stand out.

Susan Rockrise, Intel's worldwide creative director, collaborated closely with the Addis team throughout the strategic and creative development. "Susan's vision inspired us to break from the category conventions and create a mark that was as significant as the technology they were about to unveil to the world," says John Creson, executive creative director for Addis. "Intel could see that Centrino would be moving personal computing into a whole new space with a truly mobile offering. So, the company wanted to create something that would create a buzz and something they could build on. There was a lot riding on the logo."

> "We wanted to convey the notion of freedom and balance in life."

Addis had also created the design for the Intel Pentium 4 logo, so the designers were already familiar with the constraints of creating an "ingredient" identity. Because the Centrino mark would appear all over the world, the designers had to consider various language and cultural factors. The mark would be reproduced in any number of sizes (usually very small, however, and likely to grow even tinier, as applications for it continue to shrink in physical size). And it had to be able to go wherever the technology would eventually go—a road that was not yet charted.

One of the most important attributes to convey with the new identity was that the Centrino brand was developed to meet a human need. The mobile lifestyle symbolizes freedom of movement without the loss of access to content, commerce, community, and communication. Being untethered and still connected was a big step forward.

Wings? An arrow? Actually, Intel's new Centrino mark, designed by Addis, is meant to suggest many things. The reference to wings is ideal and suggests what the Centrino brand provides: mobile computer communications. Users are rewarded with freedom instead of being tethered to a desktop computer. And a precise, forward-pointing arrow looks smart and purposeful, suggesting strength and movement.

In their initial explorations, Addis designers explored building a familial connection to the Pentium 4 mark, which they also created (far right). But here, they gave the containing rectangle an italic cant. At the time, the team was working with the project code name "Banias."

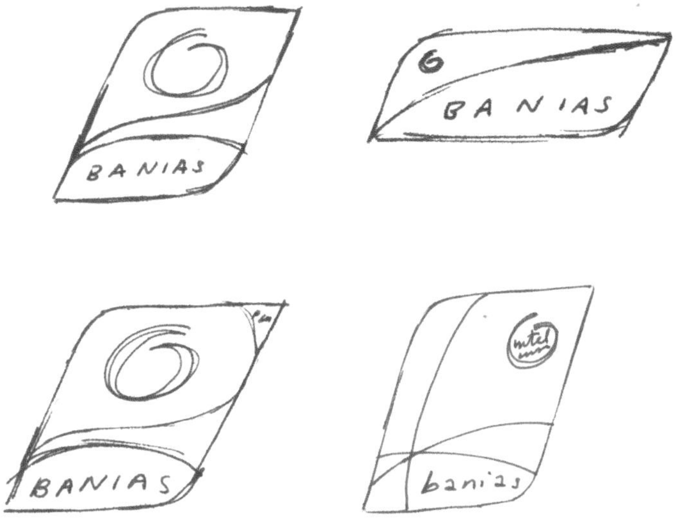

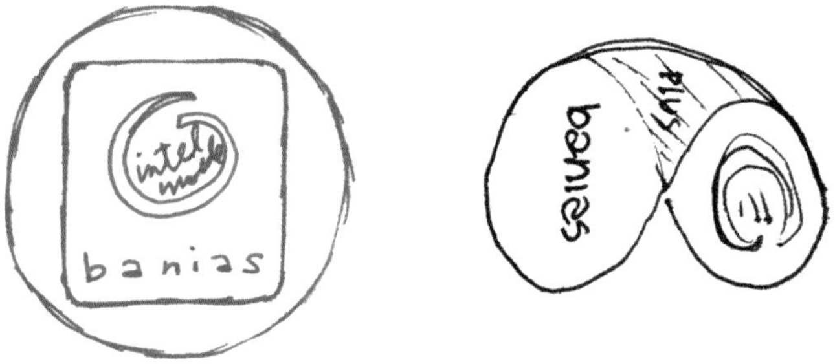

At the other end of the experimental spectrum were circular shapes. These trials were more fluid in their movement than the rectangular ones. The organic shapes were also emblematic of how mobile-computer communications would transform users' lives: the borders between work and play would certainly begin to merge.

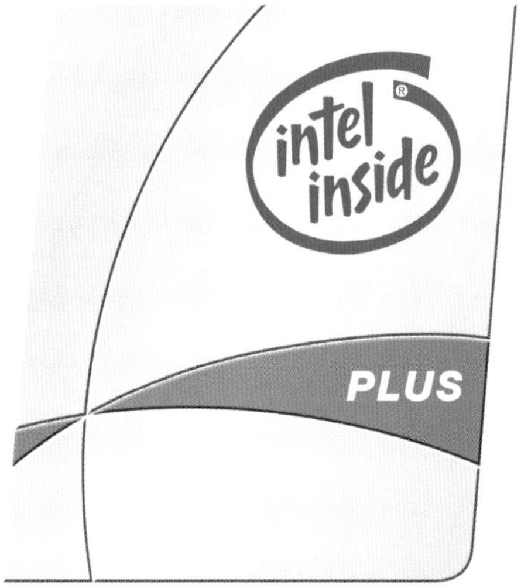

Here, the initial sketches are played out into more defined designs. In this design, rectangular and circular shapes are combined in the logo's border. The swooping, intersecting interior lines symbolize simultaneous freedom and connection.

This design is more like a flag or Rothko landscape—either connotation is appropriate. A flaglike logo could have represented the product, whereas a wide-open landscape is an apt representation of freedom.

Here, in a trial named "shimmer," a block of dots could represent people coming together (or perhaps the single dot leaving, symbolizing freedom); bits of information coming together; or even particles of air.

"We liken the technology to other major shifts in culture and history. It's potentially a seismic shift. This is where we start to blur the lines between work and play. Communication can now take place anywhere," says Creson.

Because the benefit of the product was such a human one, Creson and his team wanted to create a mark that had that feel. But because one of Intel's main attributes is precision, the identity also needed to look man-made and not entirely organic.

Preliminary market research with audiences at the IT and consumer levels revealed that end users used words like *control, comfort,* and *independence.* The designers could see that their designs would be less about performance and more about the joys of personal freedom.

To convey these highly emotional feelings to their client early in the yearlong design process, the designers created a short video with the theme "harmonic motion." The video showed how users could move seamlessly through life and still have connection and control.

"We wanted to convey the notion of freedom and balance in life," notes Creson.

Intel agreed with this concept, and the Addis team got to work. The Centrino name had not yet been chosen, so the team worked with the code name "Banias" for much of the project. Not having the product name was certainly a handicap, says Creson, but it forced the designers to focus on the essentials of the brand, and not specifics such as a single letter or typestyle.

In their first set of explorations, the designers created pencil sketches that had a familial tie to the Pentium 4 and other Intel marks: a rectangular enclosure. However, they slanted the rectangle to suggest movement. At the other end of the experimental spectrum, circular designs were suggested. These designs were fluid, opposing the constraints presented by straight-edged shapes.

It became clear in early presentations that the client wanted to move beyond the rectangular shape. But because the mark would ultimately be reproduced at such tiny sizes, everyone agreed that a recognizable shape would be a must.

"We realized that form factors are getting smaller and smaller. This ID would have to work for five to ten years out. It needed to have a form that could be recognized even without a word attached to it. You should be able to look at it and recognize it immediately, like the golden arches or the Nike swoosh," Creson says.

The designers also explored the notion of personifying the technology in the form of a small character. This idea definitely gave the identity a human touch and had other advantages in merchandising possibilities, but, in the end, this approach was too radical for Intel.

"It was at this point that the idea of wings started to emerge," explains Creson.

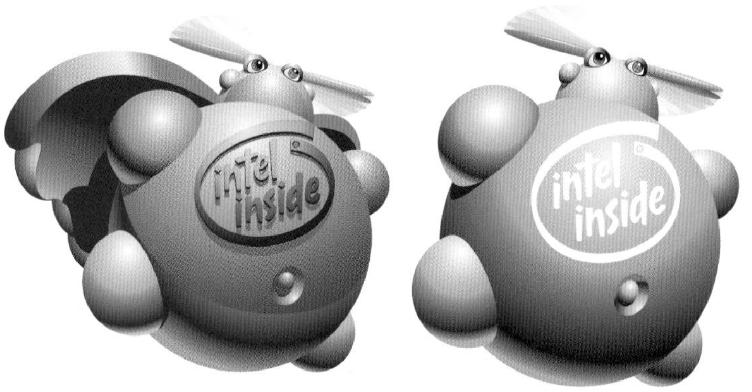

With these explorations, the designers sought to personify the brand. A cape and propeller beanie indicate the ability to fly; the rounded shape suggests a friendly personality. He is also in the style of Japanese anime characters. (Japan is a major market for Intel.)

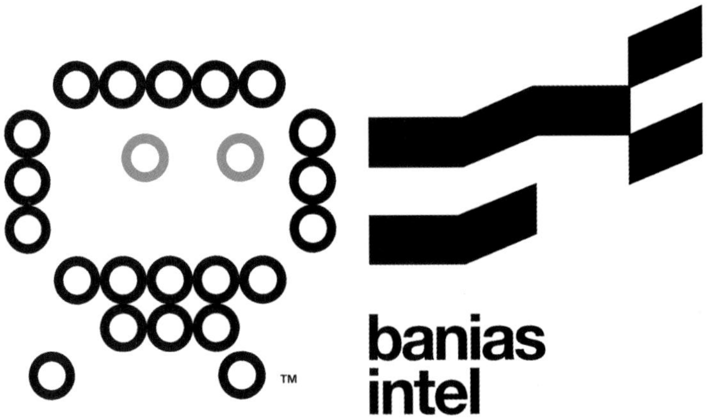

Here, the designers explored other ideas. Because the applications for the finished mark would only get smaller and smaller over the coming years, any shape the designers created needed to be well defined and identifiable at a glance. They were also trying to simplify forms as much as possible.

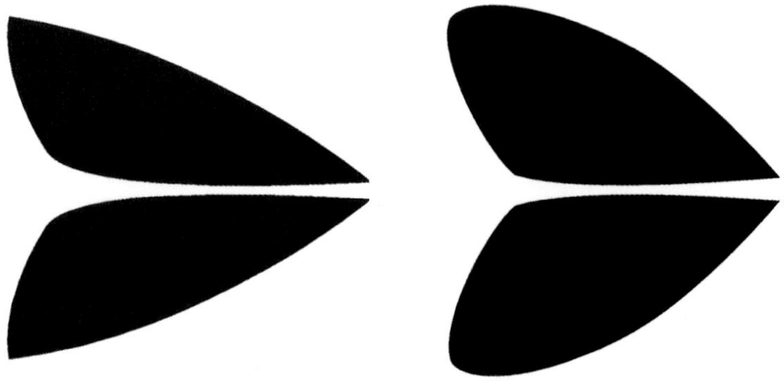

What followed was a lengthy exploration on the basic forms of wings. The designers wanted their designs to look organic yet still have the feel of something made by man. About sixty forms had been created at this point.

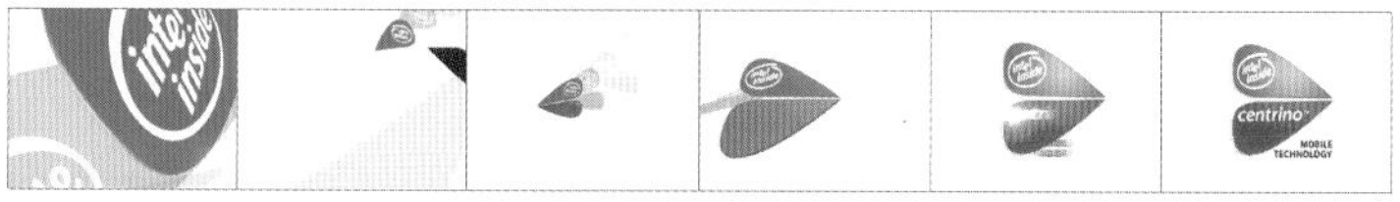

The final mark has become a very visible logo. It is a polite houseguest no matter where it lands, yet its color and shape make it stand out. It can even be animated when necessary. The designers believe that as people become more familiar with what Centrino is, the words *Mobile Technology* will eventually be removed from the mark.

Ultimately, the client and the design team kept coming back to the concept of wings.

Other experiments included a flaglike design that also suggested a landscape throughout which users might move. This trial was more about using the power of color to communicate emotion. Yet another design, which they dubbed "shimmer," used a pattern of dots that suggested a network of individuals coming together. It also suggested particles of air or information coming together.

Ultimately, the client and the design team kept coming back to the concept of wings. This approach commenced a huge series of shape explorations: What exactly are all the basic forms that can suggest the notion of wings? How could they balance the organic against something that looked man-made? How does one indicate precision in something that will for ever be changing, depending on the user's needs?

A simple pair of wings emerged as a promising form, but even this design was played out in more than sixty different trials over the period of a month. Once the perfect version had been selected, color was the next challenge. Partnering with Rockrise, the Addis team worked to develop a strong strategic and design rational for the color magenta.

"It is fashionable, energetic, and warm," says Creson. "It really was the color that fulfilled the design as a lifestyle brand." The Addis team eventually did convince the client of this direction.

The final design has strong, formal qualities but is still very warm and human. "I think we have achieved both flight and emotion for a logo that needs to be able to go anywhere technology goes," Creson says.

Archipelago
Naming and Identity Design

Addis, Berkeley, California

Archipelago was an investment group that sought to bring far-flung investors together. Its founders wanted to facilitate investment among different countries around the world, some of which were financially separated by culture, language, and even time zones. The monies were there, but investors needed an advocate to bring them together.

When the company was started, it did not have a name. Its organizers came to Addis for a name and complete identity. Principal Steven Addis and his team studied hundreds of names, carefully studying what Addis calls the "essence of the brand."

"We felt their essence was visionary, but they had a rational basis, too, of coming together and working together," he says.

The name Archipelago, meaning chain of islands, soon became the strongest direction. For this design, the designers broadened the meaning to consider the seven continents as a chain of islands that blanketed the earth. The metaphor of a chain was an effective one: The investment group wanted to connect people in different lands.

The designers searched for a way to express the same concept visually. They might have pushed all the continents back together into a massive, unwieldy, Pangaea-like land mass. Or, they might have tried to work with a conventional maplike arrangement of shapes. Instead, they found a more elegant solution: the designers assembled seven very stylized, abstracted continent shapes into the form of a swift, swimming sea turtle.

"The point of the design is if seven geographies can work together, they can form a stronger whole. We have all the continents coming together to form a new creature," Addis explains. He likes the design because it is a strong idea that integrates name and concept. "There is such a positive feeling about sea turtles. They live long, swim fast, and are friendly and intelligent. There were so many wonderful attributes that came along with a simple symbol."

The green turtle was rendered with white streaking on its body. The streaks suggest movement and give the shapes roughness and dimension. The animal has a more natural feel than if it were drawn in a solid manner. In some print applications, the logo was also embossed, again to give the animal form and stature. It is definitely an animate object.

The new mark and name garnered the company a great deal of attention in a field of competitors who had adopted largely high-tech, low-warmth identities.

"There was so much noise going on at the time. This identity had a story and a mission. People had something to talk about when they encountered it," Addis said.

ARCHIPELAGO
Greenwich Street
Francisco, CA
TEL

Design Firm **Design Guys**

Client **Target–Todd Oldham Product Line**

Project **Product Identity Redesign**

TODD OLDHAM
HOME [ROOM]

Creating identities for the retail market can be a bit like trying to stake a claim in quicksand: as soon as you get the flag posted, the ground starts to shift beneath your feet.

Such was definitely the case for Design Guys when the Minneapolis-based design firm created a new identity for the Todd Oldham line of goods that would be marketed through Target stores in the fall of 2003. The Oldham brand had already been in the stores the previous year when Target buyers and marketers decided that its original look was a bit too strong: They asked Design Guys to create a look that would be commensurate in visual strength with their revised numbers—the Oldham line would be only 30 percent of the back-to-school and dorm room goods on the shelves, as opposed to the 70 percent it held the first year.

The back-to-school market has emerged as a burgeoning category for Target, says Design Guys principal Steve Sikora. "Traditionally, it has been associated with grade- and high-school kids, but with products like those in the Todd Oldham line, it also relates to college kids and even people outfitting their first apartments," he says.

> "A designer is less likely to treat the work as precious if it's part of a larger process."

Because it is now such a meaningful category for the company, Target pays close attention to trends—which are subject to change at a moment's notice. When Design Guys started the identity design for the second year's design, it was still operating (at Target's direction) on the previous year's indicators.

"Originally, we were creating a retro, funky, '50s roadside motel look," Sikora recalls. The designers studied books on Las Vegas signage and motel marquees and tried to incorporate eclectic elements such as wood grain and neon.

"We kept working until we had something that was equal parts motel sign and logo. The creative director and upper management at Target were happy, but then the merchants changed their thinking. They felt it was much too strong and needed to be moderated," he says. "You have to get used to tectonic shifts like these in large organizations."

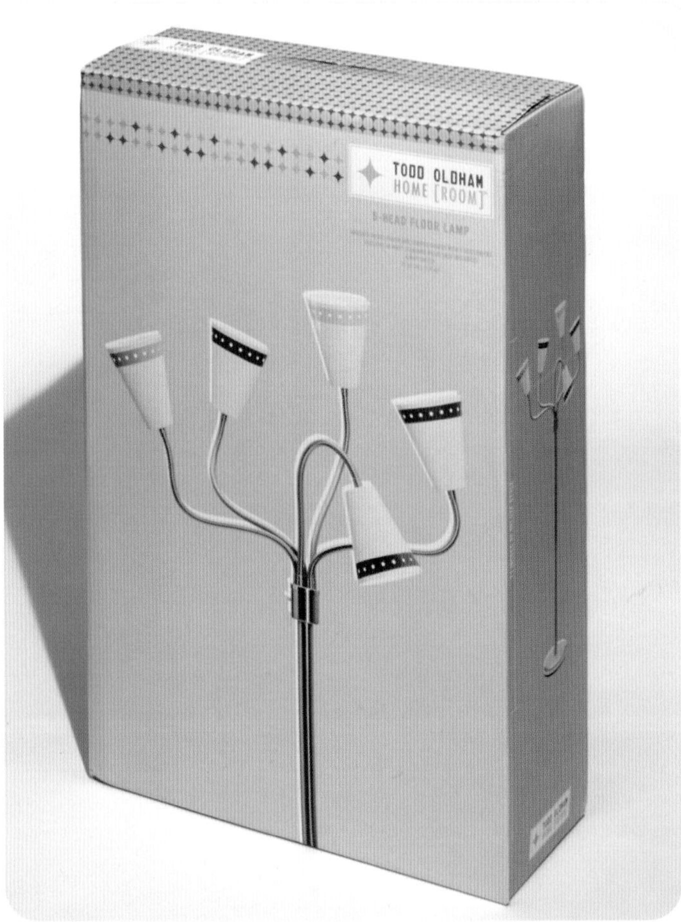

Although the Todd Oldham in-store identity for Target started its life with a retro flavor, it was toned back significantly by the designers at Design Guys (Minneapolis). The new identity shown here still has a flavor of the '50s, yet it is recessive enough to let the style of the decorating products show through.

Design Guys designers Kelly Munson and Anne Peterson developed a wide array of logo explorations for the Todd Oldham line. Influences included motel marquees and Las Vegas signage. These directions were well received by Target's creative director and upper management, but in-house merchants felt the designs were too strong. The design team had to return to square one.

The final iteration diminished the personality of the identity, thereby allowing the product to speak for itself and open the door to a slightly broader audience.

So the designers circled back to the start to rerun a race that still had to be completed in the allotted time frame. Sikora keeps his staff motivated in such instances by always having more than one person working on a project and assembling a spectrum of concepts that are all workable and practical and that can be mined deeply, if necessary.

"A designer is less likely to treat the work as precious if it's part of a larger process," he notes. "Once we have chosen a general direction, I want the designer's full personal investment in it. And we will fight for that idea, if it really is the best one."

So the design team began pulling away from the extreme retro look and experimented with marks that still had a period feel, yet were more generic. This approach was not an entirely bad thing, Sikora says, because a more neutral mark would not compete for attention with the products it would adorn, which, after all, had plenty of style already.

The broader approach also gave the designers some wiggle room. "While we are working, Todd is also working, so his colors and patterns are changing all the time," Sikora notes. "We needed to create an identity that could easily pick up his most current palette, whatever it turned out to be."

When Design Guys presented a second and more acceptable identity, the merchants pulled yet another switch: Now the Todd Oldham line would populate 50 percent of the shelf space in the category. This meant that Target's in-house brand, Room Essentials, would now occupy the remaining half of the shelves. This was relevant to Design Guys, because the firm was also creating the identity for that line.

The identity for Room Essentials was simpler to create than the Todd Oldham line because the Design Guys designers had far fewer people from which to gain approvals. But great care still had to be taken—as the low-price selection, Room Essentials had to avoid looking cheap.

"There is a real need in this market for the aesthetic to go where people don't feel they are buying something of low quality. They need to feel they are getting a good value," Sikora says.

The final identity elements were developed with the guidance of the Target creative manager, who met with the merchant staff on a regular basis. The final iteration diminished the personality of the identity, thereby allowing the product to speak for itself and open the door to a slightly broader audience.

The final design is decidedly tamer than the point at which the designers began, but it did meet the assignment by providing exactly what the client wanted.

Sikora says when combining creative issues with commerce, the latter often wins out. But that's a fact of life, he adds. A designer may never hit the target—or in this case, Target—dead on, but it's important to be as close as possible.

In addition to the final design for the Todd Oldham in-house line, Design Guys also created the logo for the Target line of back-to-school products that competed against the Todd Oldham products.

Jeune Lune
Identity Redesign

Design Guys, Minneapolis, Minnesota

Design Guys first started working with Theatre de la Jeune Lune in 1981, when the then-fledgling design firm and blossoming French/English theater were both becoming well recognized in the Minneapolis arts scene. In those days, the landscape was a much different place: It was still legal to post broadsheets and other promotional pieces in public places. For $1,000, the team would produce its one and only promotion of the year—a poster on newsprint that could be inserted in papers, handed out, or displayed around town. It was a modest but effective plan.

Over the years, things changed. The city forbade such postings. Other theaters and arts organizations in the area—all of whom competed for funds and patrons—were in the midst of multimillion-dollar building projects, increasing their local prominence. Jeune Lune would not be undertaking construction, although it had recently gone national and would be celebrating its twenty-fifth anniversary in 2003. It was time for a new identity to help the theater take a big step forward and let the public know about the heft and depth of its talent.

"Their original identity was an old-style engraving, and it was beautifully done," explains Design Guys principal Steve Sikora. "But it smacked of antiquity. Reproduction methods are really so much better now. We knew we could design something more sophisticated."

The theater's artistic director asked the design team to create something more cinematic, to match the performance style of the organization, with a clean, modern feel. All the design trials circled around images of the moon, whether it was an implication, such as a simple, solid circle, or a more defined moonlike shape, such as a crescent.

But the idea the client liked immediately was a dramatic photographic representation of the moon. Another suggestion from the designers was to shorten the theater name to simply "Jeune Lune," which was more memorable and easier for non-French speakers to confidently pronounce.

With the new identity in place, the client and designers actually returned to their roots for the twenty-fifth-season anniversary piece. They asked the printer who had originally printed the company's poster broadsheets to produce a double-wide broadsheet that unfolds to reveal the new identity and then the entire season.

The new mark reproduces beautifully, whether in tiny program ads or when projected onto the lobby wall, Sikora reports. And it's an unconventional and engaging mark for a theater that is just as unusual.

"We love their work," Sikora says. "Jeune Lune has always been a client that, for us, was not at all about the money but about doing good work in every sense of the word, just as they do."

Theatre de la Jeune Lune's original logo, created in the early 1980s to look as if it were engraved, definitely had a dated feel, not at all appropriate for a theater company that was about to literally take its shows on the road to national venues.

The new logo is dramatic, modern, and very simple. In addition, the name was shortened to make the mark more memorable and easy to pronounce.

Design Firm: **FutureBrand/Argentina**

Client: **Prestigio**

Project: **Corporate Identity Redesign**

Prestigio is a retail chain of about fifty paint stores located mainly in the Buenos Aires, Argentina, area that has a unique attraction for customers: with the help of some impressive-sounding equipment—a spectrophotometer and a tintometric machine—paint buyers can mix their own paints and get the exact color they want. It's a concept that has been popular with the metropolitan area's approximately twelve million inhabitants—so popular, in fact, that competitors quickly copied the system.

But Prestigio has other attractions. Unlike a traditional paint or hardware store that might be dirty and disorganized, its stores are well organized and offer excellent customer service. This fact alone makes the stores more attractive to female customers, a promising new customer base for the company.

Also, in 2001, Argentina was declared in default and its economy went into a nosedive. Many people's budgets then required them to stop eating out or shopping as much as they used to, and instead of throwing things out, they started to repair them.

"Home is now a refuge. Design is a boom [industry] here in Argentina, so Prestigio needed to be repositioned to be part of that design boom."

"Home is now a refuge. Design is a boom [industry] here in Argentina, so Prestigio needed to be repositioned to be part of that design boom," explains design director Julio Ferro of FutureBrand/Argentina, the design group that undertook the redesign.

Prestigio's old logo was based on multicolored arrows placed in different directions but always pointing up. This identity, which had been in use for about fifteen years, worked well on the façade of stores but not as well inside or on packaging and other print materials. The skyward orientation of the arrows was supposed to indicate excellence or superiority, but in truth, they weren't really unique enough as a symbolic device to single out Prestigio. In addition, the great numbers of colors used in the old identity confused consumers.

FutureBrand suggested a new brand proposition to its client: "Inspires the change." It was a position based on leadership, agreement, and attitude.

prestigio
Inspira el cambio

Prestigio, a chain of Argentinean paint stores, had its identity remade by FutureBrand/Argentina. What used to be simply a place to buy paint and supplies is now a place where property owners can make their decorating dreams come true.

prestigio pinturerías prestigio

Prestigio's old logo used upward-pointing arrows to suggest advancement and premier service. However, the arrows did not stand out in an urban environment and really said nothing about paint and its capabilities.

From left to right, the development of the new mark moved quickly into an entirely revamped space. After experimenting a bit with the old arrows, the designers explored prismlike or paint chip designs that suggested that Prestigio "owned" color. In later rounds, images such as flags and banners—which spoke of leadership—were studied. Finally, the pair of hands encircling color and also forming an eye was selected as not only visionary but also flexible enough to accommodate future Prestigio product expansion.

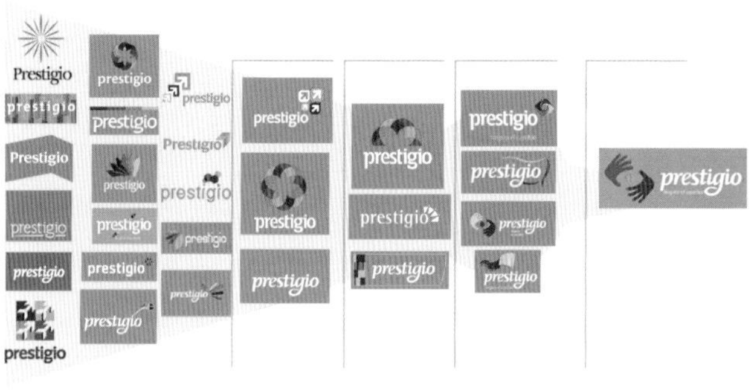

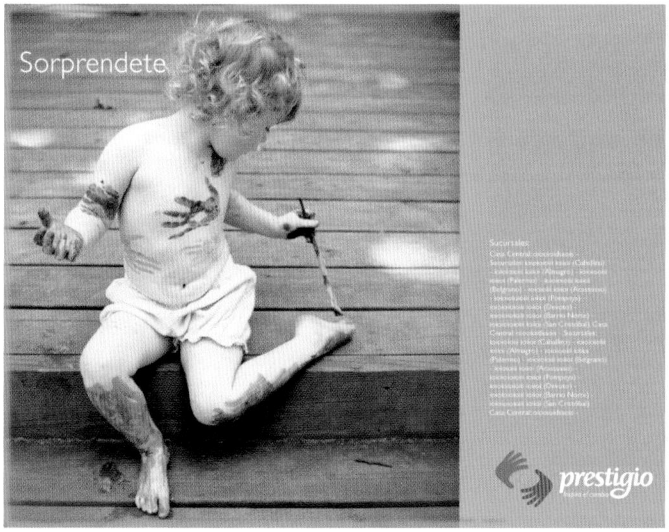

Because hands are such a common visual element, the designers were able to translate the logo or its components into photography, another hallmark of the identity system.

The public already saw Prestigio as the leader in bringing change in the form of color to customers' lives, so it needed a visual representation of that status. The new positioning statement also did not refer to paint, which opened up future product offerings and marketing opportunities.

The FutureBrand design team began by trying to work with the arrow concept. But ultimately, this approach was regarded to be a facelift and not the seismic shift in identity the client required. So the designers began searching for other solutions to illustrate that Prestigio was the owner of color. Some of these designs were prismlike, whereas others suggested flowers or paint chips. Unfortunately, these ideas didn't go far beyond the basic and preconceived notion of what a paint store might be. Prestigio needed to be more than that.

Therefore, the explorations moved into a realm of other symbols, including flags and ribbons. This new set of imagery spoke more clearly of leadership and agreement. One design from this group introduced a new concept: vision. This design featured two hands encircling a colored dot. The negative space inside the hands forms an eye. It nicely symbolizes the vision Prestigio has for its business and creative concepts. The new tagline, "Inspires the change," further empowers the customer.

Orange was selected as the institutional color, but it essentially also acts as another symbol in the system. It is an energetic color born from the combination of the two hottest primary colors: red lends strength and warmth, and yellow adds the association of the sun, life, and light (without which color would not exist). The color stands out well in an urban environment and is a beautiful complement to the blue sky above. It also works well as a backdrop color inside of the stores and as the base color for signage, vehicles, print applications, and the company's website.

"Orange as a symbol works," says Ferro. "People started to recognize the refurbished stores in a snap."

Another addition to the identity system was photography of people, meant to inspire a warm, comforting sense. Including photos as a main element also means that the overall system can be updated periodically, for reason or season.

The result of the redesign is that Prestigio has been transformed from a mere paint store to a more sophisticated shopping environment, more in the decorating world than in the hardware world. More and more female shoppers, who are far more likely to redecorate and paint at more frequent intervals, have been attracted.

The logo solution works well, says Ferro, because it sparks the imagination. "The solution of the hands forming the frame was an idea that can be extended to the gesture of imagining a new space," he adds.

The hand/eye logo is easily translatable into patterns or art.

(Opposite, Top; Bottom Right) Orange was selected as the corporate color and as an integral part of the identity. It worked equally well inside and outside the Prestigio stores.

LanChile
Identity Redesign

FutureBrand, Buenos Aries, Argentina

LanChile is one of the rare success stories in the airline industry, a business plagued with structural challenges and constant reorganizations. In the late 1990s, the airline sought to become Latin America's leading regional carrier and one of the world's top ten airlines.

To help it toward that goal, FutureBrand created a new identity for LanChile, which helped to establish it as a world-class airline. In fact, the design was so successful that it was later extended to the company's other operational brands: LanPeru, LanEcuador, LanDominicana, LanExpress, and LanCargo. The company had grown substantially—in its geographical footprint, in its coverage, and in its goal of consistently superior service.

In 2003, LanChile managers challenged FutureBrand to create a new regional brand that would signal the airline's achievements and aspirations. The recommendation was to launch a network brand, LAN, which stands for Latin American Airline Network (but which originally stood for Lineas Aereas Nacionales).

"The challenge was to create a logo that satisfied various needs. In Chile, the origin country for the company, it had to be perceived as an evolution of the LanChile brand, still reflecting national pride," says Gustavo Koniszczer, managing director of FutureBrand, Southern Cone. "In neighboring countries, it would have to convey regional coverage and not be too 'Chilean' in its content."

All the design explorations centered around the star, which was a main component of the previous identity. The shape is also an almost universal symbol of quality.

The new aircraft livery proudly showcases the star on the tail. A sweeping curve over the fuselage visually connects it to the bold LAN logotype at the front. The new identity will also be featured across all passenger items and corporate communications. The new tag line, which translates to "A Marvel in Flight," builds upon the airline's core positioning attributes of reliability and enchantment.

The identity is definitely more modern, says Koniszczer, and it clearly supports the previously established brand architecture.

LAN
CC-CEK

Design Firm: **A & Company**

Client: **Total**

Project: **Corporate Identity**

When the petrol companies Total and Fina combined forces in 1999 and then were joined by Elf in 2000, the triad created a formidable union. The new company—which adopted the name TotalFinaElf in 2000, shortened to just Total in 2003—could claim an amazing 14,700 stations around the world. But despite its far-flung geographical presence, the new company needed help with its identity.

None of the original companies had a brand identity that was worth saving, nor did the new management team want to maintain any of the former identities. Elf's original logo was somewhat contemporary but awkward. Fina's logo felt unremarkable and dated, whereas the old Total logo was more powerful but still behind the times.

A & Company, Paris, was selected to create a logo for the new team and its thousands of stations. Laurent Vincenti, design manager at A & Company, describes the design problem: "The main goals of the new identity were to give a new brand image to the new group, reposition the group to a new brand image with new value, and to give a sense of movement to the identity that expresses the group's mission to be a worldwide energy provider. Total has always been concerned about its responsibilities to the environment and to human beings."

A & Company designers considered several distinct directions in their early designs. Some trials explored the control of energy, whereas others were more based on earth or energy imagery. But the direction that was ultimately selected was one Vincenti calls "multi-energy," symbolic not only of the many ways the company served the consumer but also of the new union.

Beyond technical commitments to reproduction issues, Vincenti believes that to be successful, this and any other logo project must meet the following parameters:

- It must restore the image and the position of the brand for the consumer that the company itself set as the strategic target.
- It must be appreciated by the maximum number of customers.
- It must deliver a big impact with its history. The more stories a brand can tell, the more it is liked by consumers and is engraved into their memories.
- It must represent a global style that is easily translatable to the brand.
- It must readily become a new flag for the company. Different mergers of firms need to be able to regroup themselves around a common flag.

Total's new logo meets these goals, Vincenti says. It is formed by three intertwined and curving shapes that form a globe. Its colors were selected

The merger of three major European oil companies—Fina, Elf, and Total—necessitated a new brand identity for the organization, also named Total. Three curving, swooping lines form a globe, representing the joining of the three companies but also create an easily animated, three-dimensional form that works equally well as flat art or a sculpture.

The logos of the three separate companies were dated and uninspiring. The client did not ask A & Company to preserve any of the aspects of these marks. Still, the new identity would have to be something around which all employees worldwide—now all on the same team—could rally.

The wordmark was designed to have enough personality to stand on its own when necessary, without the logo.

The new logo is built from three pieces: a light blue swoop that represents air, a dark blue curve that symbolizes water, and a red curve that represents Earth. Together they form a synergistic globe that speaks of energy, the merging of cultures, and cooperation.

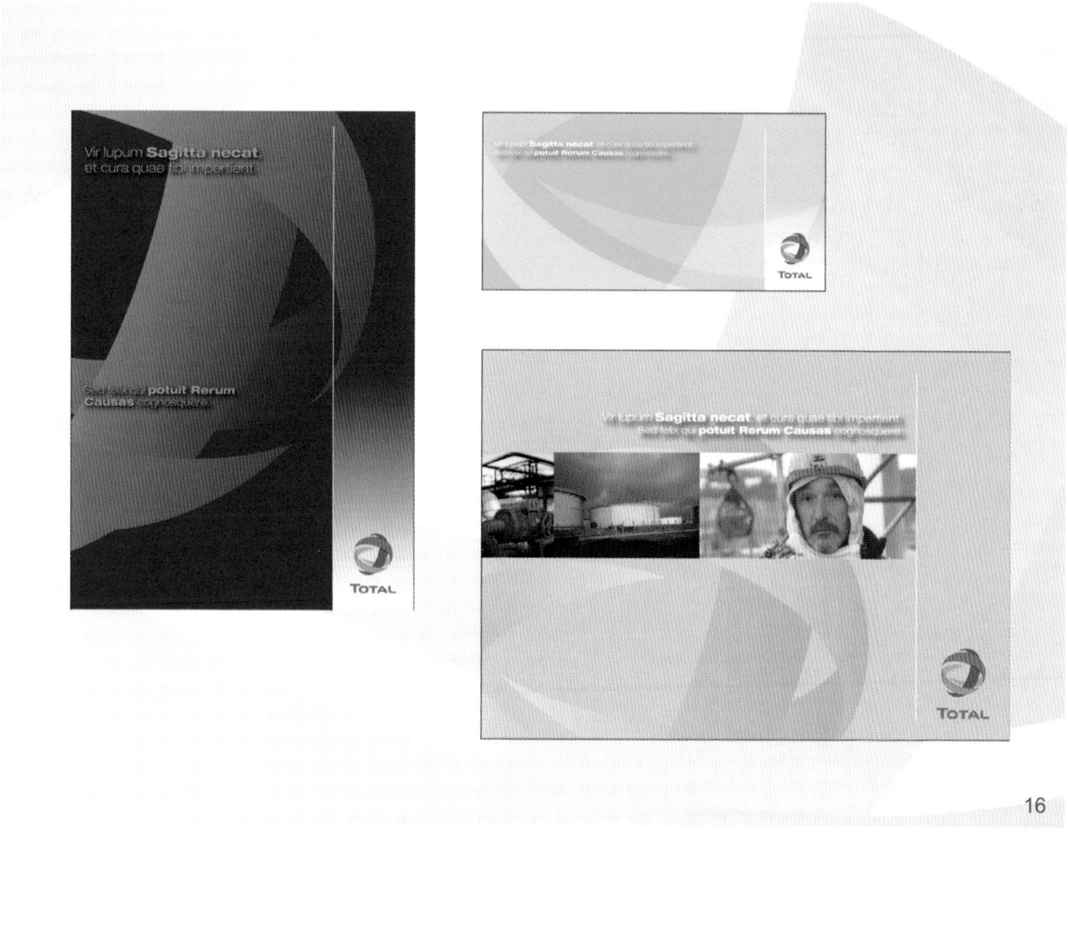

Note how the logo can be abstracted as an art or background element for collateral designs.

TotalFinaElf était l'addition des énergies de trois grandes sociétés. Trois sociétés ayant les mêmes aspirations et les mêmes objectifs.
Quand on est trois à faire le même métier, on a envie de faire partie de la même famille. Alors on prend le même nom.
Ces trois sociétés forment maintenant une seule et même famille avec un seul et même nom. Et comme toutes les additions, la nôtre a aussi un total : c'est Total.
TOTAL

The triad aspect of the new company has been played up in Total's advertising.

> A good logo must represent a global style that must be easily translatable to the brand.

to represent the elements of natural energy: dark blue for water, light blue for air, and red for the earth. Several of the curves reveal their inner sides in an even brighter color—yellow—which demonstrates that energy is at the core of the identity and of the business.

"[The colors] also show the diversity of the cultures [of Elf, Fina, and Total] that are crossing. The form actually represents many things," Vincenti says, "the earth by the sphere, and energy by the different curves. In the movement are mobility and the dynamism of progress. The fusing of the shapes displays the complexity of the world. The crossing lines symbolize exchanges and synergies between peoples, and the colors represent the diversity of cultures."

Because of its three-dimensionality, the new logo also animates quite naturally. The curving lines swoop around its suggested volume, crossing and recrossing. Vincenti says their circular movement is like an elegant waltz of energy. But the mark can also work as a sculpture and exist in real space, a quiet piece of art that can be appreciated just for its shape.

New typography was created for the project—an entirely new alphabet is now available to the client. The new letterforms are designed with curves reminiscent of the new logo: they feel steady and powerful. The wordmark was designed to have enough personality to stand on its own when necessary, without the logo.

At this writing, the new identity is being rolled out worldwide, and Vincenti has confidence in its success. Qualitative tests of the mark show that recognition rates of the new Total logo is 19 percent higher than any competing oil company and 38 percent higher than the old brand image of Total.

"The new logo is large in imagination and power. Consumers have become attached to it," he says. Just as important, the design has turned into the rallying flag for the company's employees, unifying personnel from three very different companies. "It is being welcomed with enthusiasm by 120,000 employees. The new brand is felt as a new race, a new departure for the company."

In application, the new Total logo is dynamic as well as practical. Note the new typeface that was created for the project. The client now has a complete alphabet at its disposal for future designs.

The design has turned into the rallying flag for the company's employees, unifying personnel from three very different companies.

BNP Paribas
Identity Design

A & Company, Paris, France

BNP Paribas is a bank with global reach. It has three core competencies: corporate and investment banking, retail banking, and asset management. The company as it exists today is a merger of two separate banking houses, former competitors BNP (which can trace its origins back to 1848) and Paribas (created in 1872). So, the new company has a long history of serving private and public investors as a solid, staid entity.

Therefore, in 2000, when its management decided it was time for a major identity overhaul, it was a significant event. Five large identity firms, which together submitted more than 100 design proposals, competed for the prize assignment. The winner was A & Company, of Paris, who created what is now known as the "taking flight" logo.

The company's design is appropriate on many levels. The client had asked the designers to heighten its visibility, which A & Company took literally with its ascending star design. The design also had to suggest the values of innovation and dynamism and express an international reach.

The new design does all these things and more. It evokes the stars on the European flag as well as the image of a swallow, a bird that migrates vast distances, suggesting freedom and movement. The design is certainly dynamic with its forward-moving trajectory. At the center of the logo is a suggested globe. The bird spans the globe, flying seemingly even beyond the Earth's stratosphere.

For color, A & Company designers chose green because they felt it evoked the power of imagination in creating an entirely new bank. Green is also traditionally symbolic of hope and knowledge, as well as of transparency and concern for the environment.

BNP PARIBAS

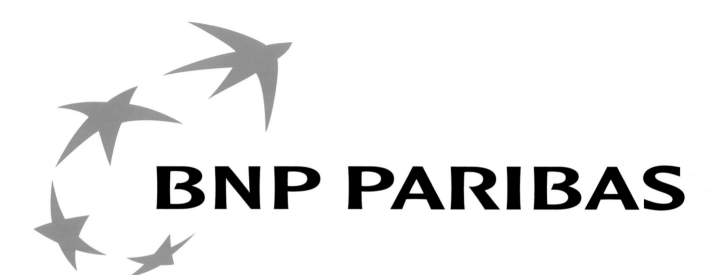

Design Firm | **Thomas Manss Design**

Client | **Atlantic Electric and Gas**

Project | **Corporate Identity**

After utilities were deregulated in the United Kingdom in 1990, a whole crop of small, young, and enthusiastic electric and gas companies sprang up—and just as quickly went away. Although many had managed to attract a number of customers who had tired of larger, corporate suppliers, the new companies just did not have the economies of scale they needed to compete effectively. Billing, customer service, and other business-to-consumer systems weren't in place to make long-term relationships possible.

This was the climate into which Atlantic Electric and Gas was born. Established by the American utility Sempra, Atlantic perhaps had a greater degree of financial backing than smaller competitors did. But time had shown that more than that would be needed. In such a complex and changeable market, it was imperative that the new company have the appearance of an established business, of being a large, stable, and financially sound organization, and one that conceivably had been around for twenty years or more.

> "Competitors include British Gas and Petroleum, London Energy, PowerGen, and Enpower—all large companies. It was important to appear to be on par with them."

Thomas Manss Design, of London and Berlin, was tapped to create the new company's identity and introduction. Clear in Atlantic's brief was the need to create a brand that was portable. Atlantic was not simply about selling electricity and gas but also about creating a brand through which a whole portfolio of products and services could potentially be offered. The company name was chosen for its American connection and suggestion of great size.

Manss explains: "Competitors include British Gas and Petroleum, London Energy, PowerGen, and Enpower—all large companies. It was important to appear to be on par with them."

Jeffrey Percival, the CEO of Atlantic, took it upon himself to guide the entire process—a somewhat unusual move, according to Manss. "Often, the job of steering the development of a new identity is delegated to a separate department, so this was a refreshing change," he says.

The new Atlantic Electric logo is very graphic and demands that the viewer get involved with the design. After some period of study, it becomes apparent that the capital letter *E* is also a lowercase *a.*

"A new identity has two tasks: It should plant a visual seed in the minds of customers, and it should weld together employees and give them something to which to aspire."

Manss's office customarily works quite closely with its client contacts. "There is no six to eight weeks of secret work, followed by lots of logos pasted onto black boards and presented to put sand in the eyes of the client. Our client saw everything we did, even initial ideas. This is a very satisfying and successful way of getting involved with a client—certainly better than just working from a brief," the designer says.

Manss and Percival started by taking a fresh look at how gas and electricity are sold to customers. Instead of spending lots of money on a huge ad campaign, the decision was made to sell direct to customers through a website and through teams of salespeople. Service was stressed, as was ease of sign-up.

Another possible attribute of the company that could have been stressed was price. With deregulation came a host of websites in which utilities customers could price-shop. Atlantic was competing against many of the old monopoly companies, who had large bureaucratic pricing systems in place. Atlantic, on the other hand, although having a markup on its services, still managed to be more competitive in its pricing.

But, as Manss points out, it is unwise if not impossible to relate a company's full list of attributes through a logo. He and his team decided to concentrate on what product the company offered and the manner in which the product was provided.

"If you had a brief asking you to create a logo for the Ten Commandments, you could never do justice to every commandment. Just showing two aspects of Atlantic would be challenging enough," he says.

Manss and his designers discussed three principal ways to brand the company: through a pictorial symbol, with a monogram, or by using a logotype. Quite quickly, the monogram was selected as the best approach. "A logo would have been clear and direct, but it could lack impact," Manss explains. "A pictorial symbol is much more suited to high visibility ad campaigns, where customer recognition and a process of learning are key."

Although some pictorial explorations were tried for the new logo, Manss designers quickly concluded that a monogram of the letters *A* and *E* would work best for this assignment. They wanted to turn the letters into art but still allow them to be readable as characters.

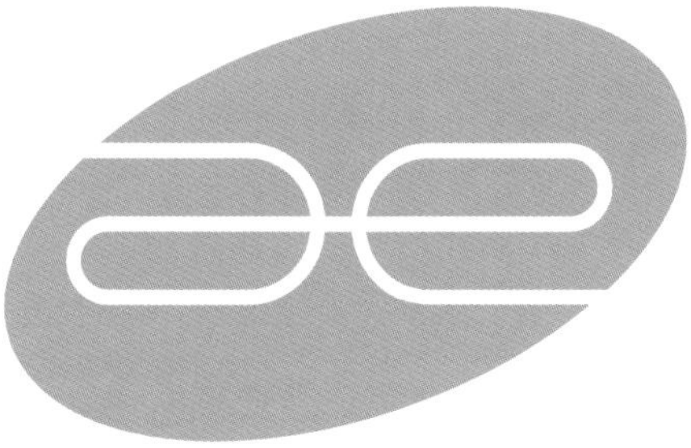

By allowing the client to take a meaningful part in and witness the design process, he or she understands how design can make a real difference in the success or failure of his or her company.

"If we had gone the route of using a pictorial symbol, we also would have had to include the name of the company for people to relate to, which could have been difficult in the design. The concern was that people may not ever have enough exposure to the symbol to make the connection to the company," the designer says.

The best balance of impact and ease of recognition would be the monogram, the team decided. A monogram has the advantage of potentially being adapted to new industry sectors, crucial in the company's plans for expansion.

On the shortlist were two particular monograms—one friendlier and cuddlier, and one that looked more established. Ultimately, the more established look was chosen. This monogram provided the most fundamental message that needed to be conveyed in a market punctuated with mergers and acquisitions.

The response to the new design was very positive, not only with customers. The new identity also had great effect in uniting the employees of Atlantic.

"A new identity has two tasks: It should plant a visual seed in the minds of customers, and it should weld together employees and give them something toward which to aspire," Manss says. "Inside Atlantic, this seems to be working. The identity has helped them bring together a strong internal team."

Working with a client right in the office during creative sessions might seem on the surface somewhat onerous, but Manss believes it is the surest way to score a successful outcome for everyone involved. His offices may have two or three clients physically on the premises, directly involved with the design process.

"Most people would find this to be a nightmare. You have to have a lot of confidence. They can see directly how we respond to their input. We can sense any insecurities they might have. And decisions can be made quickly, which has an effect on cost," Manss says. So many clients think designers are style merchants, he adds. By allowing the client to take a meaningful part in and witness the design process, he or she understands how design can make a real difference in the success or failure of his or her company. For the designer, such relationships inspire loyalty and repeat business.

"Even ten years after we have created an identity for a company, they will usually come back because they like the way we work. We give them something they can own. They won't have to exchange it for something else, something new in three years. That may be a good way to drum up new business for a design firm, but it doesn't inspire loyalty."

This design, like the final, also effectively combines the two letters, but it is a bit more "cuddly," says Thomas Manss. Although this was an appropriate design in that it was an effective counterpoint to the more cold, corporate utilities companies that already existed, the design team decided that a more staid look would work better.

The new logo is still friendly, but it has an established, strong feel that plays out well in almost any application. It works both with the Atlantic name or without it.

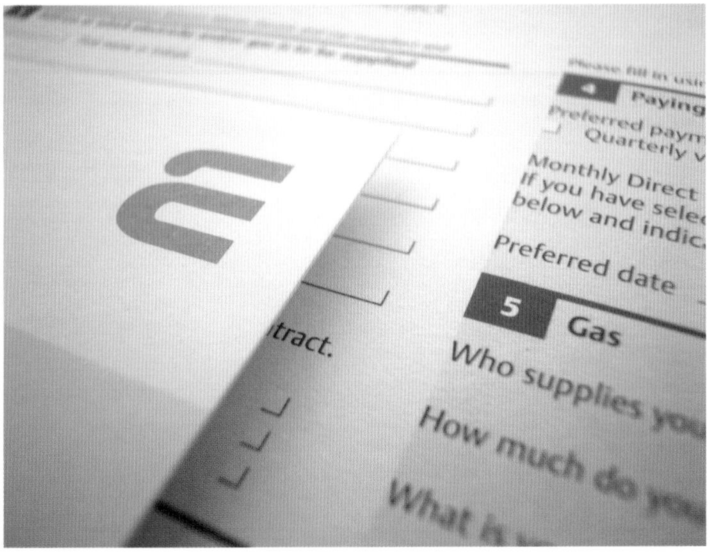

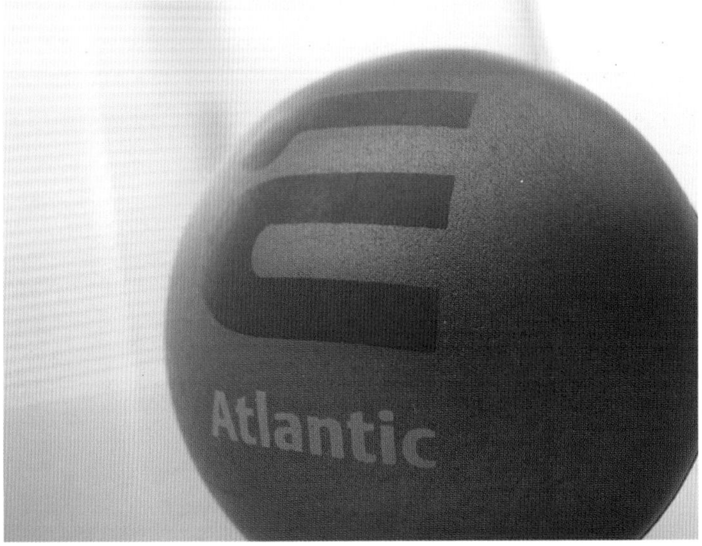

Berlin Brandenburg Express Identity Design

Thomas Manss Design, London, United Kingdom

Thomas Manss Design landed a notable and very visible public transportation project by inspiring the same type of client loyalty he describes in the main feature article on Atlantic Electric.

After establishing a close relationship with a client a decade ago, and after that client made several impressive career moves, Manss was called on again, this time as a member of a task force setting up a new regional railway company.

The Berlin Brandenburg Express needed a new identity, as well as absolutely everything else the line would need—stationery, collateral, signage, even the design for the trains. It was a project that was wide in scope but tight in parameter.

"I have never designed anything with a brief as tight as this. The new design had to be somehow related to other marks already in the family, but it couldn't be yellow, red, or blue. It had to be a monogram based on the letters *BBX*, and, like its mother company BVG, the monogram had to be placed in the bottom of a square," Manss says.

Even given these restrictions, Manss designers found a way to make the BBX logo unique—they turned the X into two facing arrows that suggested movement, speed, and the bidirectional nature of the line. But the symbol within the symbol also had another use—as art.

Even more visible than a logo in this identity system would be the trains themselves. What better way to make an impression than with very large vehicles traveling at high speeds?

"We wanted to make sure no one missed these trains. But we were not in favor of just painting them one color and putting on some 'go faster' stripes," Manss says.

Instead, his designers applied the arrow-X image to the trains in a bold, abstract pattern that is unusual and eye-catching. The pattern can also be played out on signage and print designs. A number of color variations were tried, but in the end, purple was selected for the first line. (Other colors may be selected for other lines, but they will use the same pattern.) The train is not just painted—it now appears to be a single object. Every surface is covered.

At the time of this writing, Manss was waiting for the designs to be implemented on the first line. "The Heather line runs through flat countryside where there is a lot of heather, so the color is appropriate. But a train that runs through a harsh industrial area might be bright yellow or orange. What will be common to all the designs is the treating of the whole train as a single object," Manss explains.

Sehenswertes an der
Für Fahrten ins Blaue
BBX
BBX
BBX

Groß Schönebeck
BBX
BBX
VBB
VT 005

Design Firm **Enterprise IG**

Client **Syspro**

Project **Identity Redesign**

What can be a positive attribute can also make designing a client identity difficult. Kay Nash, group managing director of Africa and the Middle East for Enterprise IG, says that was certainly the case for her firm's experience with Syspro, a software manufacturing company.

Syspro, which designs software that creates automated systems infrastructure for mid-size companies, began as a small, owner-managed company. By 2002, it found itself with offices around the world, each office being run with the same entrepreneurial spirit that the company founder possessed.

"This is a tenacious, intrepid, resourceful group of people," Nash says. "The company is one of the very few that has survived Microsoft and its products, so you know they are enterprising."

This tenacious spirit initially looked as though it might cause Nash and her design team problems: Everyone had a very different idea of what the new identity should be, and no one's vision was particularly risk-taking. The company's old identity in no way reflected its business culture, attitude, approach, or product. Enterprise IG felt it should be banished in lieu of a more appropriate and comprehensive identity system. Syspro managers were feeling differently. They wanted a new logo that felt familiar—period.

> "It is important to be on target but also to show the client dramatic directions—solutions that are relevant but that scare them."

After extensive research and interviews, Nash's team defined the brand essence in a single word—tenacious. This trait can be either positive or negative. Enterprise IG decided to take it into a positive realm: The client could be vigorous, strong, and enduring, but it could also be flexible and contemporary.

The first thing to overcome was the preexisting corporate culture and the restrictions each business unit threw in front of the project. United States team members wanted the company to stick with its U.S. product name, Impact. From the United Kingdom came the request that the identity be blue. In Africa, it had to be red.

SYSPRO

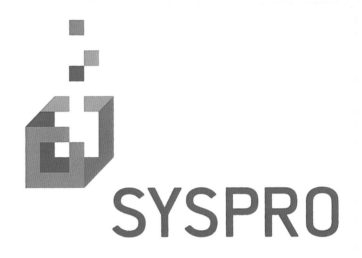

This static representation of Syspro's new logo, created by Enterprise IG, actually does not show how versatile the mark is. This is just a starting point for the new identity. Its pieces and colors present Syspro offices around the world with a tool kit with which each can form its own mark. Also, in electronic representation, the logo might unfold and/or rebuild itself.

SYSPRO 01

SYSPRO 01

SYSPRO 01

Enterprise IG designers presented a number of diverse experiments to push the client out of its comfort zone. But this simple, solid, sans serif experiment was probably the most comfortable and familiar to the client.

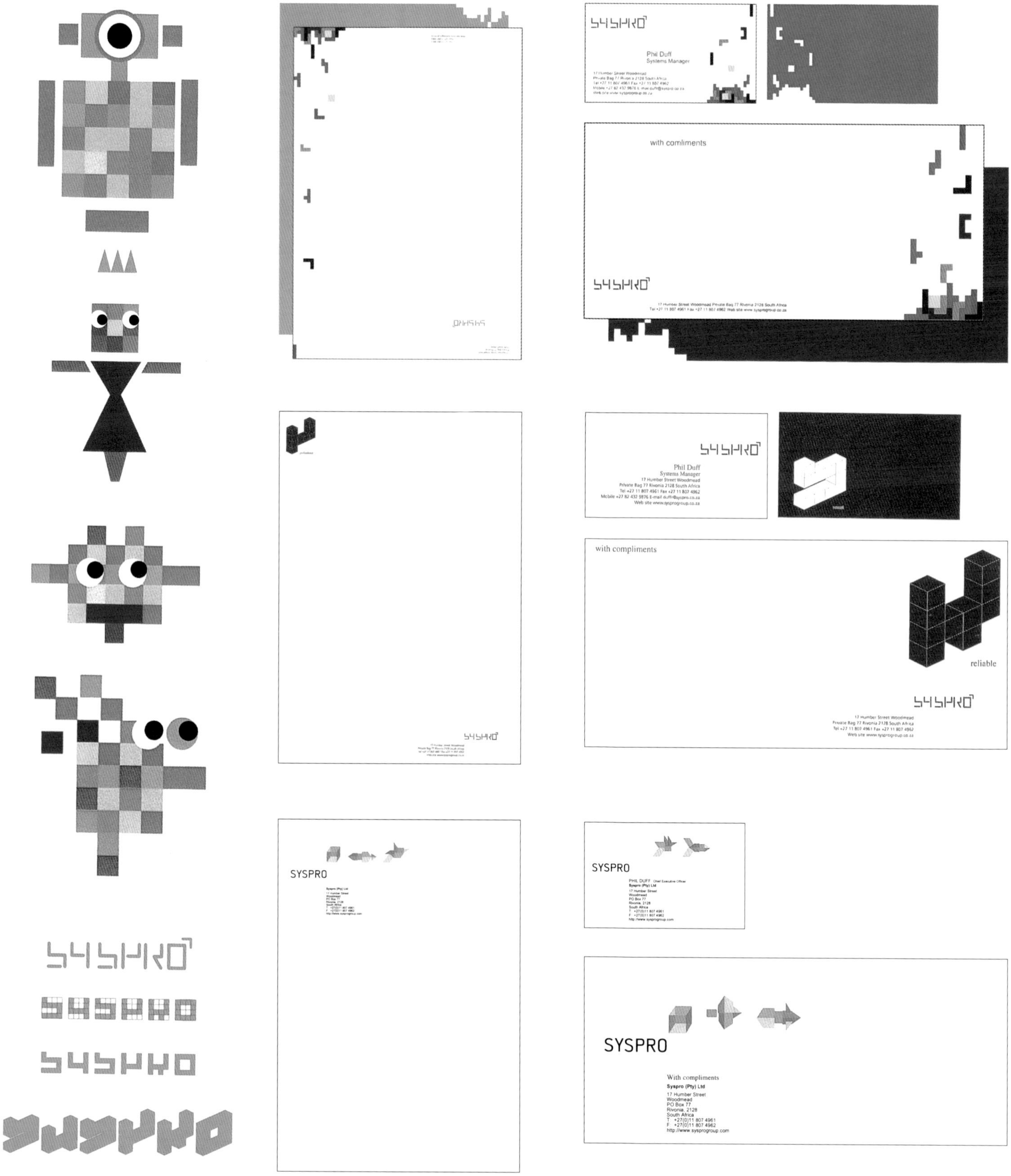

These designs represent the far-opposite end of the experimentation for the project. They were meant to fully terrify the client but also to stretch their imagination and vision. Built from pixels and parts, this approach suggested that the final logo might be a changeable thing, rebuilt for each occasion as necessary.

"There were hundreds of restrictions. We needed to listen to them, but we had to define some bombproof criteria against which the new identity could be judged around the world, or we would never get consensus. Their in-house design advisors had tried other design options before and had never been able to create the identity. So, the most important thing was to define and agree on the criteria that would guide the designers," Nash says.

The criteria that were eventually defined were:

- The new identity had to be indicative of an open organization.
- Syspro had to feel approachable, unlike, say, IBM, but it also had to feel like a professional, world-class organization.
- The new design had to signal a different way for the company to conduct business—that is, to be more flexible and agile. This signal would not be just for customers but for internal staff as well.
- The new identity had to be smart, which Nash defines as dynamic and intelligent.
- Finally, the new identity had to show that Syspro could compete as a leader in its market.

With Nash providing extensive information and running interference for the designers—to protect them from exhausting meetings and endless protests that could suck the life out of any intelligent solutions they might devise—Enterprise IG designers created a wide range of possible solutions, from conservative to over the top.

"When we design, the strategists work with the designers to determine how far the design should go along the revolution scale," explains Nash. "We create conservative options but also provide terrifying and ridiculous options. It is important to be on target but also to show the client dramatic directions—solutions that are relevant but that scare them."

The psychology behind this approach makes sense. The designers want the client to open up and take more risks. If they show how wide that risk window is and can stretch their vision, the client will be more likely to select something that is closer to the risk end than the middle: the possibilities excite their imagination.

"We have three design teams, and we ask them to push different buttons. The first team was asked to focus on producing a small, evolutionary change and draw on the stable, reliable aspect of the brand proposition. The second team focused on challenging the client's vision. They would leverage the flexible and innovative aspects of the business—this would be a real revolution. The third team balanced all the design criteria," Nash explains. Her office calls this a kinetic identity process.

For this project, the conservative direction felt safe and familiar to the client, but it proved not risk-taking enough. Solid and simple, it had a digital feel that also suggested the building blocks of manufacturing. However, the design just didn't have the legs to grow, despite the comfort the client found in it.

At the other extreme was a collection of little characters that were built from pixels or boxes. From this approach grew another approach—origami-like constructions that were endlessly changeable. Various offices could produce their own forms, using the same toolkit of shapes and colors. This design was too far out for the client, but it also suggested a new direction that informed subsequent explorations: interactivity. "What if the logo itself were interactive?" the designers wondered. A customer might click on a website version of the logo, and the logo would unfold, refold, and change. The logo could also be made into a game, a pattern, or other formats that would engage and challenge the viewer.

Designs based on boxes, which suggest manufacturing, were between the two extreme directions. Some of these were origami-like, and others were more like unfolded box patterns. All were colorful and progressive; all connoted flexibility and approachability.

The final design represents a box made from pixels. This direction emerged from a meeting with the client during which the group played with a tangram game.

"The client could actually break a box into pieces and move the pieces around. This was a critical juncture for them. We could move away from a simple box. Maybe every country could have its own box. The pixels would be a bit like Lego pieces. We might tell them they could only play with Legos, but they could still build a lot of things with that," says Nash.

This final approach was the one that was eventually selected. The new logo is endlessly changeable—it can be printed in different configurations on paper applications, and it can be animated and interactive in electronic venues. For instance, a viewer can click on the logo, and it unpacks or repacks itself.

The new logo and identity is a tailored fit for the client. It is smart, approachable, agile, competitive, and certainly indicative of the company's business. Like software, it also grows smarter the more the identity is used. Nash gives plenty of credit to her designers and also to the client.

"The designers were courageous: they just kept trying different routes and having fun with it. They lived this project for six months," she explains. The client was equally brave. "They were inexperienced and fragmented, yet they were very courageous. We wanted them to become braver and braver, not furnish them with a solution that would allow them to sneak back into a little box later. The more they have used the logo, the bolder they have become."

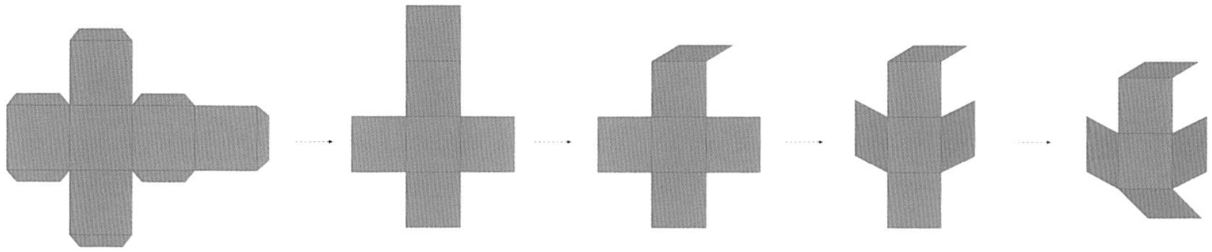

This was another kinetic design. The box was meant to represent the manufacturing process; it would fold and unfold in different manifestations.

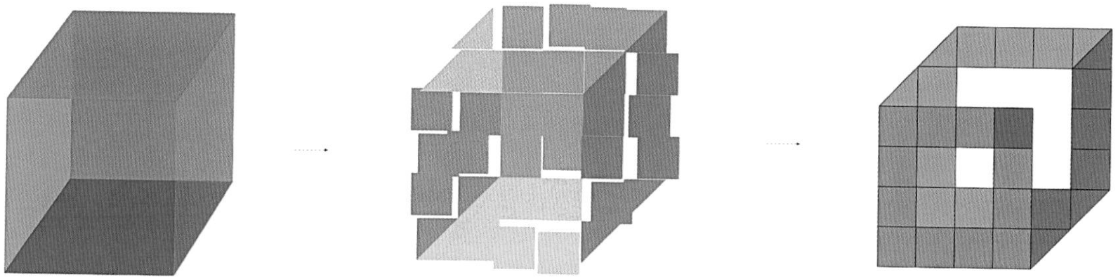

Here, the box is built from pixels, which also suggest the building blocks of manufacturing.

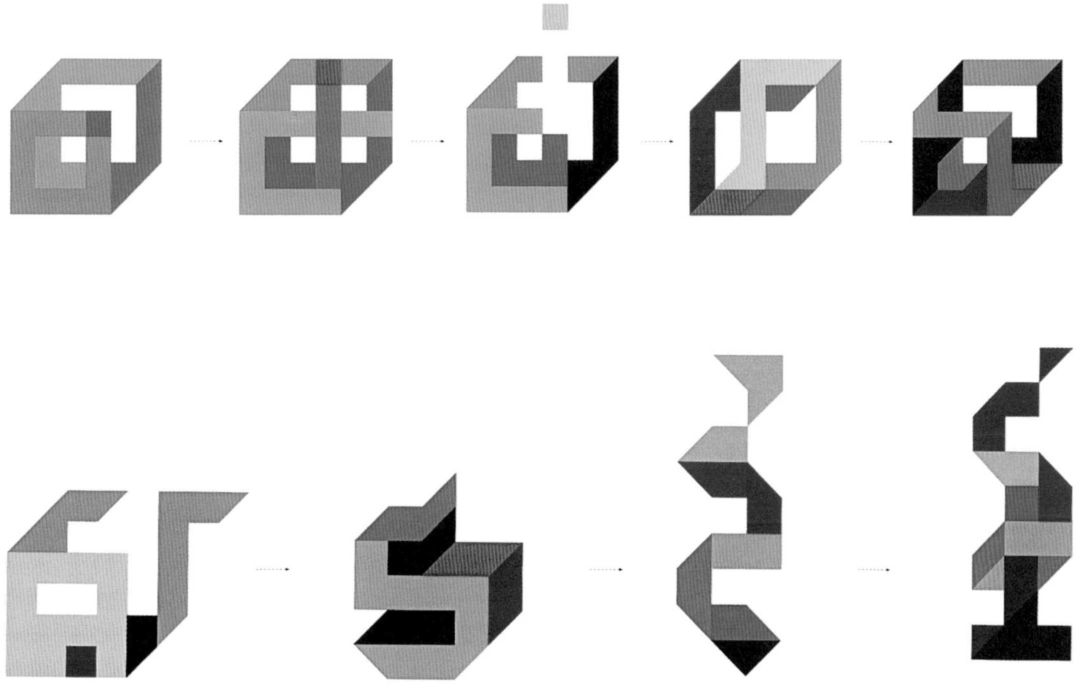

This box could be brought to life, assembled and reassembled like a tangram game. The blocks could be used to create any number of shapes, forms, or even characters. This design would encourage interaction, not just by Syspro employees, but by their clients as well. The creative license to craft a personalized logo was especially important to the many Syspro offices, each of which was highly entrepreneurial.

Sunesi
Identity Design

Enterprise IG, Johannesburg, South Africa

Sunesi was originally a company called Medixx, a start-up whose product digitized data for medical professionals. The product was unique and decidedly beneficial. It had overcome many of the failings of analog data entry and allowed medical institutions, or even patients, to have access to health files anywhere around the world.

But the company's previous identity and name said nothing about these advantages. In fact, it was quite faceless. "The old identity had no personality in terms of what a brand needs to do," explains Robert du Toit, creative director for Enterprise IG's Middle East and Africa regions. "We offered to kill quite a few holy cows with a new identity."

Enterprise IG was also quite involved with the industrial design of the product itself, which captures everything from heart rate to hearing. The equipment could not be offensive or frightening to the patient. Instead, it needed to instill confidence and look friendly. The new identity had to have the same nature.

"We had to concentrate on the consumer, not the product. What emerged had to be something to which the consumer could relate," du Toit adds.

His solution combines two ancient symbols—the ouroboros, a snake eating its tail, which symbolizes the continuity of life; and the center dot, an African symbol for the sun. The dot with the circle around it also means optimism. The name *Sunesi* is from a Latin word meaning "health," and, of course, its final letter also provides a convenient home for the dot/sun, allowing the wordmark and logo to be used together or alone: The dot established a dynamic relationship between the two.

In the beginning, it was difficult for the client to appreciate the design, du Toit recalls. But the interest that the new identity garnered from the market was phenomenal, especially when it came to investors.

"Investors identified that the company had put its money into creating a new brand. In their eyes, it emphasized that the start-up was making a wise investment," he says.

Sunesi was a new name for an old company, Medixx, which was a faceless moniker for a company whose product offered real benefit to physicians and patients. Enterprise IG designers communicated this through symbols.

The new logo for a very modern product is composed of two very old symbols: an ourobouros, a snake eating its tail, which symbolizes the continuity of life; and a dot, which is an African symbol for the sun.

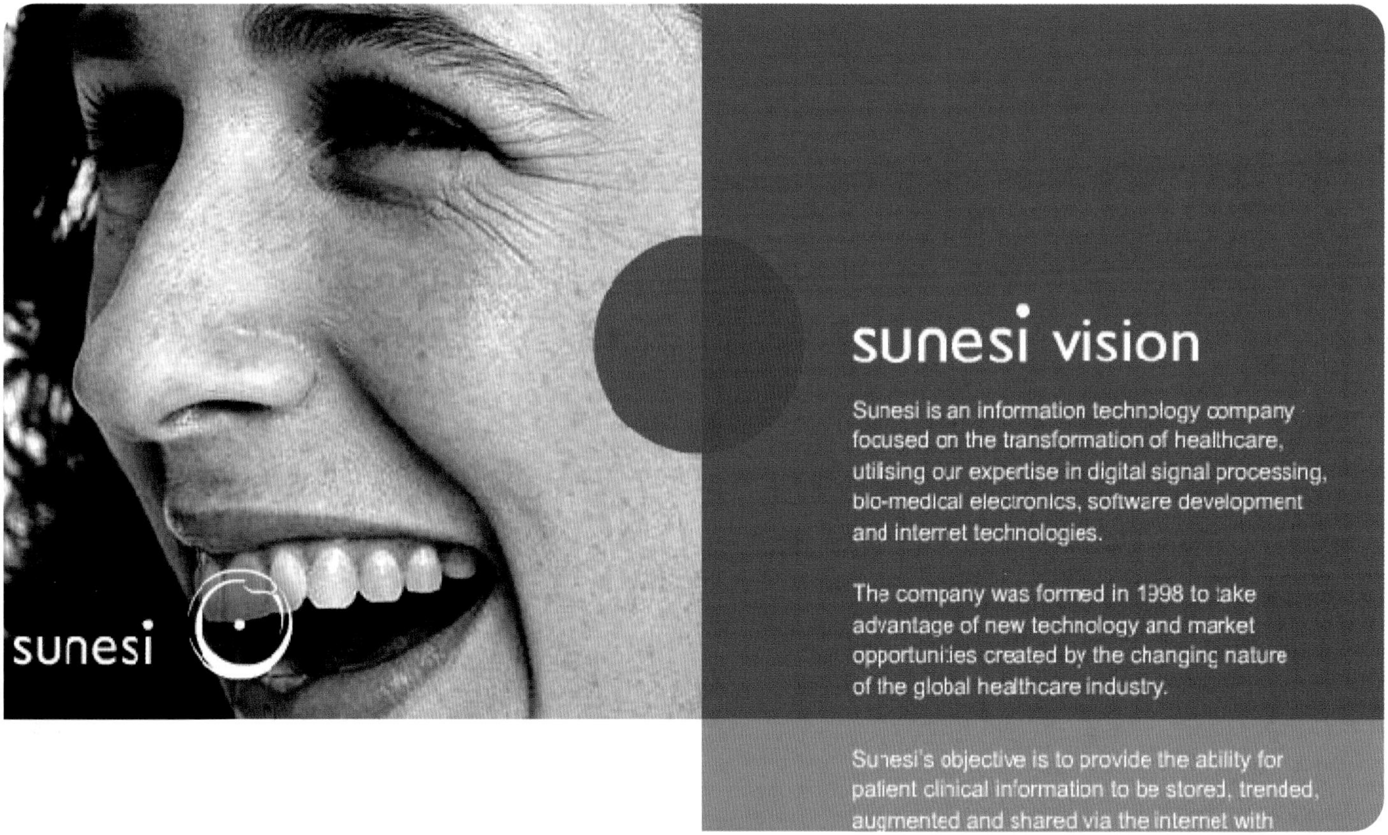

sunesi
sunesi vision
Sunesi is an information technology company focused on the transformation of healthcare, utilising our expertise in digital signal processing, bio-medical electronics, software development and internet technologies.
The company was formed in 1998 to take advantage of new technology and market opportunities created by the changing nature of the global healthcare industry.
Sunesi's objective is to provide the ability for patient clinical information to be stored, trended, augmented and shared via the internet with

The new logo, with its open center, can be placed into any layout and still remain unobtrusive and almost transparent.

collections and sketches

LOGO SEARCH

Keywords: Initials

Type: Symbol Typographic Combo All

	A	B	C	D
1	LOGO SEARCH			
2			AROMA NATURAL	aquamarine SEAFOOD
3	Ajunto® Get iT.™	ANGEL ISLAND records®	ABSA	
4	AVERY DENNISON	Alpine Oral Surgery	ASX AUSTRALIAN STOCK EXCHANGE	
5	ARCH Deluxe		AHA	

Ⓓ = Design Firm Ⓒ = Client

1C Ⓓ judson design associates Ⓒ Harris County Water District 1D Ⓓ Hornall Anderson Ⓒ Hornall Anderson Design Works 2A Ⓓ O'Connor Identity Development Ⓒ Alvin Ailey 2B Ⓓ Creative Madhouse Ⓒ Atlantis Cruises 2C Ⓓ Davidson Design Ⓒ Go Natural 2D Ⓓ Miriello Grafico, Inc. Ⓒ Aquamarine Seafood 3A Ⓓ d4 creative group Ⓒ Ajunto 3B Ⓓ Sackett Design Ⓒ Eric Johnson 3C Ⓓ Enterprise IG Ⓒ Absa 3D Ⓓ Squires & Company Ⓒ Richardson Independent School District 4A Ⓓ Landor and Associates Ⓒ Avery Dennison 4B Ⓓ BBK Studio Ⓒ Alpine Oral Surgery 4C Ⓓ Landor and Associates Ⓒ ASX 4D Ⓓ Deep Design Ⓒ Atlanta Film & Video Festival 5A Ⓓ Duffy & Partners Ⓒ McDonald's Corporation 5B Ⓓ Pure Fusion Media Ⓒ Morning Star International 5C Ⓓ Crosby Associates Ⓒ Association for Hospital Professionals 5D Ⓓ Glitschka Studios Ⓒ MacAgent.com

	A	B	C	D
1				
2		BENETONE FILMS	BLUE RIVER GOURMET	BIZZBASE
3				
4	clearly canadian.	CLINIGEN		
5			CONVERGENTENERGY	

Ⓓ = Design Firm Ⓒ = Client

1A Ⓓ Duffy & Partners Ⓒ Basin/Retail Concepts 1B Ⓓ McAndrew Kaps Ⓒ Bentley Sports 1C Ⓓ Peter Montoya Inc. Ⓒ Brent Hanson 1D Ⓓ Marius Fahrner Design Ⓒ Belvedere Vermoegensverwaltung 2A Ⓓ Dotzero Design Ⓒ Brandywine Graphics 2B Ⓓ logobyte Ⓒ Benetone Films 2C Ⓓ CAPSULE Ⓒ Blue River Gourmet 2D Ⓓ Simon & Goetz Design Ⓒ Frank Kuhlmann 3A Ⓓ Indicia Design Inc Ⓒ The Buckley Group 3B Ⓓ Howling Good Designs Ⓒ Brady & Honaski Associates 3C Ⓓ Gardner Design Ⓒ Bredar Waggoner Architects 3D Ⓓ Simon & Goetz Design Ⓒ optik meyer 4A Ⓓ karacters design group Ⓒ Clearly Canadian Beverage Corporation 4B Ⓓ What Design, Inc. Ⓒ Clinigen, Inc. 4C Ⓓ MINE Ⓒ Core Technologies 4D Ⓓ Crosby Associates Ⓒ Champion International Corporation 5A Ⓓ Kircher, Inc. Ⓒ Concept Interactive, Inc. 5B Ⓓ Essex Two Incorporated Ⓒ Catalyst Partner 5C Ⓓ judson design associates Ⓒ Convergent Energy 5D Ⓓ Peter Montoya Inc. Ⓒ Comprehensive Corporate Care

Ⓓ = Design Firm Ⓒ = Client

1A Ⓓ Carousel30 Ⓒ Carousel30 1B Ⓓ Enterprise IG Ⓒ Cell C 1C Ⓓ Methodologie Ⓒ Casey Family Programs 1D Ⓓ Howerton+White Interactive Ⓒ Cherry Creek Assisted Living 2A Ⓓ Landor and Associates Ⓒ Computer Assosiates 2B Ⓓ Glenn Sakamoto Design Ⓒ Creative Artists Agency 2C Ⓓ LeVesque Design Ⓒ Casa Decor 2D Ⓓ Glitschka Studios Ⓒ Design Logic Inc. 3A Ⓓ CDI Studios Ⓒ Connection Power 3B Ⓓ Element Ⓒ Columbia Resources 3C Ⓓ Monigle Associates Inc. Ⓒ Cole Taylor Bank 3D Ⓓ Rickabaugh Graphics Ⓒ University of Connecticut 4A Ⓓ Lewis & Son Creative Ⓒ Diverse Power 4B Ⓓ Gardner Design Ⓒ Devlin Trucking 4C Ⓓ Davidson Design Ⓒ Davidson Design 4D Ⓓ Dennis Purcell Design Ⓒ Dennis Purcell Design 5A Ⓓ five Ⓓ DKM 5B Ⓓ Creative Madhouse Ⓒ E. S. Systems 5C Ⓓ Fernandez Design Ⓒ Design Engine 5D Ⓓ John Langdon Design Ⓒ Edwards Enterprises

A B C D

1

2

3

4

5

Ⓓ = Design Firm Ⓒ = Client

1A Ⓓ thomasvasquez.com Ⓒ BMG/RCA 1B Ⓓ hendler-johnston Ⓒ Equity Bank 1C Ⓓ LIFT HERE, Inc. Ⓒ Emobile Technologies 1D Ⓓ Giraffe, Inc. Ⓒ Maternity Health
2A Ⓓ Richards Brock Miller Mitchell & Associates Ⓒ Ellis Construction 2B Ⓓ BDG Studio Ⓒ Ronin Utopia for ebuyxpress 2C Ⓓ Bernhardt Fudyma Design Group Ⓒ Electrical Digest
2D Ⓓ Gardner Design Ⓒ Flagstone Investments 3A Ⓓ Neoalchemia Design Lab Ⓒ Department of Foreign Language, San Jose State, CA 3B Ⓓ Duffy & Partners Ⓒ Fractal, LLC 3C Ⓓ Gardner Design Ⓒ Flagstone Investments
3D Ⓓ Design and Image Ⓒ Flipside Design 4A Ⓓ Brandbeat Ⓒ 3Office 4B Ⓓ Koch Business Solutions Ⓒ Flint Hills Resources 4C Ⓓ Landor and Associates Ⓒ General Electric 4D Ⓓ Landor and Associates Ⓒ Gamesa
5A Ⓓ LIFT HERE, Inc. Ⓒ Self 5B Ⓓ Landor and Associates Ⓒ GeoCities 5C Ⓓ The Bradford Lawton Design Group Ⓒ Gary Pools 5D Ⓓ Richards Brock Miller Mitchell & Associates Ⓒ Gordon & Gale

	A	B	C	D
1		THE GATHERING	G-FORCE RECRUITMENT	
2	GrupoGallegos	GOprinter		Hinge
3				
4		Hvassaleitisskóli	hp	Healtheon
5		Harrison Center *for the arts!*	HOOK-H	

Ⓓ = Design Firm Ⓒ = Client

1A Ⓓ Hubbell Design Works Ⓒ Goodrich Theaters 1B Ⓓ Tribe Design Houston Ⓒ The Gathering 1C Ⓓ Hoyne Design Ⓒ G-Force Recruitment 1D Ⓓ Tom Fowler, Inc. Ⓒ The Gegenheimer Group
2A Ⓓ Richards Brock Miller Mitchell & Associates Ⓒ Grupo Gallegos 2B Ⓓ Segura Inc. Ⓒ GoPrinetr.com 2C Ⓓ McAndrew Kaps Ⓒ Golden Lariat Film Company 2D Ⓓ Hinge Ⓒ Hinge
3A Ⓓ Intrinsic Design Ⓒ Handcrafted Constructed 3B Ⓓ dialogbox Ⓒ Hammerschon 3C Ⓓ Kern Design Group Ⓒ Hartwood Acres 3D Ⓓ BC Design Ⓒ Hamilton Consulting
4A Ⓓ Prejean LoBue Ⓒ The Richards Group / H-E-B Grocery Company 4B Ⓓ Kraftaverk - Design Studio Ⓒ School 4C Ⓓ Landor and Associates Ⓒ Hewlett Packard 4D Ⓓ Landor and Associates Ⓒ Healtheon
5A Ⓓ Kraftaverk - Design Studio Ⓒ VISION 5B Ⓓ Kristian Andersen, Inc. Ⓒ Harrison Center for the Arts 5C Ⓓ Cam Stewart Graphic Design Ⓒ Hook-H Corp. 5D Ⓓ Kraftaverk - Design Studio Ⓒ HassoTowers

	A	B	C	D
1		Intellitech	IRONHIDE™	™
2		power		IVARA WORK SMART
3	inspire music corp		J.	
4	kă·mün·ă·kāte	kalypsys		KOOCHES
5			KAMINSKI	

Ⓓ = Design Firm Ⓒ = Client

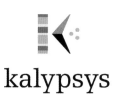

1A Ⓓ wilhelmedwardopatz Ⓒ Fotoforum international 1B Ⓓ judson design associates Ⓒ Intellitech 1C Ⓓ Stiles+co Ⓒ IronHide 1D Ⓓ Duffy & Partners Ⓒ IC Corporation, the bus subsidiary of International Truck and Engine Corporation 2A Ⓓ Deep Design Ⓒ Project IT, Inc. 2B Ⓓ Jeff Kern Design Ⓒ Igility-Noble and Associates 2C Ⓓ Gardner Design Ⓒ Info Network 2D Ⓓ Riordon Design Ⓒ Ivara Corporation 3A Ⓓ Grassroots Studios Ⓒ Inspire Music Corp. 3B Ⓓ faux koi Ⓒ joanna jahn 3C Ⓓ wilhelmedwardopatz Ⓒ IMK 3D Ⓓ thomasvasquez.com Ⓒ Kindred Kitchens 4A Ⓓ Burd & Patterson Ⓒ Kamunacate Interprises 4B Ⓓ Dept 3 Ⓒ Kalypsys 4C Ⓓ Glenn Sakamoto Design Ⓒ Krall Podiatry 4D Ⓓ Design Nut Ⓒ Kooches Hand Made Carpets 5A Ⓓ Gardner Design Ⓒ Krehbil Architects 5B Ⓓ Eskil Ohlsson Assoc. Inc. Ⓒ Kroma Lithographers Inc. 5C Ⓓ Hotdog Creative Ⓒ Karen Kaminski Fashion Design 5D Ⓓ Landor and Associates Ⓒ LG

	A	B	C	D
1	LUMINOUS			
2				MYND
3	MAXIUM financial		Mediacode	MENNTAFÉLAGIÐ
4		MINAKAMI Town & Resort	MAXUM	Maxcor
5			MELANCHRONIC	

Ⓓ = Design Firm Ⓒ = Client

1A Ⓓ Platform Creative Group Ⓒ Luminous 1B Ⓓ Jane Cameron Design Ⓒ Mindfield Books 1C Ⓓ m+ Ⓒ m7 1D Ⓓ Catapult Strategic Design Ⓒ Meadow Valley Corp. 2A Ⓓ Courtney & Co. design Ⓒ MarketQuest 2B Ⓓ thomasvasquez.com Ⓒ Miller Brewing Co. 2C Ⓓ Squires & Company Ⓒ Mission Resources 2D Ⓓ Duffy & Partners Ⓒ Policy Management Systems 3A Ⓓ Scribblers' Club Ⓒ Maxium 3B Ⓓ Eskil Ohlsson Assoc. Inc. Ⓒ Merchantile Leasing Corp. 3C Ⓓ Dept 3 Ⓒ MediaCode 3D Ⓓ Nonni & Manni/Ydda Ⓒ Menntafélagi_ 4A Ⓓ Massive Studio Ⓒ Mechanical Contractors 4B Ⓓ Landor and Associates Ⓒ Minakami 4C Ⓓ Howalt Design Studio, Inc. Ⓒ Maxum Contractors 4D Ⓓ LeVesque Design Ⓒ Maxcor Financial Group, LLC 5A Ⓓ Nestor Stermole VCG Ⓒ Millennium Pharmaceuticals 5B Ⓓ THINKMULE.com Ⓒ Melanie Pruitt Art Studio 5C Ⓓ Dept 3 Ⓒ Melancronic 5D Ⓓ Gardner Design Ⓒ Mega Metals Group

A B C D

1

2

3

4

5

(D) = Design Firm (C) = Client

1A (D) TD2, S.C. (C) A LA MEDIDA 1B (D) DDB (C) McDonald's 1C (D) Q (C) Medi Didac GmbH 1D (D) Enterprise IG (C) Maybach 2A (D) Jeff Kern Design (C) National Grant Center - Robison Gamble Creative 2B (D) Gardner Design (C) Neufeldt's Flooring 2C (D) dialogbox (C) Nicholson | NY 2D (D) Allen Creative (C) R.J. Gibson Advertising 3A (D) Mortensen Design (C) TeraStor 3B (D) Design Continuum Inc (C) Next Office 3C (D) Howalt Design Studio, Inc. (C) Nextel Communications/Martin Williams 3D (D) Landor and Associates (C) Nielsen 4A (D) Custom Art Company (C) Northland Bicycle Shop 4B (D) Hotdog Creative (C) National Diaper Laundry Service 4C (D) Landor and Associates (C) NEC 4D (D) Mortensen Design (C) NewGround Resources 5A (D) Nonni & Manni/Ydda (C) Nonni og Manni 5B (D) Crosby Associates (C) National-Louis Univerity 5C (D) Proart Graphics/Gabriel Kalach (C) NU Orbit 5D (D) Landor and Associates (C) Napa Valley

Ⓓ = Design Firm Ⓒ = Client

1A Ⓓ redinwyden osanimi Ⓒ rainforest protection 1B Ⓓ Simon & Goetz Design Ⓒ open air systems gmbh 1C Ⓓ Dotzero Design Ⓒ Pacific Crest Motel 1D Ⓓ Gardner Design Ⓒ Pivotal Athletic Training 2A Ⓓ TD2, S.C. Ⓒ PRINTEGRA 2B Ⓓ Popgun Ⓒ Popgun Design 2C Ⓓ Fernandez Design Ⓒ Penco Construction 2D Ⓓ Segura Inc. Ⓒ Pocket Card 3A Ⓓ CrossGrain Creative Studios Ⓒ Portico Church 3B Ⓓ MINE Ⓒ Paradox Media (unused) 3C Ⓓ Gardner Design Ⓒ PrintMaster Printing 3D Ⓓ Perks Design Partners Ⓒ Gandel Asset Management 4A Ⓓ Glitschka Studios Ⓒ Living Epistles 4B Ⓓ Landor and Associates Ⓒ Radio Shack 4C Ⓓ VMA Ⓒ Rogero Buckman Architects 4D Ⓓ Miriello Grafico, Inc. Ⓒ Rancho Bernardo Inn 5A Ⓓ Burd & Patterson Ⓒ Rick Mosley Hair 5B Ⓓ Glitschka Studios Ⓒ Rocket Performance 5C Ⓓ Alesce Ⓒ Zride 5D Ⓓ Mitten Design Ⓒ Philip Salaverry

A	B	C	D	
santa fe film festival	saba		STRICKLAND	1
			standard lifestyl	2
savingumoney.com	SECURUS	SILVERSEA	SimpleWare	3
	SELBY			4
sb studio besser		SHORE SCORES		5

Ⓓ = Design Firm Ⓒ = Client

1A Ⓓ the atmosfear Ⓒ Santa Fe Film Festival 1B Ⓓ Landor and Associates Ⓒ Saba 1C Ⓓ Richards Brock Miller Mitchell & Associates Ⓒ Saturn 1D Ⓓ BDG Studio Ronin Ⓒ Steve Strickland, DDS
2A Ⓓ Dotzero Design Ⓒ Standard Companies 2B Ⓓ Dotzero Design Ⓒ Standard Supply 2C Ⓓ Ames Design Ⓒ Sideline Solutions 2D Ⓓ Gardner Design Ⓒ The Standard 3A Ⓓ karacters design group Ⓒ Saving U Money
3B Ⓓ logobyte Ⓒ Securus Inc. 3C Ⓓ Typonic Ⓒ Lenco 3D Ⓓ Firewheel Design Ⓒ SimpleDevices 4A Ⓓ Richards Brock Miller Mitchell & Associates Ⓒ S3 Communications
4B Ⓓ Williams Collins Design & Development Ⓒ Bret Selby—Selby Laminated Longboard Company 4C Ⓓ Jonathan Rice & Company Ⓒ Sandra Rice 4D Ⓓ McMillian Design Ⓒ Beth Stienke
5A Ⓓ wilhelmedwardopatz Ⓒ Studio Besser 5B Ⓓ greteman group Ⓒ strange ideas 5C Ⓓ d4 creative group Ⓒ Shore Scores Inc. 5D Ⓓ Hornall Anderson Ⓒ Lincoln Square

	A	B	C	D
1	TENET	THINERGY	TradeSpark™	TOKYO GAS
2		TANDOU LIMITED		techtv
3		UB OUTFITTERS	URBAN FREEDOM ®	UMOGUL
4				VirginiaFirst
5				WINGNUT WINGS ™

Ⓓ = Design Firm Ⓒ = Client

1A Ⓓ CAPSULE Ⓒ Tenet 1B Ⓓ Mad Dog Graphx Ⓒ Thinergy 1C Ⓓ Bernhardt Fudyma Design Group Ⓒ TradeSpark 1D Ⓓ Landor and Associates Ⓒ Tokyo Gas 2A Ⓓ Essex Two Incorporated Ⓒ Tucker Gallery and Salon 2B Ⓓ Hoyne Design Ⓒ Tandou Ltd 2C Ⓓ Custom Art Company Ⓒ Typographic Printing Company 2D Ⓓ Aahbullay Ⓒ TechTV 3A Ⓓ Gardner Design Ⓒ un 3B Ⓓ Glitschka Studios Ⓒ Union Bay Sportswear 3C Ⓓ BC Design Ⓒ Mecca 3D Ⓓ Michael Doret Graphic Design Ⓒ uMogul 4A Ⓓ Gardner Design Ⓒ Viz Worx PhotoLab 4B Ⓓ Cave Ⓒ Velocity 7 4C Ⓓ Gardner Design Ⓒ versacourt 4D Ⓓ Scott Lewis Design Ⓒ Virginia First Financial Services, Inc. 5A Ⓓ Nestor Stermole VCG Ⓒ Wolper Sales Agency 5B Ⓓ Braue; Branding & Corporate Design Ⓒ Druckhaus Wuest 5C Ⓓ Kircher, Inc. Ⓒ Food Marketing Institute 5D Ⓓ HardBall Sports Ⓒ Wingnut Wings

A B C D

1

2

3

4

5

Ⓓ = Design Firm Ⓒ = Client

1A Ⓓ Glenn Sakamoto Design Ⓒ Workspaces 1B Ⓓ Duffy & Partners Ⓒ The Wieland Furniture Company 1C Ⓓ S Design, Inc. Ⓒ Women's Foundation of Oklahoma 1D Ⓓ Landor and Associates Ⓒ Xerox 2A Ⓓ greteman group Ⓒ seaXpress 2B Ⓓ Firewheel Design Ⓒ Pure Imagination Studios 2C Ⓓ ContrerasDesign Ⓒ Zdot Technology 2D Ⓓ Prejean LoBue Ⓒ Peninsula Gaming 3A Ⓓ Landor and Associates Ⓒ 3M 3B Ⓓ Blattner Brunner Ⓒ Litigation Communications 3C Ⓓ Landor and Associates Ⓒ Times Three 3D Ⓓ CRE8 communications, inc. Ⓒ H & H Services 4A Ⓓ Delikatessen Ⓒ Brau und Brunnen 4B Ⓓ Design Continuum Inc Ⓒ Studio 12 4C Ⓓ BC Design Ⓒ Mecca 4D Ⓓ Gardner Design Ⓒ Cox News 22 5A Ⓓ Segura Inc. Ⓒ T26 Digital Type Foundry 5B Ⓓ Ty Wilkins Ⓒ For Sale: ty@tywilkins.com 5C Ⓓ Methodologie Ⓒ RC Hedreen 5D Ⓓ Clive Jacobson Design Ⓒ Sigma Network LLB

Brooklyn Brewery
Identity and Package Design

Milton Glaser, Inc., New York, New York

Brooklyn was home to forty-eight breweries a century ago, each with its own culture and loyal neighborhood of customers. The taverns that sold the locally brewed products were important centerpieces in the borough's neighborhoods, and the families who started the breweries held positions of civic and social importance.

Unfortunately, in 1976, the last of these local businesses was put under by large Midwestern breweries. But in 1987, a former AP foreign correspondent, who had taken up home brewing while living in the Middle East where beer is not available, and his Brooklyn neighbor, then a lending bank officer, brought brewing back to Brooklyn.

The partners contacted Milton Glaser to create an identity for their new company, Brooklyn Brewery. Glaser liked the company for several reasons. First, he says the products taste terrific. "It's made intelligently. The brewmaster is very good, and the beer is as good as anything you can get in Europe." Second, he felt it would be a great accomplishment to bring back this piece of local history.

Originally, the client wanted to call the company The Brooklyn Bridge Brewery, but at Glaser's recommendation, dropped the "Bridge" portion to make the product feel more inclusive. In fact, the team wanted to create an identity that looked vaguely European. The beer has a very intense taste, as European varieties do.

"The labeling we created is more minimal than the national brands," Glaser says. "People remember it when they see it. They don't associate it with American beers."

But the identity he created does have one distinctly American trait. The swooshing B in the logo reminds many people of baseball—specifically, the Brooklyn Dodgers. Glaser acknowledges this reference to classic Brooklyn. It cashes in on the value of local nostalgia and history, casting a fond eye back to when the Dodgers were just as much a part of the borough as the neighborhood beer.

The gold, green, and black logo that Glaser created transfers easily to differently colored labels, accommodating the company's eight lines of beers, plus some seasonal specialties.

Creating a new mark, especially one that must thrive in a market with many prevailing products, is a balancing act. The logo must fit the product category or buyers won't understand what the packaging contains. But it can't lapse into similitude, either.

"European- or imported-beer drinkers have expectations, but there are also the expectations of American beer buyers, which might be shifted," Glaser says. "You have to consider the context of the product and be novel. It's definitely a balancing act."

	A	B	C	D	
	LOGO SEARCH Keywords: Typography — Type: ○ Symbol ○ Typographic ○ Combo ◉ All		5isters unique gifts & collectibles	slice	1
	easy hanger	erwin an american cafe and bar	Motivity	a place to grow	2
	naughty + nice	OK optimistic kids	wr!te on	Kern	3
	radius	the golden pear	interview	Ferrari	4
	Celesta luxury glass enclosures	ACQUA	SPACE	RIVERSTONE	5

Ⓓ = Design Firm Ⓒ = Client

1C Ⓓ Great Scott Design Ⓒ 5 Sisters 1D Ⓓ Chuck Pennington Ⓒ Slice Editorial 2A Ⓓ Davidson Design Ⓒ Easy Hanger 2B Ⓓ Essex Two Incorporated Ⓒ erwin 2C Ⓓ Essex Two Incorporated Ⓒ Motivity 2D Ⓓ Kiku Obata & Company Ⓒ Bloom & Grow, Inc. 3A Ⓓ The Mixx Ⓒ IBB 3B Ⓓ Jane Cameron Design Ⓒ Optimistic Kids 3C Ⓓ the atmosfear Ⓒ Write On Inc. 3D Ⓓ Kern Design Group Ⓒ Kern Design Group 4A Ⓓ Mortensen Design Ⓒ Radius, Inc. 4B Ⓓ Howling Good Designs Ⓒ The Golden Pear Cafe 4C Ⓓ John Langdon Design Ⓒ Cycle Guide Publications 4D Ⓓ Landor and Associates Ⓒ Ferrari 5A Ⓓ Lipson Alport Glass & Associates Ⓒ Basco 5B Ⓓ Hubbell Design Works Ⓒ Hawaiian Regent Resort 5C Ⓓ The Bradford Lawton Design Group Ⓒ Clear Channel Exhibition 5D Ⓓ Kern Design Group Ⓒ Riverstone Design Studio

	A	B	C	D
1	PROQUEST	TRILOGY	RED DELICIOUS	COVENANT HealthCare
2	CONSTITUTION BANK	SEVEN TENS	HARPO	WOOL LOO MOO WINES LOO
3	TEXAS BLOOMS HELPING TEXAS GROW.	SPATIQUE HEALTH & BEAUTY	PRADERA	Las Guitarras de FUEGO
4	MATADOR RANCH 50 Years of Excellence 50	ALPHABET ARM DESIGN®	BELVEDERE VERMÖGENSVERWALTUNG GMBH & CO. KG	Pastabilities UNIQUE FLAVORED PASTA
5	ManhattanTimes	STARBUCKS doubleshot™	elementsix™ ADVANCING DIAMOND	taxizone

Ⓓ = Design Firm Ⓒ = Client

1A Ⓓ Essex Two Incorporated Ⓒ ProQuest Company 1B Ⓓ FutureBrand Ⓒ Park Hyatt Hotel 1C Ⓓ BlueSpark Studios Ⓒ Red Delicious 1D Ⓓ Monigle Associates Inc. Ⓒ Covenant Health
2A Ⓓ John Langdon Design Ⓒ Constitution Bank 2B Ⓓ Clive Jacobson Design Ⓒ SevenTens Swimwear 2C Ⓓ Essex Two Incorporated Ⓒ Harpo Studios, Inc. 2D Ⓓ Emery Vincent Design Ⓒ Woolloomooloo Wines
3A Ⓓ Firewheel Design Ⓒ TexasBlooms 3B Ⓓ Scribblers' Club Ⓒ Spatique Health and Beauty Clinic 3C Ⓓ Pageworks Communication Design, Inc. Ⓒ Continental Homes 3D Ⓓ Popgun Ⓒ Las Guitarras de Fuego
4A Ⓓ Koch Business Solutions Ⓒ Matador Ranch 50th Anniversary Logo 4B Ⓓ Alphabet Arm Design Ⓒ Alphabet Arm Design 4C Ⓓ Marius Fahrner Design Ⓒ Belvedere Vermoegensverwaltung 4D Ⓓ MINE Ⓒ Pastabilities
5A Ⓓ Bonfilio Design Ⓒ David Keisman/Manhattan Times 5B Ⓓ Duffy & Partners Ⓒ North American Coffee Partnership/Starbucks 5C Ⓓ Landor and Associates Ⓒ Element Six Advanced Diamond 5D Ⓓ Doug Beatty Ⓒ Doug Beatty

	A	B	C	D	
					1
					2
					3
					4
					5

Ⓓ = Design Firm Ⓒ = Client

1A Ⓓ Landor and Associates Ⓒ Accenture 1B Ⓓ Scribblers' Club Ⓒ Just Fix It 1C Ⓓ Imatrix Ⓒ match.com 1D Ⓓ Emery Vincent Design Ⓒ Aberdeen Wine Company 2A Ⓓ Landor and Associates Ⓒ People PC 2B Ⓓ Jonathan Rice & Company Ⓒ Weary & Associates 2C Ⓓ Soloflight Design Studio Ⓒ Ed DeCastro 2D Ⓓ Glenn Sakamoto Design Ⓒ Saybrook Capital 3A Ⓓ Context Ⓒ Motive Media 3B Ⓓ Sanna Design Group, Inc. Ⓒ Taxxes.com 3C Ⓓ Landor and Associates Ⓒ Microsoft 3D Ⓓ BDG Studio Ronin Ⓒ matchbox venture capital 4A Ⓓ Michael Powell Design Ⓒ Data Guidance Group, Watkins Communications Company 4B Ⓓ Glenn Sakamoto Design Ⓒ Chops Hair Salon 4C Ⓓ Wolken communica Ⓒ Bellevue Art Museum 4D Ⓓ SD Graphic Design Ⓒ student work 5A Ⓓ Atlanta College of Art Ⓒ polka dot 5B Ⓓ Crosby Associates Ⓒ Champion 5C Ⓓ faux koi Ⓒ cinesound 5D Ⓓ Typonic Ⓒ Roxon Productions

Ⓓ = Design Firm Ⓒ = Client

1A Ⓓ Brandbeat Ⓒ FONO 1B Ⓓ Landor and Associates Ⓒ Intel 1C Ⓓ Landor and Associates Ⓒ FedEx Express 1D Ⓓ Hausch Design Agency LLC Ⓒ Vigilo 2A Ⓓ Monigle Associates Inc. Ⓒ Altus Resources 2B Ⓓ Dotzero Design Ⓒ SoMA 2C Ⓓ Device Ⓒ astralasia 2D Ⓓ Landor and Associates Ⓒ Cadence 3A Ⓓ Crosby Associates Ⓒ Journal of the Chicago Chapter of the American Institute of Graphic Arts 3B Ⓓ Bonfilio Design Ⓒ Mayor Rudolph Giuliani 3C Ⓓ Redbeard Communications Inc. Ⓒ Vote No on G Committee 3D Ⓓ Alphabet Arm Design Ⓒ Justin Morris/Skyscraper Entertainment 4A Ⓓ Landor and Associates Ⓒ Dell 4B Ⓓ Monigle Associates Inc. Ⓒ Unova Inc. 4C Ⓓ Mike Quon/Designation Ⓒ None-Available 4D Ⓓ Glenn Sakamoto Design Ⓒ Yamano Beauty College 5A Ⓓ Williams Collins Design & Development Ⓒ Bite of Bakersfield Event 5B Ⓓ Essex Two Incorporated Ⓒ Think2 5C Ⓓ Redbeard Communications Inc. Ⓒ Redbeard Communications 5D Ⓓ Graham Hanson Design Ⓒ Sun Coast Capital

	A	B	C	D	
					1
					2
					3
					4
					5

(D) = Design Firm (C) = Client

1A (D) Landor and Associates (C) San Francisco Opera 1B (D) O'Connor Identity Development (C) Kimberly Jordan 1C (D) INA SHOKAI (C) VICTOR ENTERTAINMENT 1D (D) Landor and Associates (C) Merck 2A (D) Wolken communica (C) Bellevue Art Museum 2B (D) Alesce (C) Twinx 2C (D) judson design associates (C) Clive's Grill 2D (D) Design Army (C) The Washington Ballet 3A (D) Atha Design (C) Dooley Manufacturing 3B (D) THINKMULE.com (C) Team Revolution 3C (D) Atlanta College of Art (C) trivet 3D (D) Landor and Associates (C) Reuters The Business of Information 4A (D) Smith-Boake Designwerke Inc. (C) Thomas Kofman 4B (D) Nicole Imbert Design (C) Ferquido 4C (D) Hubbell Design Works (C) Symbion 4D (D) Mitchell Design (C) The Summus Group 5A (D) Hornall Anderson (C) InSite Works 5B (D) Keyword Design (C) Keyword Design 5C (D) Bernhardt Fudyma Design Group (C) Advanced Network & Services 5D (D) Alesce (C) JPerry

	A	B	C	D
1	**LOGO SEARCH** Keywords: Enclosures; Type: Symbol / Typographic / Combo / ● All			
2				
3				
4				
5				

Ⓓ = Design Firm Ⓒ = Client

1C Ⓓ Molly Z. Illustration Ⓒ Toy Lab 1D Ⓓ Go Welsh! Ⓒ Sara Goulet Communications 2A Ⓓ karacters design group Ⓒ Good Cause 2B Ⓓ @radical.media Ⓒ The City of New York 2C Ⓓ Z-Design Ⓒ PAEN 2D Ⓓ Aahbullay Ⓒ PBS
3A Ⓓ Art Chantry Ⓒ Estrus 3B Ⓓ Prejean LoBue Ⓒ WWOZ—New Orleans 3C Ⓓ BBDO Detroit Design Group Ⓒ DaimlerChrysler 3D Ⓓ Tim Frame Design Ⓒ Graphic Design Society
4A Ⓓ thomasvasquez.com Ⓒ New York City Schools 4B Ⓓ Bonfilio Design Ⓒ Amsterdam Billiard Club 4C Ⓓ Landor and Associates Ⓒ Tide 4D Ⓓ Landor and Associates Ⓒ Circuit City
5A Ⓓ Ross Creative + Strategy Ⓒ Einstein Vodka 5B Ⓓ The David Group Ⓒ Plush Nightclub 5C Ⓓ d4 creative group Ⓒ AT&T DMC and SANZ 5D Ⓓ Neoalchemia Design Lab Ⓒ Seoul Game Festival 2002 Organization

A B C D

1

2

3

4

5

Ⓓ = Design Firm Ⓒ = Client

1A Ⓓ Watts Design Ⓒ Ancient Grains 1B Ⓓ Addis Ⓒ intel 1C Ⓓ Michael Doret Graphic Design Ⓒ Chic-A-Boom 1D Ⓓ Sibley/Peteet Design, Inc. Ⓒ Zax Pints and Plates 2A Ⓓ Modern Dog Design Co. Ⓒ K2 Snowboards 2B Ⓓ Michael Doret Graphic Design Ⓒ Chic-A-Boom 2C Ⓓ Gardner Design Ⓒ The Standard 2D Ⓓ Landor and Associates Ⓒ Old Navy 3A Ⓓ Dotzero Design Ⓒ Chit Chat Coffee Shop 3B Ⓓ redinwyden Ⓒ scribble toy design 3C Ⓓ Duffy & Partners Ⓒ Chums 3D Ⓓ the atmosfear Ⓒ Stinkweeds 4A Ⓓ Device Ⓒ Hard Time 4B Ⓓ DDB Ⓒ DDB 4C Ⓓ DDB Ⓒ DDB 4D Ⓓ Jeff Kern Design Ⓒ Campbells—Noble and Associates 5A Ⓓ Duffy & Partners Ⓒ IBP (Iowa Beef Producers) 5B Ⓓ Townsend Ⓒ Minnesota Dept. of Tourism 5C Ⓓ Gardner Design Ⓒ The Fantastic World of Gourmet Chocolate 5D Ⓓ Landor and Associates Ⓒ Royal Carribean International

	A	B	C	D
1				
2				
3		Project kNOw for drug education and prevention.		
4				
5				

Ⓓ = Design Firm Ⓒ = Client

1A Ⓓ Landor and Associates Ⓒ Hyatt 1B Ⓓ CAPSULE Ⓒ Yank, Inc. 1C Ⓓ Fernandez Design Ⓒ Beyond Communications 1D Ⓓ Ross Creative + Strategy Ⓒ Peoria Next 2A Ⓓ Howling Good Designs Ⓒ Margolin, Winer & Evens 2B Ⓓ Landor and Associates Ⓒ Gap 2C Ⓓ R&R Partners (Randy Heil) Ⓒ Insomnia Entertainment 2D Ⓓ Crosby Associates Ⓒ national association of design professionals 3A Ⓓ Marius Fahrner Design Ⓒ Boutique No 2 3B Ⓓ Crosby Associates Ⓒ Project kNOw 3C Ⓓ Landor and Associates Ⓒ Hilton International 3D Ⓓ Art Chantry Ⓒ Project Infinity 4A Ⓓ Glenn Sakamoto Design Ⓒ Umongo Online Sports 4B Ⓓ Landor and Associates Ⓒ Abertis 4C Ⓓ Landor and Associates Ⓒ Tommy Hilfiger 4D Ⓓ Duffy & Partners Ⓒ Free Arts Minnesota 5A Ⓓ d4 creative group Ⓒ E&C Medical Intelligence 5B Ⓓ The Office of Bill Chiaravalle Ⓒ XBOX Technologies 5C Ⓓ Hutchinson Associates, Inc. Ⓒ S&F 5D Ⓓ wilhelmedwardopatz Ⓒ Otto and Ehrlich

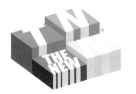

	A	B	C	D
1				
2				
3				
4				
5				

Ⓓ = Design Firm Ⓒ = Client

1A Ⓓ Matsumoto Design Ⓒ Team Sake 1B Ⓓ oakley design studios Ⓒ KINK fm 102 1C Ⓓ Wolken communica Ⓒ Oobas Mexican Grill 1D Ⓓ Newbomb Design Ⓒ Park City Diner 2A Ⓓ Enterprise IG Ⓒ SA Post Office 2B Ⓓ Alesce Ⓒ Twinx 2C Ⓓ Mires>Design for Brands Ⓒ Arena Stage 2D Ⓓ The Mixx Ⓒ Vertical Group 3A Ⓓ SPUR Ⓒ AIDS Interfaith Residential Services 3B Ⓓ Brian Blankenship Ⓒ Java Lounge 3C Ⓓ Segura Inc. Ⓒ TNN 3D Ⓓ Segura Inc. Ⓒ TNN 4A Ⓓ thomasvasquez.com Ⓒ b-nox, inc. 4B Ⓓ Device Ⓒ Touch 4C Ⓓ Art Chantry Ⓒ FISK 4D Ⓓ Tim Frame Design Ⓒ Cowboy 5A Ⓓ Proart Graphics/Gabriel Kalach Ⓒ Self 5B Ⓓ Segura Inc. Ⓒ Q101 Radio 5C Ⓓ Rickabaugh Graphics Ⓒ self promo 5D Ⓓ Proart Graphics/Gabriel Kalach Ⓒ Little Wunderbar

	A	B	C	D
1				
2				
3				
4				
5				

Ⓓ = Design Firm Ⓒ = Client

1A Ⓓ thomasvasquez.com Ⓒ New York City School District 1B Ⓓ Art Chantry Ⓒ Estrus 1C Ⓓ m+ Ⓒ orb, inc. 1D Ⓓ Methodologie Ⓒ Maxon 2A Ⓓ Dotzero Design Ⓒ Dotzero 2B Ⓓ Enterprise IG Ⓒ Super C 2C Ⓓ Gardner Design Ⓒ Cattleman's Collection Steaks 2D Ⓓ I Design Creative Group Ⓒ Motorcycle Mary 3A Ⓓ Smith Design Ⓒ Unilever Bestfoods 3B Ⓓ MINE Ⓒ Rich Steel 3C Ⓓ Duffy & Partners Ⓒ Rainforest Cafe 3D Ⓓ Jon Flaming Design Ⓒ Lone Star Frames 4A Ⓓ Delikatessen Ⓒ Fotomotel Hamburg 4B Ⓓ Frederick & Froberg Design Office Ⓒ Mattel 4C Ⓓ Michael Doret Graphic Design Ⓒ QVC 4D Ⓓ Integer Group-Midwest Ⓒ River Music Experience 5A Ⓓ Duffy & Partners Ⓒ Rainforest Cafe 5B Ⓓ Gardner Design Ⓒ Loft 150 5C Ⓓ Sayles Graphic Design, Inc. Ⓒ Wild Willy's Cycle Werks 5D Ⓓ Glenn Sakamoto Design Ⓒ Mulberry Street Pizzeria

A B C D

1 2 3 4 5

Ⓓ = Design Firm Ⓒ = Client

1A Ⓓ Integer Group-Midwest Ⓒ StageWest Theater Company 1B Ⓓ CRE8 communications, inc. Ⓒ The Dive Bar & Grill 1C Ⓓ greteman group Ⓒ choco drop 1D Ⓓ thomasvasquez.com Ⓒ Glue Brand Design 2A Ⓓ Art Chantry Ⓒ Estrus 2B Ⓓ Michael Doret Graphic Design Ⓒ Car Crazy 2C Ⓓ Blacktop Creative Ⓒ Coca-Cola 2D Ⓓ Device Ⓒ NYC Mech 3A Ⓓ Landor and Associates Ⓒ Del Monte 3B Ⓓ Hoyne Design Ⓒ Betta Foods Australia 3C Ⓓ Landor and Associates Ⓒ Frito Lay 3D Ⓓ Landor and Associates Ⓒ Levi's 4A Ⓓ Sibley/Peteet Design, Inc. Ⓒ Buddy Systems 4B Ⓓ DRAFT INDONESIA Ⓒ Lowe IMC 4C Ⓓ thomasvasquez.com Ⓒ US State Department 4D Ⓓ McAndrew Kaps Ⓒ Word Records 5A Ⓓ Planet Propaganda Ⓒ Just Coffee 5B Ⓓ Ames Design Ⓒ Pearl Jam 5C Ⓓ greteman group Ⓒ City of Wichita 5D Ⓓ Tallgrass Studios Ⓒ Topeka Advertising Federation

Podere Belvedere Identity Design

hand made group, Stia, Italy

Alessandro Esteri and his associates in hand made group—a multidisciplinary firm with offices in Florence, Milan, Paris, New York, and Bologna—believe in full integration of design and life. Their projects are selected on their capacity to make life better for others through photography, Web design, architecture, and furniture, industrial, and graphic design.

Design, Esteri believes, cannot be about just applying art. It must also ask questions about the design's intent: Is the product produced ethically? Does its production damage the earth? Is the product itself moral?

"We make our work go in a direction where it applies our art to things that we believe are good to people and the world," the designer says.

That's why he and Simona Vanzetto, his wife and business partner, began work on what could be the largest project of their careers, one that will truly combine their lives with design and its power to affect good. They purchased an 80-acre (32 hectare) plot of land in Tuscany on which to build an organic farm, a completely natural hotel, and a holistic spa. The new business, called Podere Belvedere (which means "the farm with the beautiful view"), will be thoroughly infused with manmade design and the natural beauty of Tuscany. It is a spiritual place, Esteri says, wild and full of forests and animals. This is where St. Francis lived, he adds.

This place would need a logo that could be applied to food packaging, wines, furniture, and anything else the farm would produce. It would also have to work on Podere Belvedere's stationery, promotional materials, hotel towels and furnishings, restaurant menus, and untold other items, still unimagined.

"We were looking for a logo that we could adapt to many things and one that expresses our philosophy of life," Esteri explains.

About six months into the development of the project, Esteri and his wife were surveying their property when the land itself offered up the answer. They found a piece of pottery with an unusual, flowerlike amoeba shape, almost framed by the form of the shard. The partners knew they had been given a sign.

Esteri, with the help of Davide Premuni (senior designer of hand made group), refined the shape carefully to preserve its freshness while increasing its sophistication. He ensured the new mark would work in any number of colors, as a 2-D or 3-D representation, and would be simple enough to reproduce in any manner, from embroidery to four-color printing.

"It felt right because of two things: It was found in the middle of our land, but it was also a sign that graphically represented the meaning of the project, which can be defined in a simple word: respect—for human beings, for the animals, for the earth. A friendly and happy sign with no arrows, all round shaped, and very feng shui—it was perfect," Esteri says. He acknowledges that they are building in what is a fertile archeological site—anyone who digs a hole is likely to find something interesting—but he still has the sense that the land is instructing him, whispering tales of the civilizations that walked here before him.

A B C D

LOGO SEARCH

Keywords: Display Type

Type: ○ Symbol ○ Typographic ○ Combo ◉ All

1

2

3

4

5

Ⓓ = Design Firm Ⓒ = Client

1C Ⓓ DDB Ⓒ DDB 1D Ⓓ Ames Design Ⓒ Phish 2A Ⓓ CDI Studios Ⓒ Sony Computer Entertainment America 2B Ⓓ Modern Dog Design Co. Ⓒ Publicis/Washington State Lottery 2C Ⓓ oakley design studios Ⓒ exotic magazine 2D Ⓓ Device Ⓒ icandy 3A Ⓓ GOLDFINGER c.s. Ⓒ Hothouse Inc for Nike 3B Ⓓ Modern Dog Design Co. Ⓒ K2 Snowboards 3C Ⓓ Modern Dog Design Co. Ⓒ Blue Q 3D Ⓓ Modern Dog Design Co. Ⓒ K2 Snowboards 4A Ⓓ Element Ⓒ Inside Out Youth 4B Ⓓ Landor and Associates Ⓒ Kool-Aid 4C Ⓓ Marius Fahrner Design Ⓒ Fork unstable media 4D Ⓓ Michael Doret Graphic Design Ⓒ Mammoth Records 5A Ⓓ CDI Studios Ⓒ Natasha Doll 5B Ⓓ Marius Fahrner Design Ⓒ Pleasure Snowboard Magazine 5C Ⓓ Duffy & Partners Ⓒ Rick Webb 5D Ⓓ Michael Doret Graphic Design Ⓒ Astrolux Records

A B C D

1

2

3

4

5

Ⓓ = Design Firm Ⓒ = Client

1A Ⓓ Duffy & Partners Ⓒ Stroh Brewery 1B Ⓓ Artomat Design Ⓒ The Rocket 1C Ⓓ Sayles Graphic Design, Inc. Ⓒ Metrojam 1D Ⓓ Art Chantry Ⓒ Art Chantry Design Co. 2A Ⓓ Art Chantry Ⓒ Estrus 2B Ⓓ Art Chantry Ⓒ The Breeders 2C Ⓓ Art Chantry Ⓒ The X-Rays! 2D Ⓓ Art Chantry Ⓒ The Cramps 3A Ⓓ Device Ⓒ Thrill Killers3B Ⓓ BLANK, Inc. Ⓒ The Adrenaline Group 3C Ⓓ Pennebaker Ⓒ Hindsight 3D Ⓓ Stephen Averitt Ⓒ Pinnacle Entertainment 4A Ⓓ Art Chantry Ⓒ Budweiser 4B Ⓓ McAndrew Kaps Ⓒ IMG 4C Ⓓ Device Ⓒ Galaxy 5 4D Ⓓ Modern Dog Design Co. Ⓒ K2 Snowboards 5A Ⓓ Gardner Design Ⓒ Cattleman's Collection Steaks 5B Ⓓ Rickabaugh Graphics Ⓒ self promo 5C Ⓓ Union Design & Photo Ⓒ Crush 5D Ⓓ Dotzero Design Ⓒ Dotzero

	A	B	C	D	
					1
					2
					3
					4
					5

Ⓓ = Design Firm Ⓒ = Client

1A Ⓓ Williams Collins Design & Development Ⓒ The Mint 1B Ⓓ O'Connor Identity Development Ⓒ True Magazine 1C Ⓓ b5 Marketing & Kommunikation GmbH Ⓒ qood GmbH 1D Ⓓ thomasvasquez.com Ⓒ BMG/RCA 2A Ⓓ Device Ⓒ Teen Titans 2B Ⓓ Ames Design Ⓒ MTV 2C Ⓓ Duffy & Partners Ⓒ Hart Ski 2D Ⓓ Device Ⓒ kenetic 3A Ⓓ Device Ⓒ Halo 3B Ⓓ Landor and Associates Ⓒ Mylo 3C Ⓓ Duffy & Partners Ⓒ Sub-Zero 3D Ⓓ Landor and Associates Ⓒ Alfa Laval 4A Ⓓ Segura Inc. Ⓒ Tiaxa 4B Ⓓ antoa Ⓒ maze a 4C Ⓓ O'Connor Identity Development Ⓒ Meoshe 4D Ⓓ the atmosfear Ⓒ Muse Music 5A Ⓓ Felixsockwell.com Ⓒ wahoo 5B Ⓓ Device Ⓒ Puss Puss 5C Ⓓ Duffy & Partners Ⓒ The Coca-Cola Company 5D Ⓓ DDB Ⓒ Anheuser Busch

	A	B	C	D
1	LOGO SEARCH			
2				
3				
4				
5				

LOGO SEARCH

Keywords: Calligraphy

Type: ○ Symbol ○ Typographic ○ Combo ● All

Ⓓ = Design Firm Ⓒ = Client

1C Ⓓ Marius Fahrner Design Ⓒ Montegro Food 1D Ⓓ Marius Fahrner Design Ⓒ Marius Fahrner 2A Ⓓ Artomat Design Ⓒ Frye Art Museum 2B Ⓓ Essex Two Incorporated Ⓒ Ariel Mutual Fund 2C Ⓓ John Langdon Design Ⓒ Victoria Maloney 2D Ⓓ Scribblers' Club Ⓒ Mreal—Jeff Tapping 3A Ⓓ bp360 Ⓒ Hualalai Rental Group 3B Ⓓ logobyte Ⓒ Scorpio Rising 3C Ⓓ MEDICIbrands Ⓒ pacha imports 3D Ⓓ Newbomb Design Ⓒ Lilacs & Lemonade 4A Ⓓ Enterprise IG Ⓒ Sugar Mill Casino 4B Ⓓ Rickabaugh Graphics Ⓒ CAPA 4C Ⓓ Eskil Ohlsson Assoc. Inc. Ⓒ The Rouse Company 4D Ⓓ Compass Design Ⓒ Great Waters Brewing Company 5A Ⓓ John Langdon Design Ⓒ Dan Brown 5B Ⓓ Compass Design Ⓒ August Schell Brewing Company 5C Ⓓ John Langdon Design Ⓒ Crown Vantage Paper Co. 5D Ⓓ Burd & Patterson Ⓒ Windsor Marketing Group

A	B	C	D	
				1
				2
				3
				4
				5

Ⓓ = Design Firm Ⓒ = Client

1A Ⓓ Nestor Stermole VCG Ⓒ Cucina Antica 1B Ⓓ Duffy & Partners Ⓒ Smartwool Socks 1C Ⓓ O'Connor Identity Development Ⓒ Cubop Records 1D Ⓓ Duffy & Partners Ⓒ LaMadeleine 2A Ⓓ Hoyne Design Ⓒ Fosters Group 2B Ⓓ redinwyden Ⓒ Pastafina 2C Ⓓ Soloflight Design Studio Ⓒ Self brew 2D Ⓓ Landor and Associates Ⓒ Hilton 3A Ⓓ Stuph Clothing Ⓒ Monroe FBC 3B Ⓓ TD2, S.C. Ⓒ NESTLÉ CHOCOLATES 3C Ⓓ Sabingrafik, Inc. Ⓒ Adra Soaps 3D Ⓓ Digital Soup Ⓒ Red9 4A Ⓓ Essex Two Incorporated Ⓒ Spiegel, Inc. 4B Ⓓ Landor and Associates Ⓒ Coca-Cola 4C Ⓓ Creative FX Communications Ⓒ Snow Masters, Inc. 4D Ⓓ Landor and Associates Ⓒ Kellogg's 5A Ⓓ Landor and Associates Ⓒ Miller 5B Ⓓ Landor and Associates Ⓒ Coors Brewing Company 5C Ⓓ Landor and Associates Ⓒ Disney 5D Ⓓ Landor and Associates Ⓒ Johnson & Johnson

Ⓓ = Design Firm Ⓒ = Client

1A Ⓓ Gardner Design Ⓒ Nature's Choice 1B Ⓓ Davidson Design Ⓒ Sugar & Spice 1C Ⓓ Cirque de Darmon Ⓒ self (student work) 1D Ⓓ Modern Dog Design Co. Ⓒ K2 Snowboards 2A Ⓓ Essex Two Incorporated Ⓒ Miller Brewing, Inc. 2B Ⓓ oakley design studios Ⓒ crystal pictures 2C Ⓓ DDB Ⓒ delilah 2D Ⓓ Art Chantry Ⓒ King of Hawii 3A Ⓓ karacters design group Ⓒ Sun-Rype Products Ltd. 3B Ⓓ Duffy & Partners Ⓒ Rick Webb 3C Ⓓ m+ Ⓒ american express 3D Ⓓ switchfoot creative Ⓒ Garden Variety 4A Ⓓ Landor and Associates Ⓒ Lilly 4B Ⓓ The Bradford Lawton Design Group Ⓒ Williams Landscaping 4C Ⓓ Atlanta College of Art Ⓒ eye frame 4D Ⓓ Davidson Design Ⓒ Myer Grace Bros 5A Ⓓ dialogbox Ⓒ tokyo 5B Ⓓ Jeff Kern Design Ⓒ SEF-Robison Gamble Creative 5C Ⓓ John Langdon Design Ⓒ The Norman & Rina Indictor Library of Islamic Art 5D Ⓓ Enterprise IG Ⓒ Madinat Jumeirah

Luxi
Identity Design

Liska & Associates, New York, New York

A new hybrid of logo or wordmark has emerged in the past few years: designs that are essentially URLs. The mark for Luxi, a new online retailer for high-end jewelry and watches, fits this description. The New York City office of Liska & Associates created its wordmark and also named the new service in 2003.

The new name needed to convey that quality merchandise was available at discount prices—but the look and sound of the name had to be decidedly highbrow. The name needed to be gender-neutral—strong enough to appeal to men (who still make up the majority of the online buying audience) yet friendly enough to welcome the female shopper.

From a long list of names, Luxi was selected because it was short, memorable, and easy to spell—crucial for a URL.

"The *I* at the end also suggests a nickname," explains Liska designer Tanya Quick. "It's like you are hearing an insider's secret."

When the name was selected, the design team began exploring how to visualize it. One direction involved using images of constellations, because watching the stars was an ancient way of mapping time. Stars in the sky could also represent diamonds.

Another exploration used the universal symbol for a hand. This concept worked well for what would eventually become two sister Luxi sites—one for jewelry and one for watches—because the hand could be shown wearing either a ring for one URL and a timepiece on the other, for example.

"This direction was more playful and could be played out throughout the site—as a directional, as a helping hand, and so on," Quick says. The client liked this approach but wanted something that was a bit stronger, much bolder, and a bit less casual. "Balancing friendliness and masculinity was important," she adds.

So the designers developed the idea of a simple and direct wordmark. The final design uses an elegant, elongated set of letters with plenty of presence. But balancing the letters, especially the slight *I* at the end of the word, was tricky. Stretching the word turned it into more of a unified shape that included the *I* as part of its form.

The wordmark also worked well for Luxi's primary applications—displayed online and stamped on gift boxes. "Going with the simple mark allows for much more play in packaging and online," Quick says. Refining elements such as colors and thick-thin weights in typography is more difficult in online display than it is in print, she adds.

But the electronic environment also offers advantages. For instance, for another Liska project, a line of teen skin-care products that would be sold only online, Liska designers discovered that they were not bound by a strict requirement of in-store packaging: a powerful shelf face.

"We could think about all sides of the bottle, not just its face. For this particular design, we let the logo wrap all the way around the bottle and circle it," Quick explains. Logos can also be animated, taken apart, and repurposed in new ways on websites.

"It definitely gives us the ability to have more play," she adds.

	A	B	C	D
1	LOGO SEARCH			
2				
3				
4				
5				

LOGO SEARCH

Keywords: Crests

Type: ○ Symbol ○ Typographic ○ Combo ◉ All

Ⓓ = Design Firm Ⓒ = Client

1C Ⓓ DDB Ⓒ Anheuser Busch 1D Ⓓ Williams Collins Design & Development Ⓒ Buck Owens Productions 2A Ⓓ Perks Design Partners Ⓒ King Island Bakehouse 2B Ⓓ Michael Doret Graphic Design Ⓒ Margarethe Hubauer GmbH 2C Ⓓ McArtor Design Ⓒ Charles' BBQ 2D Ⓓ Gardner Design Ⓒ Morrison Farms Popcorn 3A Ⓓ Michael Doret Graphic Design Ⓒ Event Media 3B Ⓓ Michael Doret Graphic Design Ⓒ Graphic Artists Guild 3C Ⓓ Webb Scarlett Ⓒ Plymouth Gin 3D Ⓓ Sayles Graphic Design, Inc. Ⓒ Jimmy's 4A Ⓓ Sayles Graphic Design, Inc. Ⓒ Beaverdale Business Coalition 4B Ⓓ Sayles Graphic Design, Inc. Ⓒ Good Burrito Company 4C Ⓓ Glitschka Studios Ⓒ Integrity First Financial 4D Ⓓ Sayles Graphic Design, Inc. Ⓒ Outside the Box Promotions 5A Ⓓ Gardner Design Ⓒ Tote Cuisine 5B Ⓓ Gardner Design Ⓒ CS Walter's 5C Ⓓ Michael Doret Graphic Design Ⓒ General Amusements 5D Ⓓ Delikatessen Ⓒ Maras Icecream

A	B	C	D	
				1
				2
				3
				4
				5

Ⓓ = Design Firm Ⓒ = Client

1A Ⓓ Alphabet Arm Design Ⓒ Messiah Records/Quion Sneed 1B Ⓓ Creative FX Communications Ⓒ Kaye Communications 1C Ⓓ Squires & Company Ⓒ Lightning Couriers 1D Ⓓ Alphabet Arm Design Ⓒ Tyler Fischer 2A Ⓓ Landor and Associates Ⓒ Ferrari 2B Ⓓ Dotzero Design Ⓒ Longbottom Coffee 2C Ⓓ McArtor Design Ⓒ Perfection Carpet Cleaning 2D Ⓓ Gardner Design Ⓒ LS Frazey 3A Ⓓ Gardner Design Ⓒ Saxon 3B Ⓓ Gardner Design Ⓒ Cox Digital Cable 3C Ⓓ Gardner Design Ⓒ Gates Enterprises 3D Ⓓ McArtor Design Ⓒ Midwest Sports Syndicators 4A Ⓓ Ross Creative + Strategy Ⓒ Peoria Chamber of Commerce 4B Ⓓ Gardner Design Ⓒ Great Lodge 4C Ⓓ Enterprise IG Ⓒ The Boardwalk 4D Ⓓ Webb Scarlett Ⓒ Pernod Ricard 5A Ⓓ Gardner Design Ⓒ BG Bolton's Bar and Grill 5B Ⓓ BC Design Ⓒ Pyramid Breweries 5C Ⓓ Sayles Graphic Design, Inc. Ⓒ Beaverdale Village 5D Ⓓ Tim Frame Design Ⓒ American Hog Classic

A B C D

1

2

3

4

5

(D) = Design Firm (C) = Client

1A (D) Indicia Design Inc (C) Countryside Bistro 1B (D) Glitschka Studios (C) Cardwell Creative 1C (D) Tim Frame Design (C) Hoosier Soap Company 1D (D) Michael Doret Graphic Design (C) Hollywood Dell Civic Association
2A (D) On Duty Design (C) Gigabeats 2B (D) Brian Blankenship (C) FC Erdinger 2C (D) McAndrew Kaps (C) Camelback Motors 2D (D) BBDO Detroit Design Group (C) DaimlerChrysler Corporation
3A (D) Oxide Design Co. (C) River City Roundup 3B (D) MLS Creative Services (C) Anheuser-Busch and Major League Soccer 3C (D) GOLDFINGER c.s. (C) Outkast 3D (D) Blacktop Creative (C) Durham School Buses
4A (D) Gardner Design (C) Kansas Masonic Home 4B (D) Williams Collins Design & Development (C) Mark Szymborski—GBI 4C (D) Tim Frame Design (C) Clutch Graphic 4D (D) CDI Studios (C) Caesars Palace
5A (D) Burd & Patterson (C) Highways To Adventure, Inc. 5B (D) Blacktop Creative (C) Twisters Frozen Custard 5C (D) Sabingrafik, Inc. (C) Harcourt & Co. 5D (D) Gardner Design (C) BG Bolton's Grille and Tavern

A B C D

1

2

3

4

5

Ⓓ = Design Firm Ⓒ = Client

1A Ⓓ Michael Doret Graphic Design Ⓒ Books 1B Ⓓ Michael Doret Graphic Design Ⓒ ViaWest 1C Ⓓ Michael Doret Graphic Design Ⓒ Wonderful World 1D Ⓓ Michael Doret Graphic Design Ⓒ Chronicle Books
2A Ⓓ Michael Doret Graphic Design Ⓒ Capitol Records 2B Ⓓ Howalt Design Studio, Inc. Ⓒ Expressions 2C Ⓓ Michael Doret Graphic Design Ⓒ Toronto Blue Jays 2D Ⓓ Michael Doret Graphic Design Ⓒ Casablanca Records
3A Ⓓ greteman group Ⓒ zombie party 3B Ⓓ Duffy & Partners Ⓒ Dickson's 3C Ⓓ greteman group Ⓒ piping and equipment 3D Ⓓ Landor and Associates Ⓒ 20th Century Fox
4A Ⓓ MLS Creative Services Ⓒ RiCH Levy Productions 4B Ⓓ Gardner Design Ⓒ BG Bolton's Bar and Grille 4C Ⓓ Tim Frame Design Ⓒ Sater Industries 4D Ⓓ Soloflight Design Studio Ⓒ Talia! Quality Foods
5A Ⓓ Sayles Graphic Design, Inc. Ⓒ The Shag Brag Tour 5B Ⓓ McAndrew Kaps Ⓒ Belles Brewing Company 5C Ⓓ Squires & Company Ⓒ Jack's Guitars 5D Ⓓ McArtor Design Ⓒ Master Builders

	A	B	C	D
1	LOGO SEARCH Keywords: Sports Type: Symbol Typographic Combo All			
2				
3				
4				
5				

Ⓓ = Design Firm Ⓒ = Client

1C Ⓓ Landor and Associates Ⓒ 2002 Olympics 1D Ⓓ Landor and Associates Ⓒ Nagano 1998 2A Ⓓ Rickabaugh Graphics Ⓒ The Ohio State University 2B Ⓓ Clive Jacobson Design Ⓒ NFL Properties Inc. 2C Ⓓ Compass Design Ⓒ WPFL—Women's Professional Football League 2D Ⓓ Popgun Ⓒ Electronic Arts 3A Ⓓ Device Ⓒ Maxim's NFL Smackdown 3B Ⓓ Sabingrafik, Inc. Ⓒ Amerisports Bar & Grill 3C Ⓓ Rickabaugh Graphics Ⓒ Providence College 3D Ⓓ Rickabaugh Graphics Ⓒ Western Kentucky University 4A Ⓓ Rickabaugh Graphics Ⓒ University of Wisconsin 4B Ⓓ Compass Design Ⓒ WPFL—Women's Professional Football League 4C Ⓓ Rickabaugh Graphics Ⓒ University of Connecticut 4D Ⓓ Rickabaugh Graphics Ⓒ Old Dominion University 5A Ⓓ McAndrew Kaps Ⓒ NCAA 5B Ⓓ Glitschka Studios Ⓒ Upper Deck Company 5C Ⓓ Michael Doret Graphic Design Ⓒ 3com 5D Ⓓ Michael Doret Graphic Design Ⓒ Toronto Blue Jays

	A	B	C	D	
	BALLGREEN golf is everything	AustinGolf	zonafoot	GOLF MADE SIMPLE	1
	PAYNE STEWART	GOLFOTO	TOP THIS A GOLFING GAME OF SKILL		2
		BIGEASY	GOLF DOLLARS		3
					4
	CRICKET AUSTRALIA	Outletics TENNIS	BOOKSTORE	US SKI TEAM GOLD CUP LAKE PLACID '98	5

Ⓓ = Design Firm Ⓒ = Client

1A Ⓓ Simon & Goetz Design Ⓒ ballgreen gmbh & co. kg 1B Ⓓ Tribe Design Houston Ⓒ Austin Golf 1C Ⓓ cesart.com Ⓒ Zonafoot 1D Ⓓ HardBall Sports Ⓒ Golf Made Simple 2A Ⓓ Platform Creative Group Ⓒ Vintage Golf 2B Ⓓ greteman group Ⓒ golfoto 2C Ⓓ MarketSource Ⓒ M. Levine 2D Ⓓ R&R Partners (Randy Heil) Ⓒ unused 3A Ⓓ Glenn Sakamoto Design Ⓒ Golf Education Inc 3B Ⓓ R&R Partners (Randy Heil) Ⓒ Billy Vassiliadis 3C Ⓓ Popgun Ⓒ Golf Dollars 3D Ⓓ Gardner Design Ⓒ The Oaks Golf Course 4A Ⓓ Cave Ⓒ Andrea Decof Foundation 4B Ⓓ Rick Johnson & Company Ⓒ Santa Ana Golf Club, New Mexico 4C Ⓓ Gardner Design Ⓒ Crestview Plaza 4D Ⓓ Gardner Design Ⓒ Crestview Plaza 5A Ⓓ FutureBrand Ⓒ Cricket Australia 5B Ⓓ Freemind Studio Ⓒ Outletics Inc. 5C Ⓓ Tharp Did It Ⓒ TDCTJHTBIPC.org 5D Ⓓ substance151 Ⓒ U.S. Ski Team

	A	B	C	D
1	MLS	FIFA WOMEN'S WORLD CUP USA 99	DEFIANCE SOCCER	CAROLINA Courage
2	MLS Futbolito! ¡Es Nuestro Juego!	BLITZ UNITED	MLS CUP 2003	FanHome
3		KRISTI YAMAGUCHI Holiday ICE RINK at EMBARCADERO CENTER	RodriguezSurfboards	
4	WNBA	HOUSTON COMETS	100 SETON HALL BASKETBALL 1903 • 2003	
5	NBA LIVE X-LARGE	SEATTLE SONICS	NEW YORK KNICKS	NBA HERITAGE COLLECTION ESTD 1946

Ⓓ = Design Firm Ⓒ = Client

1A Ⓓ MLS Creative Services Ⓒ Major League Soccer (MLS) 1B Ⓓ Duffy & Partners Ⓒ FIFA 1999 Women's World Cup Organizing Committee 1C Ⓓ Rickabaugh Graphics Ⓒ Defiance College 1D Ⓓ Michael Doret Graphic Design Ⓒ Women's United Soccer Association 2A Ⓓ MLS Creative Services Ⓒ Major League Soccer (MLS) 2B Ⓓ Prejean LoBue Ⓒ Blitz United 2C Ⓓ MLS Creative Services Ⓒ Major League Soccer (MLS) 2D Ⓓ VMA Ⓒ FanHome.com 3A Ⓓ Sabingrafik, Inc. Ⓒ Amerisports Bar & Grill 3B Ⓓ Popgun Ⓒ Boston Properties 3C Ⓓ Lapada Visual Ⓒ Rodriguez Surfboards 3D Ⓓ Popgun Ⓒ Popgun Design 4A Ⓓ Frederick & Froberg Design Office Ⓒ WNBA 4B Ⓓ Frederick & Froberg Design Office Ⓒ WNBA 4C Ⓓ Rickabaugh Graphics Ⓒ Seton Hall University 4D Ⓓ Glitschka Studios Ⓒ Upper Deck Company 5A Ⓓ Popgun Ⓒ Electronic Arts 5B Ⓓ Hornall Anderson Ⓒ Seattle Sonics 5C Ⓓ Michael Doret Graphic Design Ⓒ NBA 5D Ⓓ Michael Doret Graphic Design Ⓒ NBA

Phish
Identity Design

Ames, Seattle, Washington

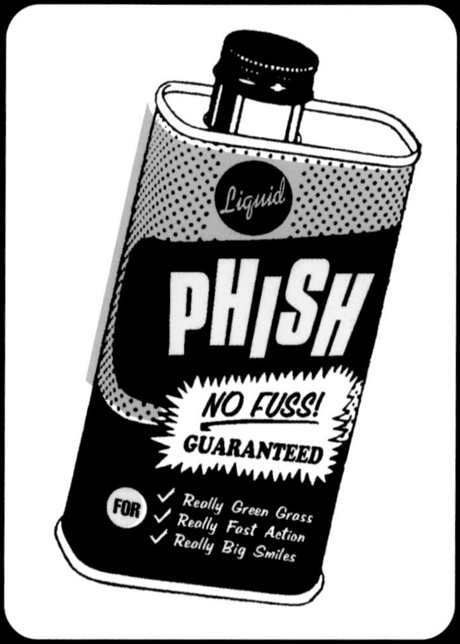

Creating an identity for an entertainment client is a never-ending cycle of renewal. As the artist constantly reinvents him- or herself, creates new work, or even performs in a different venue, design must keep pace. For a contemporary music client whose "logo" is essentially the sound it records, there can no longer be such a thing as a single visual mark that can carry the full weight of the performance. Today's brutal marketing environment requires a more fluid visual identity.

Ames's relationship with the band Phish dates back to 1996, when the Seattle-based design office created T-shirts for a U.S. tour. Since then, the two-person firm has worked with the band on a number of projects, and each has been very different. Ames also creates graphics for Pearl Jam, MTV, House of Blues, MOE, Sting, John Mayer, and Nancy Wilson, to name a few artists and groups.

Phish actually has a real logo—an uninspiringly literal aquarium-variety fish built from the letters in the band's name. But Ames and the other design companies with whom Phish works are not required to honor or use it in any way.

"Bands constantly reinvent themselves, but without design they can't do it. Even though they don't work with just one logo or look all the time, they are very concerned with their identity. Bands make a load of money on posters and T-shirts," says Ames designer Coby Schultz. The art and identity that designers create is essentially the for-sale product. "Each piece we create is completely unique. Each can stand on its own."

For a Las Vegas appearance in 2003, Ames focused on the quirky nature of the place for a poster design. Ames is known for its strong silkscreen design and production. Schultz took advantage of the process to create what he calls "large colors on big paper." This design shows a washout, complete with high-waisted pants, white belt and shoes, giant lapels, and bad glasses and hair.

"He's in his mid-40s and is still driving a Gremlin," Schultz explains. "He's still trying to hit it big."

The designer's goal is to tell a compelling story in every design. He believes that is why Ames' work appeals to bands: Like a song, their art has something to say. "There is always a deeper message, not just a cool-looking something," he adds. Here, the message is one of humor. From the arcade colors to the dimensional type to the content of the art, the designer uses the over-the-top reputation of Las Vegas to put Phish into context for this appearance.

	A	B	C	D
1	LOGO SEARCH Keywords: Heads Type: Symbol / Typographic / Combo / All			
2				
3				
4				
5				

Ⓓ = Design Firm Ⓒ = Client

1C Ⓓ Felixsockwell.com Ⓒ usa 1D Ⓓ Glitschka Studios Ⓒ Sports NW 2A Ⓓ Mike Quon/Designation Ⓒ n/a 2B Ⓓ Glitschka Studios Ⓒ RCR Suspensions 2C Ⓓ Glitschka Studios Ⓒ Pacific Security Inc. 2D Ⓓ thomasvasquez.com Ⓒ BMG/RCA 3A Ⓓ GOLDFINGER c.s. Ⓒ Mandingo Warriors 3B Ⓓ GOLDFINGER c.s. Ⓒ Soul Chemistry 3C Ⓓ Landor and Associates Ⓒ KFC 3D Ⓓ Chuck Pennington Ⓒ Pettersen & Pettersen 4A Ⓓ Felixsockwell.com Ⓒ spot 4B Ⓓ Duffy & PartnersⒸ Matt's Hats 4C Ⓓ Rickabaugh Graphics Ⓒ Hasbro 4D Ⓓ Stacy Bormett Design, LLC Ⓒ Tanaka/Sagebrush 5A Ⓓ Glitschka Studios Ⓒ Glitschka Studios 5B Ⓓ Insight Design Ⓒ Tanya's Soup Kitchen 5C Ⓓ Duffy & Partners Ⓒ Rick Webb 5D Ⓓ Art Chantry Ⓒ Estrus

	A	B	C	D
1				
2				
3				
4				
5				

Ⓓ = Design Firm Ⓒ = Client

1A Ⓓ Felixsockwell.com Ⓒ apple 1B Ⓓ THINKMULE.com Ⓒ Jeremy Pruitt 1C Ⓓ Ty Wilkins Ⓒ Ty Wilkins 1D Ⓓ Duffy & Partners Ⓒ D'Amico & Partners 2A Ⓓ John Langdon Design Ⓒ Hodgson Design 2B Ⓓ STUART ROWLEY DESIGN Ⓒ ETS 2C Ⓓ Howling Good Designs Ⓒ Imaginif Toys 2D Ⓓ Tom Fowler, Inc. Ⓒ Inua Gallery 3A Ⓓ Jeff Kern Design Ⓒ Tyson-Noble and Associates 3B Ⓓ Howling Good Designs Ⓒ One Good Turn 3C Ⓓ Pennebaker Ⓒ Red Head Hunter 3D Ⓓ Essex Two Incorporated Ⓒ Motorola 4A Ⓓ The Office of Bill Chiaravalle Ⓒ Numbers@Work 4B Ⓓ Nancy Wu Ⓒ Paul Wu & Associates Ltd. 4C Ⓓ Duffy & Partners Ⓒ Jim Beam Brands 4D Ⓓ Jon Flaming Design Ⓒ Rosen Jewelry 5A Ⓓ Art Chantry Ⓒ A. Chantry Design w/ Mark Zingarelli 5B Ⓓ THINKMULE.com Ⓒ Jeremy Pruitt 5C Ⓓ Dotzero Design Ⓒ fetish kings 5D Ⓓ THINKMULE.com Ⓒ Jeremy Pruitt

	A	B	C	D
1		one good turn	INFANT RECORDS	
2	tatico.	brainchild SOFTWARE	shady sisters kid's sun protection	
3			DANONE	goodnight moon
4			ExtendedPresence Outsourced Sales Professionals	
5	FRUIT CAPSULE		NATIONAL CAMPAIGN AGAINST YOUTH VIOLENCE	FLORIDA MUNICIPAL WASTE & WATER TREATMENT SERVICES WESTERN REGION

Ⓓ = Design Firm Ⓒ = Client

1A Ⓓ Hubbell Design Works Ⓒ Mason Elizabeth Hubbell 1B Ⓓ Howling Good Designs Ⓒ One Good Turn 1C Ⓓ Tenacious Design Ⓒ Infant Records 1D Ⓓ Proart Graphics/Gabriel Kalach Ⓒ Abeille Proposal 2A Ⓓ redinwyden Ⓒ tatico 2B Ⓓ Glitschka Studios Ⓒ Brian Child Software 2C Ⓓ Hubbell Design Works Ⓒ Shady Sisters 2D Ⓓ ADD [art dirction + design] Ⓒ Chun Kim 3A Ⓓ Duffy & Partners Ⓒ Faith Popcorn 3B Ⓓ bob neace graphic design, inc Ⓒ associates in women's health 3C Ⓓ Landor and Associates Ⓒ Danone 3D Ⓓ CAPSULE Ⓒ Goodnight Moon 4A Ⓓ Kircher, Inc. Ⓒ Alliance Service Network 4B Ⓓ Dotzero Design Ⓒ BIA 4C Ⓓ Convexus Consulting, Inc. Ⓒ Extended Presence 4D Ⓓ Chuck Pennington Ⓒ Secret Weapon Marketing 5A Ⓓ Howalt Design Studio, Inc. Ⓒ Nature's Healthy Essentials 5B Ⓓ Howalt Design Studio, Inc. Ⓒ Nature's Healthy Essentials 5C Ⓓ Howalt Design Studio, Inc. Ⓒ President Bill Clinton 5D Ⓓ Howalt Design Studio, Inc. Ⓒ Expressions

	A	B	C	D	
					1
					2
					3
					4
					5

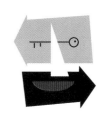

Ⓓ = Design Firm   Ⓒ = Client

1A Ⓓ Molly Z. Illustration Ⓒ Gretchen Knopf 1B Ⓓ Marius Fahrner Design Ⓒ Skin Biology Center 1C Ⓓ Simon & Goetz Design Ⓒ ritzenhoff 1D Ⓓ BC Design Ⓒ Gift 2A Ⓓ BC Design Ⓒ Gift 2B Ⓓ Neoalchemia Design Lab Ⓒ Joy Mandoo, San Jose, CA 2C Ⓓ Device Ⓒ Dolly Bird 2D Ⓓ Design Nut Ⓒ Cyber Stylist 3A Ⓓ MocaLoca Inc. Ⓒ MocaLoca 3B Ⓓ Crosby Associates Ⓒ Carol DeLong 3C Ⓓ Glitschka Studios Ⓒ Joe Mochas 3D Ⓓ Born to Design Ⓒ self 4A Ⓓ Glitschka Studios Ⓒ Zombie Citizens 4B Ⓓ Landor and Associates Ⓒ Rica 4C Ⓓ Gardner Design Ⓒ Excel 4D Ⓓ Dotzero Design Ⓒ Emberland's 5A Ⓓ Art Chantry Ⓒ Estrus 5B Ⓓ helium.design Ⓒ helium.design 5C Ⓓ Paul Black Design Ⓒ Deep Ellum Association 5D Ⓓ Felixsockwell.com Ⓒ fast co - security

	A	B	C	D
1			mind bender	KIDS NIGHT OUT LOS CERRITOS CENTER
2	CHIEF TOMMY HAWK'S SOUVENIR STANDS	Big Sam's INLET CAFE & RAW BAR	The DOLE PLANTATION	KING MAYA
3	North Star PEDIATRICS, P.C.	JAVA coffee house	c.ch@nge	
4		packet eye resources	SurfnTalk	GNF
5	IRIS BALL		CENTRAL EYEWORKS	buckminsta

Ⓓ = Design Firm Ⓒ = Client

1A Ⓓ Glitschka Studios Ⓒ NW Sports 1B Ⓓ Soloflight Design Studio Ⓒ Talia! Quality Foods 1C Ⓓ Kendall Creative Shop, Inc. Ⓒ Mind Bender 1D Ⓓ Dotzero Design Ⓒ Davis Agency
2A Ⓓ Howalt Design Studio, Inc. Ⓒ Chief Tommy Hawk's 2B Ⓓ Russell Design Co. Ⓒ Big Sam's Restaurant 2C Ⓓ Howalt Design Studio, Inc. Ⓒ Dole Plantations, Hawaii 2D Ⓓ Glitschka Studios Ⓒ Jungle Jack Palms
3A Ⓓ Born to Design Ⓒ North Star Pediatrics 3B Ⓓ SD Graphic Design Ⓒ student work 3C Ⓓ Perks Design Partners Ⓒ QBE Mercantile Mutual 3D Ⓓ Paragon Design International Ⓒ Chicago Futures Trading Group
4A Ⓓ R&R Partners (Randy Heil) Ⓒ Ministry of Technology 4B Ⓓ Cam Stewart Graphic Design Ⓒ Packet Eye 4C Ⓓ Hot Chilli Ⓒ SurfnTalk 4D Ⓓ Design Continuum Inc Ⓒ Genomics Institute of the Novartis Foundation
5A Ⓓ Richards Brock Miller Mitchell & Associates Ⓒ Iris Ball 5B Ⓓ Gardner Design Ⓒ Virtual Focus Internet 5C Ⓓ Hubbell Design Works Ⓒ Central Eyeworks Optical Shops 5D Ⓓ Basic Function Ⓒ Buckminsta Production Company

Union of European Football Identity Design

Design Bridge, London, United Kingdom

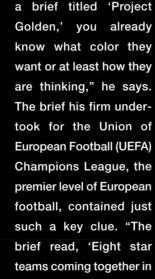

A good client brief, says Rod Petrie, founding partner of Design Bridge, London, usually has the project's design solution already embedded in it.

"If the client gives you a brief titled 'Project Golden,' you already know what color they want or at least how they are thinking," he says. The brief his firm undertook for the Union of European Football (UEFA) Champions League, the premier level of European football, contained just such a key clue. "The brief read, 'Eight star teams coming together in a championship league.' Six design companies had this same information, but we were the only ones who spotted the opportunity."

UEFA has a long history, and in 1955, it created the Champion's Club's Cup, held to determine the best club team in Europe. What became known as the European Cup gained plenty of prestige, but by the 1980s, its format and identity needed a revamp to reflect the nature of the now larger clubs and the changing face of football, and to take better advantage of the vast TV coverage and sponsorship that had become available. Finally, in 1992, the UEFA Champions League was created.

UEFA asked Design Bridge to create an identity that was modern and classical—every match branded with the new identity should look like a championship event. Although the designers presented a number of alternatives, their favorite—and, as it turned out, the client's favorite—was the "starball."

The designers had also commissioned the TV opening sequence using the starball. This was an identity that would live or die on the television screen, and they wanted to show their idea in the proper context. This step incurred additional cost and a leap of faith for the Design Bridge team before the job was even awarded, but Petrie feels that it is important to go the extra mile when he really believes in an idea.

Petrie and his group suggested a color palette of black, white, and silver. It would stand out and interact with the bright colors participating teams already used and with the general background of a football environment. Of course, the palette also mimicked the normal coloration of a football, with some additional shine.

The logo had the unique ability to be either two- or three-dimensional with little problem. It could be stamped onto a player's shirt as a flat mark, painted as a pitch decoration, or printed as a wallpaper pattern to cover up any elements in stadiums that are irrelevant to an event and should not be shown on TV.

In a three-dimensional manifestation, the logo can be an imprinted football or even a beautiful silver award, the Starball Trophy, which would be given to all the key partners in a UEFA Champions League season, including the leading goal scorer of the league.

Petrie feels the logo is one of those classics that is still as valid today as it was when it was first created.

"As designers and creative people," he says, "we always need to look and see further than our clients."

	A	B	C	D
1	LOGO SEARCH — Keywords: People — Type: Symbol, Typographic, Combo, All			
2	ALL ABOARD!	FULLY LICENSED FontPimp psst..!	SMASHGOLF™	
3	TEXPROMPT	A		
4				
5		Helping Kids Win Against Cancer		Sydney 2000

Ⓓ = Design Firm Ⓒ = Client

1C Ⓓ Creative Madhouse Ⓒ Resume Courier 1D Ⓓ Glitschka Studios Company Ⓒ now defunct 2A Ⓓ Jon Flaming Design Ⓒ Watermark Church 2B Ⓓ Device Ⓒ Font Pimp 2C Ⓓ Brad Norr Design Ⓒ Smashgolf 2D Ⓓ Gardner Design Ⓒ PrintMaster Printing 3A Ⓓ Paul Black Design Ⓒ Aqua Star Pools 3B Ⓓ Deep Design Studio Ⓒ A 3C Ⓓ Deep Design Studio Ⓒ A 3D Ⓓ Deep Design Studio Ⓒ A 4A Ⓓ Dotzero Design Ⓒ Peddler Bakery 4B Ⓓ Dotzero Design Ⓒ Bridgeport 4C Ⓓ Dotzero Design Ⓒ Bridgeport 4D Ⓓ Dotzero Design Ⓒ Bridgeport 5A Ⓓ Richards Brock Miller Mitchell & Associates Ⓒ WinStar Outreach 5B Ⓓ Richards Brock Miller Mitchell & Associates Ⓒ Hyundai Motor America 5C Ⓓ Gardner Design Ⓒ Bank of America 5D Ⓓ FutureBrand Ⓒ SOCOG

A	B	C	D	
				1
				2
				3
				4
				5

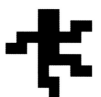

Ⓓ = Design Firm Ⓒ = Client

1A Ⓓ Gardner Design Ⓒ Excel 1B Ⓓ Eskil Ohlsson Assoc. Inc. Ⓒ Pfizer Inc. 1C Ⓓ Intrinsic Design Ⓒ Wilderness Works 1D Ⓓ Gardner Design Ⓒ Insherpa, out-take, no client, available 2A Ⓓ greteman group Ⓒ above & beyond 2B Ⓓ What Design, Inc. Ⓒ Instrument for Change 2C Ⓓ Mitre Design Ⓒ Children's Museum of Winston-Salem 2D Ⓓ wedge.a&d Ⓒ Calgary Girls Choir 3A Ⓓ Felixsockwell.com Ⓒ none 3B Ⓓ Fernandez Design Ⓒ Court Appointed Special Advocates (CASA) 3C Ⓓ Felixsockwell.com Ⓒ berkeley 3D Ⓓ Mortensen Design Ⓒ Handspring, Inc. 4A Ⓓ TD2, S.C. Ⓒ EMYCO 4B Ⓓ Dotzero Design Ⓒ Bridgeport 4C Ⓓ dialogbox Ⓒ bitman 4D Ⓓ Landor and Associates Ⓒ Rand McNally 5A Ⓓ Felixsockwell.com Ⓒ felix sockwell 5B Ⓓ Dotzero Design Ⓒ Unicru 5C Ⓓ Renata Graw Ⓒ Ibô—a creative clothing store 5D Ⓓ Born to Design Ⓒ Sylvia Griggs for Flack Design

	A	B	C	D
1	Standard. LIFESTYLE ELEMENTS	mlife		STANDARD
2	LESSONS	STANDARD™ LIFESTYLE EQUIPMENT	BESTCLONE	
3	MTV	tribeside .com		Dr. Winnie Su FAMILY MEDICINE & OBSTETRICS
4			THE HEALERS ALTERNATIVE MEDICINE	Lindaskóli
5	Single Parent Family Outreach			

Ⓓ = Design Firm Ⓒ = Client

1A Ⓓ Gardner Design Ⓒ The Standard 1B Ⓓ Howalt Design Studio, Inc. Ⓒ AT&T 1C Ⓓ Rick Johnson & Company Ⓒ New Mexico Traffic Safety Bureau 1D Ⓓ Gardner Design Ⓒ The Standard 2A Ⓓ Tharp Did It! Ⓒ TDCTJHTBIPC.org 2B Ⓓ Gardner Design Ⓒ The Standard 2C Ⓓ Q Zanders Ⓒ M Real 2D Ⓓ Glitschka Studios Ⓒ NW Sports 3A Ⓓ BC Design Ⓒ MTV 3B Ⓓ BC Design Ⓒ Tribeside.com 3C Ⓓ Squires & Company Ⓒ Uptown Association 3D Ⓓ Nancy Wu Ⓒ Dr. Winnie Su, MD 4A Ⓓ The Bradford Lawton Design Group Ⓒ Hart Work 4B Ⓓ Felixsockwell.com Ⓒ berkeley 4C Ⓓ Proart Graphics/Gabriel Kalach Ⓒ Healers 4D Ⓓ Nonni & Manni/Ydda Ⓒ Lindaskoli, elementary school 5A Ⓓ What Design, Inc. Ⓒ Single Parent Family Outreach 5B Ⓓ Squires & Company Ⓒ State Street Spirits 5C Ⓓ Blacktop Creative Ⓒ Corbin Bronze 5D Ⓓ greteman group Ⓒ celestial massage

	A	B	C	D	
					1
					2
					3
					4
					5

Ⓓ = Design Firm Ⓒ = Client

1A Ⓓ Popgun Ⓒ Media Distribution Corporation 1B Ⓓ Newbomb Design Ⓒ Wilbert's Bar & Grille 1C Ⓓ Deep Design Ⓒ Cherokee Mud Records 1D Ⓓ Brad Norr Design Ⓒ First Person Design 2A Ⓓ Elevation Ⓒ Edwardsville Arts Center 2B Ⓓ Gardner Design Ⓒ Viziworx 2C Ⓓ Glitschka Studios Ⓒ Adidas America 2D Ⓓ William Herod Design Ⓒ West Sound Taekwondo 3A Ⓓ Felixsockwell.com Ⓒ none 3B Ⓓ Felixsockwell.com Ⓒ clios 3C Ⓓ Brad Norr Design Ⓒ Whirlpool Corporation 3D Ⓓ Lomangino Studio Inc. Ⓒ Georgetown Yoga 4A Ⓓ STUART ROWLEY DESIGN Ⓒ CVPH Medical Center 4B Ⓓ Go Welsh! Ⓒ Children's Health Achievement and Motivational Program 4C Ⓓ dialogbox Ⓒ TYPo. 4D Ⓓ Jon Flaming Design Ⓒ Breast Care Consultants 5A Ⓓ Nestor Stermole VCG Ⓒ Akron Regional Perinatal Care 5B Ⓓ Blacktop Creative Ⓒ Kansas City Health Department 5C Ⓓ Miriello Grafico, Inc. Ⓒ Harcourt 5D Ⓓ Whitney Edwards LLC Ⓒ Midshore Women's Health Clinic

	A	B	C	D
1				
2				
3				
4				
5				

Ⓓ = Design Firm Ⓒ = Client

1A Ⓓ Jeff Kern Design Ⓒ The Window Cleaner Guy 1B Ⓓ Delikatessen Ⓒ Mayo Delicatessen 1C Ⓓ CAPSULE Ⓒ Society of American Fight Directors 1D Ⓓ Sabingrafik, Inc. Ⓒ Amerisports Bar & Grill 2A Ⓓ Whitney Edwards LLC Ⓒ Dance Harrison Street 2B Ⓓ Associated Advertising Agency, Inc. Ⓒ The Fusion 2C Ⓓ d4 creative group Ⓒ All Ball Inc. 2D Ⓓ Capital Associated Industries Ⓒ Evolution Technology, Inc. 3A Ⓓ James Ross Advertising Ⓒ James Ross Advertising 3B Ⓓ Scott Lewis Design Ⓒ Scott Lewis Design 3C Ⓓ thomasvasquez.com Ⓒ tnn 3D Ⓓ Thielen Designs Ⓒ The Eyeliners 4A Ⓓ Delikatessen Ⓒ Brau und Brunnen 4B Ⓓ Stephen Averitt Ⓒ The Greenbrier 4C Ⓓ Sabingrafik, Inc. Ⓒ Harcourt & Co. 4D Ⓓ BrandLogic Ⓒ Target Graphics 5A Ⓓ Scribblers' Club Ⓒ Uptown Waterloo 5B Ⓓ Integer Group - Midwest Ⓒ River Music Experience 5C Ⓓ Art Chantry Ⓒ The Beach Boys 5D Ⓓ Art Chantry Ⓒ Some People Can't Surf

A B C D

1

2

3

4

5

Ⓓ = Design Firm Ⓒ = Client

1A Ⓓ Born to Design Ⓒ Red Ella for Bonneau Production Services 1B Ⓓ GOLDFINGER c.s. Ⓒ TidyTime Cleaning 1C Ⓓ Howalt Design Studio, Inc. Ⓒ Little Deputies 1D Ⓓ Rick Johnson & Company Ⓒ Crusty Underwear 2A Ⓓ Richards Brock Miller Mitchell & Associates Ⓒ Tonman Entertainment 2B Ⓓ Landor and Associates Ⓒ Vinea 2C Ⓓ Brad Norr Design Ⓒ Provis Corporation 2D Ⓓ Molly Z. Illustration Ⓒ Landor 3A Ⓓ Gardner Design Ⓒ Backpacks To Briefcases 3B Ⓓ Element Ⓒ Industrial Wood Machinery 3C Ⓓ BC Design Ⓒ Bugle Boy 3D Ⓓ Simon & Goetz Design Ⓒ ritzenhoff 4A Ⓓ Newbomb Design Ⓒ Packy Malley 4B Ⓓ Newbomb Design Ⓒ Euro USA 4C Ⓓ Huber Design Office Ⓒ Baby Cakes 4D Ⓓ CAPSULE Ⓒ D'Amico & Sons 5A Ⓓ Gardner Design Ⓒ Scone on the Range 5B Ⓓ greteman group Ⓒ Cubano Coffee 5C Ⓓ Gardner Design Ⓒ Anastasia Marie Cosmetics 5D Ⓓ Duffy & Partners Ⓒ D'Amico & Partners

	A	B	C	D
1		MyChefJon Bringing a World of Cuisine to your Door.	STALKER	AIGA
2			Le PETIT CHEF LPC BRAND	
3	SALES DREAM OPPORTUNITY	ExpedIT™	Personology find yourself.	YOUTH IN SCIENCE S J S U
4				POKASJÓÐUR
5	Telenor	V T V		FIDELIS CARE

Ⓓ = Design Firm Ⓒ = Client

1A Ⓓ Gardner Design Ⓒ newlook landscape 1B Ⓓ Union Design & Photo Ⓒ My Chef Jon 1C Ⓓ Gardner Design Ⓒ Advanced Outdoor Products 1D Ⓓ Tharp Did It Ⓒ The Design Conference That Just Happens To Be In Park City 2A Ⓓ Gardner Design Ⓒ SomnoGraph 2B Ⓓ Jeff Kern Design Ⓒ Iams-Noble and Associates 2C Ⓓ Insight Design Ⓒ Le Petit Chef 2D Ⓓ The Bradford Lawton Design Group Ⓒ Alamo Heights Pool 3A Ⓓ Born to Design Ⓒ SaveItNow! 3B Ⓓ Imatrix Ⓒ ExpedIT Solutions 3C Ⓓ Union Design & Photo Ⓒ Personology 3D Ⓓ Redbeard Communications Inc. Ⓒ College of Science San Jose State University 4A Ⓓ Artomat Design Ⓒ Auburn Arts Commission 4B Ⓓ Moonlit Creative Group Ⓒ Florida Hospital 4C Ⓓ Alesce Ⓒ Your Way Home 4D Ⓓ Nonni & Manni/Ydda Ⓒ Pokasjodur 5A Ⓓ Landor and Associates Ⓒ Telenor 5B Ⓓ Fernandez Design Ⓒ Varsity Television 5C Ⓓ Brian Blankenship Ⓒ Shelton 5D Ⓓ Mike Quon/Designation Ⓒ Fidelis Care

A B C D

1

2

3

4

5

Ⓓ = Design Firm Ⓒ = Client

1A Ⓓ Gardner Design Ⓒ Pivotal Athletic Training 1B Ⓓ Lewis & Son Ⓒ Creative Willing Learner 1C Ⓓ BC Design Ⓒ ASTAR 1D Ⓓ Chute Gerdeman Retail Ⓒ Kodak Moments 2A Ⓓ Essex Two Incorporated Ⓒ Civitas and the City of Chicago 2B Ⓓ Idea Bank Marketing Ⓒ Moscati Health Center 2C Ⓓ The Bradford Lawton Design Group Ⓒ Creative Club of San Antonio 2D Ⓓ Cognition Design Ⓒ Mercy Covenant Church 3A Ⓓ Blattner Brunner Ⓒ Public Health 3B Ⓓ The Bradford Lawton Design Group Ⓒ University Physicians Group 3C Ⓓ Dotzero Design Ⓒ NPF 3D Ⓓ Ben Schwabauer Ⓒ Voices of Praise 4A Ⓓ Sabingrafik, Inc. Ⓒ Creative Learning Systems 4B Ⓓ Compass Design Ⓒ General Mills 4C Ⓓ G&G Advertising Ⓒ Native American Alliance Foundation 4D Ⓓ Proart Graphics/Gabriel Kalach Ⓒ Arrso Restaurants Inc. 5A Ⓓ Squires & Company Ⓒ The Court House Recreational Center 5B Ⓓ Kiku Obata & Company Ⓒ Maritz 5C Ⓓ CAPSULE Ⓒ Kitzu Discs 5D Ⓓ Tom Fowler, Inc. Ⓒ Unilever Home and Personal Care USA

	A	B	C	D
1				
2			Cultivating A Living Treasure	
3				PIN MONEY
4	CHURCH & PEACE 2002 CAIRO EGYPT	A Bid for HOPE	OVATION	
5			ST JOHN HEALTH	

Ⓓ = Design Firm Ⓒ = Client

1A Ⓓ Richards Brock Miller Mitchell & Associates Ⓒ RBMM 1B Ⓓ greteman group Ⓒ greteman group 1C Ⓓ LIFT HERE, Inc. Ⓒ Hand Entertainment Group 1D Ⓓ stay gold creative Ⓒ Wyndham Resorts Miami Beach
2A Ⓓ Gardner Design Ⓒ Frontier Farm Credit 2B Ⓓ John VanCleaf, Rutgers Univ. Ⓒ Livingston College 2C Ⓓ Design One Ⓒ North Carolina Arboretum 2D Ⓓ Scott Lewis Design Ⓒ Unused
3A Ⓓ Dotzero Design Ⓒ Burdell ALS Foundation 3B Ⓓ Tom Fowler, Inc. Ⓒ Ross Products Division/Abbott Laboratories 3C Ⓓ Blattner Brunner Ⓒ American Society of Civil Engineers 3D Ⓓ Dotzero Design Ⓒ PinMoney
4A Ⓓ Creative Development Associates, Inc. Ⓒ Third World Mission Association 4B Ⓓ switchfoot creative Ⓒ City of Hope 4C Ⓓ Sabingrafik, Inc. Ⓒ Ovation 4D Ⓓ Garfinkel Design Ⓒ University of Georgia OISPO
5A Ⓓ Howling Good Designs Ⓒ University Physicians 5B Ⓓ Tom Fowler, Inc. Ⓒ St. Luke's Life Works 5C Ⓓ Monigle Associates Inc. Ⓒ St. John Health System 5D Ⓓ Dotzero Design Ⓒ SCA

A B C D

1

2

3

4

5

Ⓓ = Design Firm Ⓒ = Client

1A Ⓓ Gardner Design Ⓒ self 1B Ⓓ Gardner Design Ⓒ INSHERPA 1C Ⓓ Felixsockwell.com Ⓒ apple 1D Ⓓ BC Design Ⓒ Bugle Boy 2A Ⓓ Dotzero Design Ⓒ Human Rights 2B Ⓓ Dotzero Design Ⓒ Human Rights 2C Ⓓ Howalt Design Studio, Inc. Ⓒ Florence Crittendon 2D Ⓓ bob neace graphic design, inc Ⓒ Rural Health/KU Med Center 3A Ⓓ Dotzero Design Ⓒ OCSA 3B Ⓓ Dotzero Design Ⓒ BIA 3C Ⓓ Dotzero Design Ⓒ BIA 3D Ⓓ Wolken communica Ⓒ Seward Park Clay Studio 4A Ⓓ Felixsockwell.com Ⓒ feluxe 4B Ⓓ Squires & Company Ⓒ ProColor Imaging 4C Ⓓ Hubbell Design Works Ⓒ Tina Casey/Photographer 4D Ⓓ Dotzero Design Ⓒ Unicru 5A Ⓓ Glitschka Studios Ⓒ Handyman Solutions of Oregon 5B Ⓓ Segura Inc. Ⓒ Spontaneous Combustion 5C Ⓓ THINKMULE.com Ⓒ Boyarm 5D Ⓓ redinwyden Ⓒ helping hands

	A	B	C	D
1	Perfect Pix			
2				GIFT
3				
4	WORLD OUTREACH			Bugle Boy Factory Outlet
5				

Ⓓ = Design Firm Ⓒ = Client

1A Ⓓ Sabingrafik, Inc. Ⓒ Perfect Pix 1B Ⓓ Gardner Design Ⓒ Flagstone Investments 1C Ⓓ Gardner Design Ⓒ Cibola 1D Ⓓ Gardner Design Ⓒ DataEdge 2A Ⓓ Gardner Design Ⓒ rti 2B Ⓓ Gardner Design Ⓒ VizWorx PhotoLab 2C Ⓓ Gardner Design Ⓒ Virtual Focus Internet 2D Ⓓ BC Design Ⓒ Gift 3A Ⓓ Felixsockwell.com Ⓒ landor/ coke 3B Ⓓ Felixsockwell.com Ⓒ landor/coke 3C Ⓓ Braue; Branding & Corporate Design Ⓒ White Heart 3D Ⓓ VINE360 Ⓒ Hope Preschool 4A Ⓓ Jeff Kern Design Ⓒ World Outreach—Robison Gamble Creative 4B Ⓓ E-Dcube Ⓒ Golden Hands Construction Inc. 4C Ⓓ Gardner Design Ⓒ MegaFab 4D Ⓓ BC Design Ⓒ bugle boy 5A Ⓓ Kraftaverk - Design Studio Ⓒ Strax 5B Ⓓ greteman group Ⓒ Art Aid 5C Ⓓ switchfoot creative Ⓒ switchfoot creative 5D Ⓓ O'Connor Identity Development Ⓒ UCLA Childrens Hopital

Born Furniture
Identity Design

Wallace Church Design, New York, New York

Born Furniture is a company whose product is inspired by design. Its molded plastic furniture is smooth and organic in shape; its curves have a modern, clean bent.

In fact, its design was so clean that any logo applied to the furniture would be best embossed into its surface, so as not to interrupt its flow. The company's creators, Frederic Debackere and Catherine Douthett, asked design director Lawrence Hagarty of Wallace Church Design for a mark that would not only work in one-color—or, in the case of embossing, no-color—applications, but also in personality.

"This furniture is really beautiful stuff," says Hagarty. "The designers took me through all the work they had produced. I started to think about interpreting the shapes of the actual furniture in the logo."

Hagarty explored several directions. One design trial referred to the new company's fledgling status while also communicating its modern sensibilities. The designer used a modified Avant Garde typeface to set the company's name but embedded an orange circle inside the counter of the letter *o*. This treatment transforms the round letter into something like an egg or an embryo. It can also be interpreted as a rising sun or a target.

"The idea was to talk about how the product was something new that was being created," Hagarty says.

Other experiments were more related to the shapes of the furniture. These two-dimensional representations also felt very modern, but whereas the furniture certainly could have a thin profile, the logo could not: These designs did not have the heft they needed to stand out, especially in an embossing application.

But Hagarty liked the idea of the logo adopting the form of the furniture. In his preliminary trials, it looked as though the viewer could actually sit on the letter b in the company name. He pushed this idea, transforming the logo into a three-dimensional object, so it appears as though the viewer could sit on ny of the letters in the company name. In fact, the collection of letters looks as if they might be comfortable to recline upon, like a chaise lounge.

The client loved the solution. The interplay of positive and negative space requires the participation of the viewer, not just placid observation. "The shapes of the letters become sculpture, a freeform element that creates the mark," Hagarty says. "The logo's success comes from two sides—one is a great idea, and the other is the execution of the design. You need the brains and the beauty."

Rob Wallace, principal of Wallace Church, concurs. When properly designed and implemented, logos are the visual catalysts of experience.

"For a corporation, a logo is an icon of its culture. For a product, a logo is the icon of its brand essence. Logos synthesize type, color, texture, and symbols into a single image that drives all perceptions. As a result, logos are design's DNA," he says.

(Top) The final logo plays off the shape of the furniture while creating an elegant interplay of positive and negative space.

(Bottom) An early direction explored the idea of embedding an orange circle inside the counter of the letter o*, suggesting an egg or embryo.*

	A	B	C	D
1	LOGO SEARCH Keywords: Mythology Type: Symbol / Typographic / Combo / All			
2				
3				
4				
5				

Ⓓ = Design Firm Ⓒ = Client

1C Ⓓ Felixsockwell.com Ⓒ limbo 1D Ⓓ THINKMULE.com Ⓒ Good vs. Evil 2A Ⓓ MINE Ⓒ Red Devils 2B Ⓓ Alesce Ⓒ Airo Skateboards 2C Ⓓ Art Chantry Ⓒ Red Rocket Records 2D Ⓓ Ross Creative + Strategy Ⓒ Gridiron 3A Ⓓ Boelts/Stratford Associates Ⓒ AOPA 3B Ⓓ switchfoot creative Ⓒ AleSmith Brewing Co. 3C Ⓓ Creative Devil Design Ⓒ Creative Devil Design 3D Ⓓ thomasvasquez.com Ⓒ Pepsi Cola 4A Ⓓ Modern Dog Design Co. Ⓒ Blue Q 4B Ⓓ Howalt Design Studio, Inc. Ⓒ Junkhead 4C Ⓓ Howalt Design Studio, Inc. Ⓒ Junkhead 4D Ⓓ Felixsockwell.com Ⓒ feluxe 5A Ⓓ THINKMULE.com Ⓒ THINKMULE 5B Ⓓ Glitschka Studios Ⓒ Glitschka Studios 5C Ⓓ Betactive Ⓒ Betactive GmbH 5D Ⓓ Richards Brock Miller Mitchell & Associates Ⓒ Dallas Children's Advocacy Center

	A	B	C	D	
					1
					2
					3
					4
					5

Ⓓ = Design Firm Ⓒ = Client

1A Ⓓ VMA Ⓒ Airborne 1B Ⓓ Art Chantry Ⓒ Insane Clown Posse 1C Ⓓ Richards Brock Miller Mitchell & Associates Ⓒ RBMM 1D Ⓓ Simon & Goetz Design Ⓒ ritzenhoff 2A Ⓓ Art Chantry Ⓒ Gasoline 2B Ⓓ judson design associates Ⓒ Gremlin Games LTD 2C Ⓓ Art Chantry Ⓒ Estrus 2D Ⓓ Glitschka Studios Ⓒ Ascending Technologies 3A Ⓓ Platform Creative Group Ⓒ BMG Music 3B Ⓓ CRE8 communications, inc. Ⓒ Stage One Supply 3C Ⓓ Taylor George Ⓒ Spicygrrl;) Clothing Company 3D Ⓓ CONCEPTiCONS Ⓒ CONCEPTiCONS 4A Ⓓ Glitschka Studios Ⓒ Unionfonts.com 4B Ⓓ Gardner Design Ⓒ pixiemoth 4C Ⓓ Synergy Graphix Ⓒ Siren Bar & Lounge 4D Ⓓ Jonathan Rice & Company Ⓒ Mercy Flight 5A Ⓓ Pennebaker Ⓒ Gilbert & Bel Valdez 5B Ⓓ Jonathan Rice & Company Ⓒ Bethesda Community Church 5C Ⓓ Richards Brock Miller Mitchell & Associates Ⓒ Office Angels 5D Ⓓ Molly Z. Illustration Ⓒ Crayons to Computers

	A	B	C	D
1	AIRLITE			IDENTITY
2				
3			ST. GEORGE'S GRYPHONS	
4				
5		PAUL KÖRNER gegründet 1831	INSTANT READERS	einhorn

Ⓓ = Design Firm Ⓒ = Client

1A Ⓓ greteman group Ⓒ airlite 1B Ⓓ Glenn Sakamoto Design Ⓒ Eagle Software 1C Ⓓ Bonfilio Design Ⓒ Angels In Waiting 1D Ⓓ McAndrew Kaps Ⓒ McAndrew Kaps 2A Ⓓ Gardner Design Ⓒ Athens 2004 Olympic Games 2B Ⓓ Gardner Design Ⓒ BigDog Motorcycles 2C Ⓓ oakley design studios Ⓒ angela 2D Ⓓ Felixsockwell.com Ⓒ limbo 3A Ⓓ Glitschka Studios Ⓒ Garden Stone 3B Ⓓ VMA Ⓒ United States Air Force Museum 3C Ⓓ Rickabaugh Graphics Ⓒ St. George's High School 3D Ⓓ greteman group Ⓒ greteman group 4A Ⓓ Glitschka Studios Ⓒ BAM Agency 4B Ⓓ Design Nut Ⓒ Griffin Group 4C Ⓓ Delikatessen Ⓒ Hanseatische Brauerei Rostock 4D Ⓓ greteman group Ⓒ greteman group 5A Ⓓ thomasvasquez.com Ⓒ Grooming Products for Men 5B Ⓓ Delikatessen Ⓒ Paul Körner Gruppe 5C Ⓓ Sabingrafik, Inc. Ⓒ Harcourt & Co. 5D Ⓓ OPEN Ⓒ Srulik Einhorn

	A	B	C	D	
					1
					2
					3
					4
					5

Ⓓ = Design Firm Ⓒ = Client

1A Ⓓ thomasvasquez.com Ⓒ Starwood Hotel Group 1B Ⓓ Union Design & Photo Ⓒ Realms of Adventure 1C Ⓓ THINKMULE.com Ⓒ Christy Elson 1D Ⓓ thomasvasquez.com Ⓒ the national network 2A Ⓓ Brandon Tabiolo Ⓒ Tom Terry 2B Ⓓ VMA Ⓒ Char-Broil 2C Ⓓ Jon Flaming Design Ⓒ The Covenant School 2D Ⓓ Synergy Graphix Ⓒ Chimera Media 3A Ⓓ Richards Brock Miller Mitchell & Associates Ⓒ Demon Season 3B Ⓓ Gardner Design Ⓒ ARES 3C Ⓓ Fernandez Design Ⓒ Protrader 3D Ⓓ greteman group Ⓒ Aviation Festival 4A Ⓓ Sayles Graphic Design, Inc. Ⓒ Neptune's Seagrill 4B Ⓓ switchfoot creative Ⓒ Triton Pools 4C Ⓓ Sabingrafik, Inc. Ⓒ Rubios Baja Grill 4D Ⓓ Sabingrafik, Inc. Ⓒ Coastal Plastic Surgery 5A Ⓓ Dennis Purcell Design Ⓒ King Clothing 5B Ⓓ StrategyBase Ⓒ Hi Life Restaurant 5C Ⓓ Monigle Associates Inc. Ⓒ Winterthur 5D Ⓓ Monigle Associates Inc. Ⓒ Winterthur

	A	B	C	D
1	LOGO SEARCH Keywords: Birds Type: Symbol Typographic Combo All			
2				
3				
4				
5				

Ⓓ = Design Firm Ⓒ = Client

1C Ⓓ Glitschka Studios Ⓒ BAM Agency 1D Ⓓ Landor and Associates Ⓒ JAL 2A Ⓓ Gardner Design Ⓒ Gold and Numismatics 2B Ⓓ bob neace graphic design, inc Ⓒ Wichita Crime Commission 2C Ⓓ Gardner Design Ⓒ un-used, for sale, available 2D Ⓓ Michael Doret Graphic Design Ⓒ United States Postal Service 3A Ⓓ Perks Design Partners Ⓒ Beringer Blass 3B Ⓓ Landor and Associates Ⓒ Union Bank 3C Ⓓ Gardner Design Ⓒ American Airfoil Corporation 3D Ⓓ Landor and Associates Ⓒ Times Mirror 4A Ⓓ Delikatessen Ⓒ Paul Körner Gruppe 4B Ⓓ Doug Beatty Ⓒ Arendscor Development 4C Ⓓ Landor and Associates Ⓒ Garuda 4D Ⓓ Landor and Associates Ⓒ Singapore Airlines 5A Ⓓ Gardner Design Ⓒ The Lord's Diner 5B Ⓓ The Bradford Lawton Design Group Ⓒ Family Violence Prevention Service 5C Ⓓ The Bradford Lawton Design Group Ⓒ New Heights Methodist Church 5D Ⓓ Monigle Associates Inc. Ⓒ American Humane Association

	A	B	C	D	
	WESTIN HOTELS	lifehouse serving people with developmental disabilities	CATHAY PACIFIC	TULIQI	1
	tucson AZ		olivia FEEL FREE		2
	Almaden Resident	songwriter records		h	3
	ODYSSEY	BirdSight bringing home the experience		trade mark FERGUSON PHILLIPS	4
		START UP	pop!con		5

Ⓓ = Design Firm Ⓒ = Client

1A Ⓓ Landor and Associates Ⓒ Westin Hotels 1B Ⓓ Landor and Associates Ⓒ LIfehouse 1C Ⓓ Landor and Associates Ⓒ Cathay Pacific 1D Ⓓ Mad Dog Graphx Ⓒ Tuliqi 2A Ⓓ Howalt Design Studio, Inc. Ⓒ BrandLab 2B Ⓓ Burd & Patterson Ⓒ IT Communications 2C Ⓓ Addis Ⓒ Olivia Cruises 2D Ⓓ Sibley/Peteet Design, Inc. Ⓒ Tequila Mockingbird 3A Ⓓ Tharp Did It Ⓒ Silicon Valley Community Newspapers 3B Ⓓ What Design, Inc. Ⓒ Songwriter Records 3C Ⓓ thomasvasquez.com Ⓒ Uptown Village Apartments 3D Ⓓ Duffy & Partners Ⓒ Hayward Hawks 4A Ⓓ Sabingrafik, Inc. Ⓒ Harcourt & Co. 4B Ⓓ PM & Co Ⓒ BirdSight 4C Ⓓ Soloflight Design Studio Ⓒ Take Home Cooking 4D Ⓓ Gardner Design Ⓒ Ferguson Phillips 5A Ⓓ Colin Gearing/Design Ⓒ Taylor Homes 5B Ⓓ Design Continuum Inc Ⓒ startup 5C Ⓓ Duffy & Partners Ⓒ Pop!con Lifestyle 5D Ⓓ Tom Fowler, Inc. Ⓒ United Methodist Homes

	A	B	C	D
1	chicken republic	Chick a ditos	W W W W	PARADOX
2		KANSAS STATE FAIR	Cockadoodles	PATHÉ!
3	FEATHERFEST	BELITO ISLAND		
4	Tele Atlas	Canadi›n		IDNÓ
5		SOLITAIRE	Sitmar Cruises	

D = Design Firm C = Client

1A D Enterprise IG C Chicken Republic 1B D Jeff Kern Design C Tyson-Noble and Associates 1C D The Bradford Lawton Design Group C Wing Basket 1D D MINE C Paradox Media
2A D The Bradford Lawton Design Group C Wing Basket 2B D greteman group C Kansas State Fair 2C D Jeff Kern Design C Tyson-Noble and Associates 2D D Landor and Associates C Pathé
3A D judson design associates C Dancie Perugini Ware Public Relations 3B D MINE C Desilva Properties 3C D Howling Good Designs C Ed O'Reilly 3D D Squires & Company C Prime Retail
4A D Landor and Associates C Tele Atlas 4B D Landor and Associates C Canadian Airlines 4C D The Bradford Lawton Design Group C Creative Surgeons 4D D Kraftaverk - Design Studio C Idno Theatre
5A D Hotdog Creative C Silver Swan 5B D Q C Bergal, Nico & Solitaire GmbH 5C D Landor and Associates C Sitmar 5D D Gardner Design C Plastic Surgery Center

ProTrader
Identity Design

Fernandez Design, Austin, Texas

High-risk tolerance. Professional. Knowledgeable. Egocentric. $100,000 of risk capital available.

All these attributes were required of potential customers of ProTrader, an online trading service that also maintained retail locations and offered proprietary trading software. (The business has since been bought out by a larger agency.) ProTrader traders were usually former brokers, far ahead of the curve in experience and information and very independent.

“This was an elite group of professionals,” explains Carlos Fernandez of Fernandez Design, the designer who was brought on to create a logo for the firm.

The client wanted to stress its retail and software offerings and how these extra perks helped maximize traders' success. So, Fernandez began considering concepts that involved a bow and arrow. “These traders must make precise decisions,” he explains.

Another direction was in trying to convey the notion of conquering the market. A flag planted at the top of a mountain suggested success—overcoming the challenge of the stock market—while also referencing another risky activity: climbing.

But the approach that the client liked best was the image of Hermes, the mythological god of commerce. Strongly rendered, the profile of the character would likely appeal to the target audience, which was very driven by power and money. This was the solution that was taken to the final round of presentations.

While waiting for final approval, Fernandez's thoughts moved on to other matters. “I wasn't thinking about the project as much; it was just marinating in the back of my mind. That's when the metaphor of the matador hit me,” he says.

The relationship between the matador and bull is the same as that between the customer and the market—right down to the notion of a bull market. Instead of just talking about ProTrader's services, this concept positioned the company's identity in a place of control and command, a much more confident position. “The artistry of working the market is very much like a bullfight, including its high risk,” the designer adds.

To both simplify and visually enhance the mark, Fernandez played with positive and negative space, creating a bull that emerged from the red cape. This, he felt, spoke of the revelation of information and of knowing where to look for both danger and opportunity.

As the Hermes solution approached approval, the matador concept was quickly brought to the table. Fortunately, the client favored the idea immediately. With approval, the matador logo was finalized and development of ProTrader's new business material began.

Unfortunately, just as the identity process proceeded, the successful company was bought out. It was too bad, the designer says, that the logo wasn't commissioned at an earlier stage of the company's existence so that it might have earned some airplay. “It's that unforgiving side of business that makes or breaks you—timing,” he says.

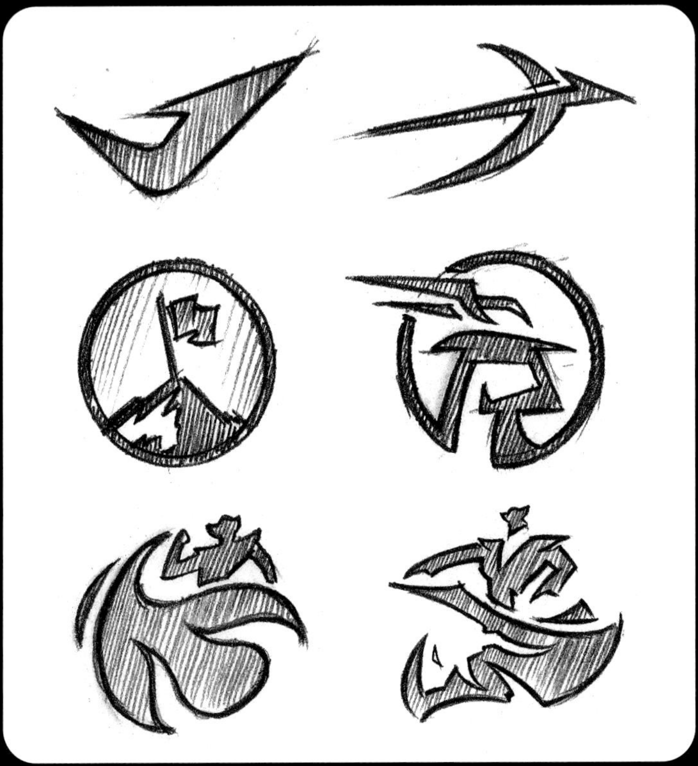

LOGO SEARCH

Keywords: Fish/Bugs/Reptiles

Type: ◯ Symbol ◯ Typographic ◯ Combo ◉ All

	A	B	C	D
1			HAMILTON ISLAND Great Barrier Reef Australia	digitalfish
2			PESCE	SPANISH PEAKS BIG SKY MONTANA
3		EXOFISHIO	SILKS	ZINS
4	C K Y M Y	Estrus	LOW COUNTRY CHARTERS	PLEASANT VALLEY FISH FARM McCOOK, NEB
5	WEST COAST AQUATICS		SeaWorld. ADVENTURE PARKS	The Maritime Aquarium AT NORWALK

Ⓓ = Design Firm Ⓒ = Client

1C Ⓓ FutureBrand Ⓒ Hamilton Island Resort 1D Ⓓ Design Continuum Inc Ⓒ DigitalFish Inc 2A Ⓓ Gardner Design Ⓒ Piranha Metal Workers 2B Ⓓ Hornall Anderson Ⓒ OneWorld Challenge 2C Ⓓ judson design associates Ⓒ Damian Mandola and Johnnie Carrabba 2D Ⓓ Sabingrafik, Inc. Ⓒ Spanish Peaks 3A Ⓓ Garfinkel Design Ⓒ Trinity Gear 3B Ⓓ judson design associates Ⓒ Coastal Billiards 3C Ⓓ FutureBrand Ⓒ Crown Casino 3D Ⓓ Soloflight Design Studio Ⓒ Chef Zin Smith 4A Ⓓ CRE8 communications, inc. Ⓒ Minnesota Print Services 4B Ⓓ Art Chantry Ⓒ Estrus 4C Ⓓ StrategyBase Ⓒ Community BrainTrust 4D Ⓓ THINKMULE.com Ⓒ Pleasant Valley Fish Farm 5A Ⓓ Hornall Anderson Ⓒ West Coast Aquatics 5B Ⓓ greteman group Ⓒ Talent Point 5C Ⓓ Landor and Associates Ⓒ Sea World 5D Ⓓ Tom Fowler, Inc. Ⓒ Maritime Aquarium of Norwalk

A B C D

1

2

3

4

5

Ⓓ = Design Firm Ⓒ = Client

1A Ⓓ judson design associates Ⓒ Coastal Billiards 1B Ⓓ Lewis & Son Ⓒ Creative Sea Horse Renovations 1C Ⓓ Landor and Associates Ⓒ Crystal 1D Ⓓ Pump Graphic Ⓒ Ultimate Players Association 2A Ⓓ Redbeard Communications Inc. Ⓒ Pacific Shores 2B Ⓓ Landor and Associates Ⓒ Shell 2C Ⓓ Tom Fowler, Inc. Ⓒ CPS Caribnet 2D Ⓓ Watts Design Ⓒ Tom Freeman 3A Ⓓ Sayles Graphic Design, Inc. Ⓒ Blue Crab Lounge 3B Ⓓ Davidson Design Ⓒ Lynton Crabb 3C Ⓓ R&R Partners (Randy Heil) Ⓒ unused 3D Ⓓ Kiku Obata & Company Ⓒ RIC Design 4A Ⓓ Ty Wilkins Ⓒ Ty Wilkins 4B Ⓓ Blattner Brunner Ⓒ Coquico 4C Ⓓ Davidson Design Ⓒ Bullfrog 4D Ⓓ Typonic Ⓒ IT Outpost 5A Ⓓ Gardner Design Ⓒ ouroclime 5B Ⓓ Enterprise IG Ⓒ Sunesi 5C Ⓓ Howalt Design Studio, Inc. Ⓒ BrandLab 5D Ⓓ Richards Brock Miller Mitchell & Associates Ⓒ Fayetteville Strikers Hockey Team

	A	B	C	D
1			TOBABY	Metabolife
2	brand new you!	ascendent	SURLY BUTTERFLY BROADCASTING CO.	mystic gardens
3	clear NEON	HONEY DESIGN, MARKETING & COMMUNICATIONS		fatcricketmedia
4		ladybug	conco CONSTRUCTION	
5				BATTLE STIKXX

Ⓓ = Design Firm Ⓒ = Client

1A Ⓓ Gardner Design Ⓒ Wichita Montessori School 1B Ⓓ Design Army Ⓒ Boutique @ U 1C Ⓓ Landor and Associates Ⓒ Tobaby 1D Ⓓ Landor and Associates Ⓒ Metabolife 2A Ⓓ Molly Z. Illustration Ⓒ Jana Currie 2B Ⓓ Pennebaker Ⓒ Ascendent 2C Ⓓ THINKMULE.com Ⓒ Surly Butterfly 2D Ⓓ Design Army Ⓒ MYSTIC GARDENS 3A Ⓓ Gardner Design Ⓒ ClearNeon 3B Ⓓ Honey Design Ⓒ Honey Design, Marketing & Communications 3C Ⓓ Glitschka Studios Ⓒ Loui Loui Sportswear 3D Ⓓ Go Welsh! Ⓒ Fat Cricket Media 4A Ⓓ Gardner Design Ⓒ Dragonfly Creek Development 4B Ⓓ Firewheel Design Ⓒ Seth Livingston 4C Ⓓ Gardner Design Ⓒ Conco Construction 4D Ⓓ angela tu Ⓒ Bughouse Production 5A Ⓓ Q Ⓒ Desinfektion und Schaedlingsbekaempfung 5B Ⓓ Soloflight Design Studio Ⓒ Grasshopper Roofing 5C Ⓓ SPUR Ⓒ Arachnatech 5D Ⓓ Richards Brock Miller Mitchell & Associates Ⓒ Battle Stikxx

A	B	C	D	
Ⓓ = Design Firm Ⓒ = Client	**LOGO SEARCH** Keywords: Animals Type: ◯ Symbol ◯ Typographic ◯ Combo ◉ All	trick dog cAfe iRvington VA	petswelcome.com	1
dogtrick creative		BIG DOG MOTOR CYCLES	A PET'S LIFE	2
Digital Dog Studios				3
Sabingrafik INCORPORATED	BARK PARK CENTRAL			4
			walk the dog!	5

Ⓓ = Design Firm Ⓒ = Client

1C Ⓓ Duffy & Partners Ⓒ Trick Dog Cafe 1D Ⓓ Zenarts Design Studio Ⓒ Petswelcome.com 2A Ⓓ Dogtrick Creative Ⓒ Dogtrick Creative 2B Ⓓ Fernandez Design Ⓒ Protrader 2C Ⓓ Gardner Design Ⓒ BigDog Motorcycles 2D Ⓓ Insight Design Ⓒ The Hayes Company, Inc. 3A Ⓓ Doug Chatham Design Ⓒ Digital Dog Studios 3B Ⓓ Glitschka Studios Ⓒ Wilsonville Highschool 3C Ⓓ Frederick & Froberg Design Office Ⓒ Edmonton Oilers 3D Ⓓ Gardner Design Ⓒ BigDog Motorcycles 4A Ⓓ Sabingrafik, Inc. Ⓒ Sabingrafik, Inc. 4B Ⓓ Squires & Company Ⓒ Deep Ellum Association 4C Ⓓ Kendall Creative Shop, Inc. Ⓒ Big Bark Bakery 4D Ⓓ Diana Graham Ⓒ Tierklinik, Diessen, Germany 5A Ⓓ Felixsockwell.com Ⓒ grey dog's coffee 5B Ⓓ Sabingrafik, Inc. Ⓒ Teen Center Cafe 5C Ⓓ greteman group Ⓒ Woofstock 2003 5D Ⓓ helium.design Ⓒ no:blind

	A	B	C	D
1				
2				
3				
4				
5				

Ⓓ = Design Firm Ⓒ = Client

1A Ⓓ bp360 Ⓒ PetStop 1B Ⓓ McMillian Design Ⓒ Leashes and Lovers 1C Ⓓ Dept 3 Ⓒ Winkie Dog 1D Ⓓ Glitschka Studios Ⓒ Lui Lui Sportswear 2A Ⓓ Richards Brock Miller Mitchell & Associates Ⓒ Windsor Wild Animal Refuge 2B Ⓓ Howalt Design Studio, Inc. Ⓒ CritterGear 2C Ⓓ bob neace graphic design, inc Ⓒ Skaer Veterinarian 2D Ⓓ R&R Partners (Randy Heil) Ⓒ unused 3A Ⓓ logobyte Ⓒ Black Cat 3B Ⓓ William Herod Design Ⓒ The Classy Cat 3C Ⓓ CDI Studios Ⓒ Victoria Hart 3D Ⓓ THINKMULE.com Ⓒ Crispy 4A Ⓓ Diana Graham Ⓒ Tierklinik Diessen, Germany 4B Ⓓ Gabriela Gasparini Design Ⓒ Gato Mia (Cat's Miow) 4C Ⓓ Richards Brock Miller Mitchell & Associates Ⓒ Cat Jugglers Inc. 4D Ⓓ Dreigestalt Ⓒ selma&louis 5A Ⓓ Sabingrafik, Inc. Ⓒ Lion 5B Ⓓ greteman group Ⓒ Zoo Zone ID Mountain Lion 5C Ⓓ Gardner Design Ⓒ The Tux Shop 5D Ⓓ judson design associates Ⓒ Weimer ISD

	A	B	C	D
1	CHATHAM AREA TRANSIT	LionessMartialArts		FOXRIVER PAPERCO
2		COYOTE RIDGE RANCH	IOWA CHRISTIAN ACADEMY BLAZERS	
3	LLAMA BEAN RANCH™			IDYLLWILDE
4	trade mark	JOHN DEERE		
5		UNIQUE VENTURES A MASS MEDIA COMPANY	PAINTED RIDGE Farms	

Ⓓ = Design Firm Ⓒ = Client

1A Ⓓ StrategyBase Ⓒ Chatham Area Transit 1B Ⓓ Mona MacDonald Design Ⓒ Lioness Martial Arts Inc. 1C Ⓓ Gardner Design Ⓒ The Oaks Golf Course 1D Ⓓ Duffy & Partners Ⓒ Fox River Paper Company 2A Ⓓ Tom Fowler, Inc. Ⓒ Ocean Fox Dive Shop 2B Ⓓ elf design Ⓒ Coyote Ridge Ranch 2C Ⓓ Burd & Patterson Ⓒ Iowa Christian Academy 2D Ⓓ Communique Ⓒ FoxHorn Estates 3A Ⓓ Great Scott Design Ⓒ Llama Bean Ranch 3B Ⓓ Gardner Design Ⓒ Total Lawn Care Inc. 3C Ⓓ Eskil Ohlsson Assoc. Inc. Ⓒ T Rowe Price 3D Ⓓ Sabingrafik, Inc. Ⓒ Idyllwilde 4A Ⓓ Gardner Design Ⓒ Great Lodge 4B Ⓓ Landor and Associates Ⓒ John Deere 4C Ⓓ Sabingrafik, Inc. Ⓒ Idyllwilde 4D Ⓓ thomasvasquez.com Ⓒ tracey locke partnership 5A Ⓓ Rickabaugh Graphics Ⓒ Phillip Morris 5B Ⓓ GOLDFINGER c.s. Ⓒ Unique Management 5C Ⓓ Squires & Company Ⓒ Painted Ridge Farms 5D Ⓓ Mitre Design Ⓒ Black Horse Photography

Ⓓ = Design Firm Ⓒ = Client

1A Ⓓ bob neace graphic design, inc Ⓒ Empress Arabians 1B Ⓓ O'Connor Identity Development Ⓒ Stoneridge Stables 1C Ⓓ Mires>Design for Brands Ⓒ Air Equine 1D Ⓓ Howalt Design Studio, Inc. Ⓒ Polaris Watercraft
2A Ⓓ ErikArt Design Ⓒ Austin Wranglers/Feste Capital 2B Ⓓ Richards Brock Miller Mitchell & Associates Ⓒ Sunshine Millions 2C Ⓓ Tharp Did It Ⓒ Sedona Rouge 2D Ⓓ bob neace graphic design, inc Ⓒ Power Link
3A Ⓓ Richards Brock Miller Mitchell & Associates Ⓒ ChildCareGroup 3B Ⓓ judson design associates Ⓒ The Warwick Hotel 3C Ⓓ judson design associates Ⓒ Texas Racing Agri-Industry Council 3D Ⓓ Design MG Ⓒ for sale
4A Ⓓ Art Chantry Washington Ⓒ State Dept. of Tourism 4B Ⓓ Popgun Ⓒ Bulletproof Jeans 4C Ⓓ Landor and Associates Ⓒ Ferrari 4D Ⓓ Felixsockwell.com Ⓒ castle repair + maintenece 5A Ⓓ Gardner Design Ⓒ Cibola
5B Ⓓ Richards Brock Miller Mitchell & Associates Ⓒ Plains Capital Bank 5C Ⓓ Fernandez Design Ⓒ Protrader 5D Ⓓ JCharlier Communication Design Ⓒ Toro Tapas Bar

A	B	C	D	
MEZCAL	BAREFOOT RANCH		ELMERS	1
		COUNTRY FAIR		2
WWF				3
ZOO AM MEER	GREAT LODGE	armadillo BY WALRUS	U.S. MINK	4
Kelling	NAPIER HILL Interior Design	Disney	milkey mouse	5

Ⓓ = Design Firm Ⓒ = Client

1A Ⓓ Estudio Ray Ⓒ Mezcal Restaurant 1B Ⓓ Jon Flaming Design Ⓒ Barefoot Ranch 1C Ⓓ CRE8 communications, inc. Ⓒ H & H Services 1D Ⓓ Eskil Ohlsson Assoc. Inc. Ⓒ Borden Corp.
2A Ⓓ Felixsockwell.com Ⓒ cream n bean 2B Ⓓ Diana Graham Ⓒ Tierklinik, Diessen, Germany 2C Ⓓ Kendall Creative Shop, Inc. Ⓒ Drive 2D Ⓓ Blattner Brunner Ⓒ Supon Design Group
3A Ⓓ Landor and Associates Ⓒ World Wildlife Foundation 3B Ⓓ THINKMULE.com Ⓒ THINKMULE 3C Ⓓ Martini Time Design Ⓒ Oso Durado Beer 3D Ⓓ greteman group Ⓒ Mannys Heating and Cooling
4A Ⓓ Braue; Branding & Corporate Design Ⓒ Zoo am Meer 4B Ⓓ Gardner Design Ⓒ Great Lodge 4C Ⓓ Platform Creative Group Ⓒ Armadillo 4D Ⓓ Art Chantry Ⓒ U.S. MINK
5A Ⓓ Eskil Ohlsson Assoc. Inc. Ⓒ Kelling Nut Co. 5B Ⓓ Williams Collins Design & Development Ⓒ Napier Hill Interior Design 5C Ⓓ Landor and Associates Ⓒ Disney 5D Ⓓ Simon & Goetz Design Ⓒ sieger design/ritzenhoff

A B C D

1

2

3

4

5

Ⓓ = Design Firm Ⓒ = Client

1A Ⓓ Eagle Imagery (PhotoGraphics) Ⓒ RabbitWurx 1B Ⓓ THINKMULE.com Ⓒ THINKMULE 1C Ⓓ Howling Good Designs Ⓒ Magicris Productions 1D Ⓓ Richards Brock Miller Mitchell & Associates Ⓒ Ratchet/The Richards Group 2A Ⓓ Blattner Brunner Ⓒ Supon Design Group 2B Ⓓ Sabingrafik, Inc. Ⓒ Tamansari Beverage 2C Ⓓ Glitschka Studios Ⓒ Chinese New Year 2D Ⓓ Glitschka Studios Ⓒ Pixel Monkey Studios 3A Ⓓ Digital Soup Ⓒ Trunk LTD 3B Ⓓ judson design associates Ⓒ The Chinquapin School 3C Ⓓ Howling Good Designs Ⓒ MemoryConcepts 3D Ⓓ Dotzero Design Ⓒ Queen of Sheba 4A Ⓓ Sabingrafik, Inc. Ⓒ Beithan Hessler Corporate Communications 4B Ⓓ Squires & Company Ⓒ Black Rhino Graphics 4C Ⓓ Richards Brock Miller Mitchell & Associates Ⓒ Blue Rhino Studio 4D Ⓓ Fernandez Design Ⓒ Lincoln Park Zoo 5A Ⓓ Diana Graham Ⓒ Mars Petcare 5B Ⓓ Rickabaugh Graphics Ⓒ Animal Connection 5C Ⓓ Gardner Design Ⓒ StackShack 5D Ⓓ Chaney, Nieman, Munson & Son Ⓒ Rescue

Elvis
Identity Design

cYclops, New York, New York

No matter how acclaimed Elvis Presley may be, there are few people who would lend any praise whatsoever to his album covers. Designer Thomas Vasquez, creative director of cYclops, a design and production firm, thinks he knows why the designs were so pedestrian.

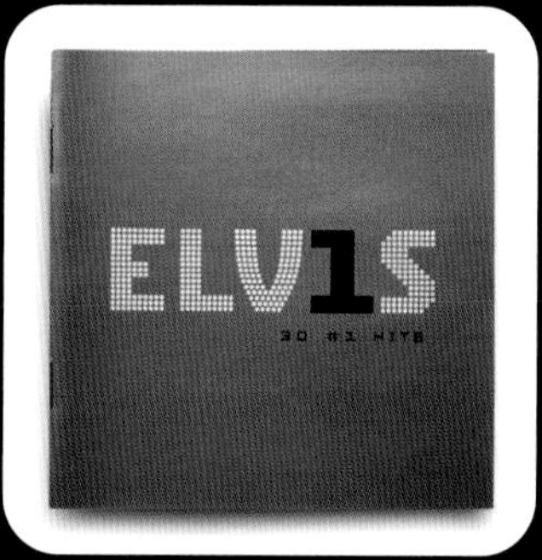

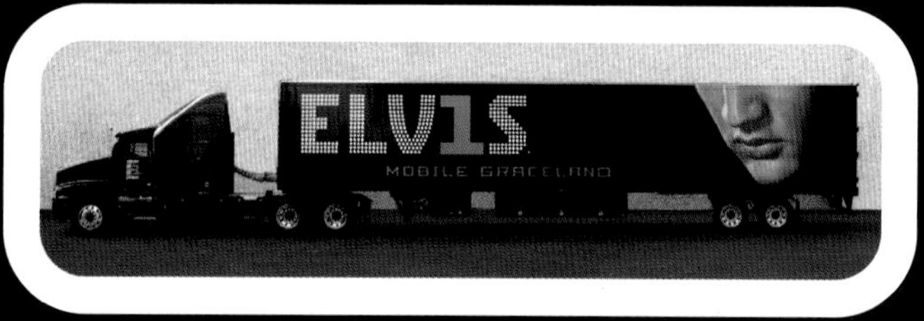

"Colonel Tom Parker, Elvis's manager, carried with him a toolbox full of photos and other elements that he called his 'instant album cover design kit.' Parker would sit down and literally in two minutes design a cover. He'd say, 'The type goes here, put some stripes on here, use this photo, print *Elvis* in big letters,' and that would be it," Vasquez says.

Elvis fans, somehow, chose to embrace this poor design and hold it almost sacred, as a crucial component of the Elvis mystique.

So Vasquez's task in creating a cover design for a new RCA collection of Elvis hits was made all the more difficult. Not only would he have to please the client, he would also have to placate a fan base that might not be all that receptive to the change.

When Vasquez, himself a long-time Elvis fan, began working on the first project, a CD cover, he was freelancing. As more and more hours were poured into the work, he was invited to join the cYclops staff as creative director. What began as a single mark for a CD cover soon became an extensive branding program, complete with a TV special and mobile exhibit.

"The client wanted this program to be so comprehensive that wherever the mark and its accompanying visual language would be seen, it would feel like it came from the same voice," he says.

The design challenge would be to depict Elvis's entire career, from his rockabilly roots in the 1950s to his last hit in 1977, representing his music, movies, and lifestyle.

The initial approach boiled the concept of Elvis down to its essence. Because of his nicknames was "E," and this CD was a compilation of his number-one hits, the idea naturally led to the creation of an "E1" logo. Vasquez liked this approach very much, but the client felt it was too reductive. (Ultimately, this design was used on the CD itself, as well as on the driver's door of the truck that transported the mobile exhibit.)

Vasquez's solution for the worldwide advertising campaign focused on the "delivery mechanism" for all of Elvis's number-one hits: his mouth. The curled lip and squared chin are recognized around the world. Vasquez simplified the message further by running the photo as a black and gold duotone to complement the already established program color palette of gold, black, and white.

The new CD, with its modern representation of Elvis, quickly became a number-one best seller, surpassing earlier Elvis releases. But the design of a compilation CD was not as warmly received. This design also employed the photo cropping Vasquez used for the first design. It resembles the "E1" mark, because it works the numeral 2 into a photo of the face of the star.

The mark soon became the topic of many online chat groups, where Vasquez's work was blasted from all directions and even reworked by those who were particularly outraged. Redesigns were posted on the Internet, voted on by fans, and submitted to RCA as bona fide alternatives. One critic compared Vasquez's design to "a coffee mug."

Vasquez admits that the criticism stung, but he believes the bile arose from his violating the established visual language of Elvis. "Without a challenge, people will feel comfortable just regurgitating the past. The language will not advance," he says.

	A	B	C	D
1	LOGO SEARCH Keywords: Nature Type: Symbol Typographic Combo All			
2				
3				
4				
5				

Ⓓ = Design Firm Ⓒ = Client

1C Ⓓ FutureBrand Ⓒ Boroondara Council 1D Ⓓ The Office of Bill Chiaravalle Ⓒ Multnomah Publishers 2A Ⓓ EM Design Ⓒ City of Decatur Environmental Committee 2B Ⓓ Be Design Ⓒ Mighty Leaf Tea Company 2C Ⓓ judson design associates Ⓒ HEB 2D Ⓓ TD2, S.C. Ⓒ PATRICIA PELAEZ 3A Ⓓ yellow dog design Ⓒ Gardens of Eden 3B Ⓓ SO/Sullivan Office Ⓒ George Fox University 3C Ⓓ Q Ⓒ l'auberge 3D Ⓓ cesart.com Ⓒ Zoo Sauvage St-Félicien 4A Ⓓ Gardner Design Ⓒ refined technologies, inc. 4B Ⓓ Gardner Design Ⓒ US AG BANK 4C Ⓓ Allen Creative Ⓒ Ivy Creek Church 4D Ⓓ Union Design & Photo Ⓒ Aquaria Canada 5A Ⓓ Tharp Did It Ⓒ The Mountain Winery 5B Ⓓ Offbeat Design Ⓒ Cornell University 5C Ⓓ Metroparks of the Toledo Area Ⓒ Metroparks Toledo 5D Ⓓ KENNETH DISENO Ⓒ La Guadalupe Nursery

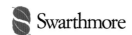

	A	B	C	D	
	SHARIBE	Swarthmore		trade mark GARDENS	1
		RIOS LANDSCAPING	ILLINOIS RIVER COUNTRY SO MANY WAYS TO PLAY	WEED WATCHERS	2
	LIVING POLICY	Penlan Perennials	CIVISTA Health	YOGASA	3
	AHBL		EVERLAND		4
	PAT AVETTA	BIRCH	McKelvey Foundation	GROUNDWORKS INC	5

Ⓓ = Design Firm Ⓒ = Client

1A Ⓓ bp360 Ⓒ ShariBe 1B Ⓓ Go Welsh! Ⓒ Borough of Swarthmore, PA 1C Ⓓ Gardner Design Ⓒ The Oaks Golf Course 1D Ⓓ Gardner Design Ⓒ Gardens 2A Ⓓ Gardner Design Ⓒ Plastic Surgery Center_2 2B Ⓓ Glitschka Studios Ⓒ RIOS Landscaping 2C Ⓓ Ross Creative + Strategy Ⓒ Illinois River Country 2D Ⓓ Howling Good Designs Ⓒ The Nature Conservancy 3A Ⓓ Scribblers' Club Ⓒ Intellitactics 3B Ⓓ Eagle Imagery (PhotoGraphics) Ⓒ www.PenlanPerennials.co.uk 3C Ⓓ Monigle Associates Inc. Ⓒ Civista Health 3D Ⓓ Glenn Sakamoto Design Ⓒ Yogasa 4A Ⓓ Platform Creative Group Ⓒ AHBL 4B Ⓓ Gardner Design Ⓒ US AgBank 4C Ⓓ Landor and Associates Ⓒ Everland 4D Ⓓ Gardner Design Ⓒ US AgBank 5A Ⓓ Mitre Design Ⓒ Pat Avetta 5B Ⓓ Insight Design Ⓒ Birch 5C Ⓓ LeVesque Design Ⓒ McKelvey Foundation 5D Ⓓ Cam Stewart Graphic Design Ⓒ Groundworks

	A	B	C	D
1				
2				
3				
4				
5				

Ⓓ = Design Firm Ⓒ = Client

1A Ⓓ Frontmedia Ⓒ LDJ Services Ltd. 1B Ⓓ Design Army Ⓒ Dolce Video 1C Ⓓ Howling Good Designs Ⓒ Daisy's Daycare 1D Ⓓ Mad Dog Graphx Ⓒ Abused Women's Aid in Crisis (AWAIC) 2A Ⓓ Matsumoto Design Ⓒ Silk and Oil Galleries 2B Ⓓ Kraftaverk - Design Studio Ⓒ The Deli 2C Ⓓ Sabingrafik, Inc. Ⓒ Taralon 2D Ⓓ Mike Quon/Designation Ⓒ Aveda 3A Ⓓ Howalt Design Studio, Inc. Ⓒ Trick Daisy 3B Ⓓ hand made group Ⓒ Podere Belvedere 3C Ⓓ Stacy Bormett Design, LLC Ⓒ Pearsons Florist & Greenhouse 3D Ⓓ Simon & Goetz Design Ⓒ world model association 4A Ⓓ Deep Design Ⓒ Frazer Center 4B Ⓓ Communications Nemesis Inc. Ⓒ Alison Silcoff Events 4C Ⓓ Gardner Design Ⓒ The Greens 4D Ⓓ greteman group Ⓒ Horn o Plenty 5A Ⓓ Landor and Associates Ⓒ Cotton 5B Ⓓ Art Chantry Ⓒ Washington State Dept. of Tourism 5C Ⓓ Simon & Goetz Design Ⓒ berghotel zirmerhof 5D Ⓓ Indicia Design Inc Ⓒ Señor Esposo

Ⓓ = Design Firm Ⓒ = Client

1A Ⓓ Alexander Isley Inc. Ⓒ The Stone Barns Center for Food & Agriculture 1B Ⓓ Perks Design Partners Ⓒ So Natural Foods & Just Squeezed Juices 1C Ⓓ Rottman Creative Group, LLC Ⓒ Calvert Country Market 1D Ⓓ octane inc. Ⓒ GG&T
2A Ⓓ Compass Design Ⓒ Courtier's Pepin Heights 2B Ⓓ Aahbullay Ⓒ The Health Network 2C Ⓓ KENNETH DISENO Ⓒ Global Frut avocado exporters, Michoacan Mexico 2D Ⓓ Sabingrafik, Inc. Ⓒ Tamansari Beverage
3A Ⓓ HardBall Sports Ⓒ World Golf Foundation 3B Ⓓ Hubbell Design Works Ⓒ Delicato Family 3C Ⓓ Nicole Imbert Design Ⓒ Chinola Card Design 3D Ⓓ Williams Collins Design & Development Ⓒ Josie Bowman—Tangerine
4A Ⓓ Chuck Pennington Ⓒ Larson Casteel 4B Ⓓ Insight Design Ⓒ Home National Bank 4C Ⓓ Dotzero Design Ⓒ Green Copier Project 4D Ⓓ Methodologie Ⓒ Plum Creek Timber Company
5A Ⓓ CRE8 communications, inc. Ⓒ Maui Radio Network 5B Ⓓ Glenn Sakamoto Design Ⓒ Landscape Designers 5C Ⓓ Delikatessen Ⓒ Greensands, United Arabic Emirates 5D Ⓓ Sabingrafik, Inc. Ⓒ The Buie Family

	A	B	C	D
1		CIGNA	h	L
2	OHIO GREEN		BOTANICAL PSYCHIATREE	FOR HARDWOODS' SAKE
3	KINGS HILL	Backyard	the GROVE at APPELDOORN	kirlin foundation
4	VALLES CALDERA NATIONAL PRESERVE	AUTUMN ADVENTURE 2002	WATERRIDGE	CROSSROADS WYOMING INITIATIVE FOR LIVING WITH DISABILITIES
5	BEECHWOOD WINES GOULBURN VALLEY	SAN JOSE SILICON VALLEY CHAMBER OF COMMERCE	GREEN SANDS	Camp Jeep

Ⓓ = Design Firm Ⓒ = Client

1A Ⓓ Landor and Associates Ⓒ Abril 1B Ⓓ Landor and Associates Ⓒ Cigna 1C Ⓓ Kraftaverk - Design Studio Ⓒ HvassoSchool 1D Ⓓ STUART ROWLEY DESIGN Ⓒ H. Leggett & Sons 2A Ⓓ DeShetler Design Ⓒ Ohio Green 2B Ⓓ Sabingrafik, Inc. Ⓒ Grove Church 2C Ⓓ Howling Good Designs Ⓒ Botanical Psychiatree 2D Ⓓ Dotzero Design Ⓒ Healthy Forest Initiative 3A Ⓓ John Langdon Design Ⓒ Willard Rouse Associates 3B Ⓓ Digital Soup Ⓒ Backyard Film Festival 3C Ⓓ Design One Ⓒ Downtown Diversified Investments 3D Ⓓ Methodologie Ⓒ Kirlin 4A Ⓓ Jeff Fisher LogoMotives Ⓒ Valles Caldera Natl. Preserve/USDA Forest Service 4B Ⓓ Metroparks of the Toledo Area Ⓒ Metroparks Toledo 4C Ⓓ Sabingrafik, Inc. Ⓒ WaterRidge 4D Ⓓ Catalyst Creative, Inc. Ⓒ Wyoming Initiative for Living with Disabilities 5A Ⓓ Watts Design Ⓒ Beechwood Wines 5B Ⓓ Redbeard Communications Inc. Ⓒ San Jose Silicon Valley Chamber of Commerce 5C Ⓓ Delikatessen Ⓒ Greensands, United Arabic Emirates 5D Ⓓ BBDO Detroit Design Group Ⓒ DaimlerChrysler

A	B	C	D	
				1
				2
				3
				4
				5

Ⓓ = Design Firm Ⓒ = Client

1A Ⓓ Wages Design Ⓒ Agreturns 1B Ⓓ Eagle Imagery (PhotoGraphics) Ⓒ WCS Enviro 1C Ⓓ McAndrew Kaps Ⓒ Alternatives, Inc. 1D Ⓓ Richards Brock Miller Mitchell & Associates Ⓒ GuideStone Financial Resources
2A Ⓓ Q Ⓒ Industrie Verband Agrar 2B Ⓓ Eagle Imagery (PhotoGraphics) Ⓒ Hannam Vale Community Hall 2C Ⓓ Delikatessen Ⓒ Greensands, United Arabic Emirates 2D Ⓓ LeVesque Design Ⓒ Tri-State Rent a Car
3A Ⓓ Indicia Design Inc Ⓒ Rock Clay 3B Ⓓ Peter Montoya Inc. Ⓒ Ted Prechter 3C Ⓓ Landor and Associates Ⓒ Stepstone 3D Ⓓ Pickard Advertising & Design Ⓒ Singapore Mediation Centre
4A Ⓓ angela tu Ⓒ Land Rover North America 4B Ⓓ Rick Johnson & Company Ⓒ Rick Johnson & Company 4C Ⓓ BC Design Ⓒ adidas 4D Ⓓ BC Design Ⓒ adidas 5A Ⓓ Tom Fowler, Inc. Ⓒ Eventra
5B Ⓓ Hubbell Design Works Ⓒ Hanes/USA 5C Ⓓ Firewheel Design Ⓒ Basic Laboratory 5D Ⓓ TMCA, Inc. Ⓒ Muthig Environmental Services

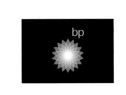

	A	B	C	D
1	south african jewish museum	Seagate We turn on ideas		NORTH SOUND CAPITAL
2		LakeChamplain.com	akopia™	Cloud9
3	COASTAL TOWER	ROCKFIRE AT · THE · LAKE	SOUTHERN SPECIALTIES	SUNDANCE
4	fest	bp	HIGH NOON SALOON LIVE MUSIC AND COLD BEER	LOVEDAY PRODUCTIONS
5	moro restaurant	VANILLA MOON CAFE	A Night at the Movies	

Ⓓ = Design Firm Ⓒ = Client

1A Ⓓ Enterprise IG Ⓒ South African Jewish Museum 1B Ⓓ Landor and Associates Ⓒ Seagate 1C Ⓓ Custom Art Company Ⓒ Surfrider Foundation 1D Ⓓ Synergy Graphix Ⓒ North Sound Capital 2A Ⓓ Kraftaverk - Design Studio Ⓒ Centrum 2B Ⓓ STUART ROWLEY DESIGN Ⓒ LakeChamplain.com 2C Ⓓ The Office of Bill Chiaravalle Ⓒ Akopia 2D Ⓓ LeVesque Design Ⓒ RCI/ G2 3A Ⓓ Design MG Ⓒ P.H. Coastal Tower 3B Ⓓ Tallgrass Studios Ⓒ Rockfire at the Lake 3C Ⓓ Cave Ⓒ Southern Specialties 3D Ⓓ Sabingrafik, Inc. Ⓒ Sundance 4A Ⓓ Mitre Design Ⓒ Whitaker Elementary 4B Ⓓ Landor and Associates Ⓒ Bio Petroleum 4C Ⓓ Planet Propaganda Ⓒ High Noon Saloon 4D Ⓓ Williams Collins Design & Development Ⓒ Mimi Dorsey—Loveday Productions 5A Ⓓ KFDunn Ⓒ Moro Restaurant 5B Ⓓ Creative Madhouse Ⓒ Vanilla Moon Cafe 5C Ⓓ Graham Hanson Design Ⓒ AIGA New York 5D Ⓓ The Bradford Lawton Design Group Ⓒ Luna C Restaurant

WRQ
Identity Redesign

Factor Design, San Francisco, California

For twenty years, WRQ had one core product, which treated the privately owned company well throughout those years. But the 900-plus-employee firm had to do a self-evaluation on the advent of its two-decade anniversary. Purchases of its single product—a software program called Reflection that allowed PCs to connect to mainframe computers to retrieve information—were in steep decline, due to the fact that not many people purchased mainframes anymore, and most who did were already satisfied Reflection customers.

WRQ had to find a way to leverage its technology and expertise to open up new opportunities. Eventually, the company purchased a firm in the Netherlands that had a complementary product—software that would eventually be marketed under the name WRQ Verastream. It provided a critical link to an emerging software market called Enterprise Application Integration, which allows disparate and proprietary mission-critical systems to be connected to one another—an important ability when companies find that the new inventory management system can't share useful data with its e-commerce application, for example.

It was a time of dramatic transition for WRQ. It moved into a new product space, and a new culture was moving in—literally. There was new leadership and a new product, as well as a rash of layoffs due to the technology bubble beginning to burst. If WRQ was going to thrive, management realized it needed a new approach to how it managed its corporate identity and a strategy for how it spoke about its products.

The company's old logo, a triangle built from bars representing earth, air, and water—all representative and appropriate to its Seattle home—had little as it pushed further into the global marketplace.

Jeff Zwerner, partner and creative director of Factor Design, a design firm with offices in San Francisco and Hamburg, Germany, says his firm was called in to develop a symbol that embodied the new business strategy related to its transition toward Enterprise Application Integration—of companies, of employees, of management, of product, and of technology. It was an interesting challenge, he notes, because although Factor Design is known for its high-touch, emotional work, WRQ is a company that deals with the intangible and often impersonal world of technology and software.

Factor's solution was pure: two interconnecting forms that could be used alongside the WRQ name, the two product names, or any future product names to strongly connect the corporate source brand with the sibling product brand. Through use of color, separate products could be distinguished. Even better, the secondary design language could be taken apart and extrapolated into myriad design applications, furthering the brand's visual identity through artistry.

"The identity was designed to be flexible," Zwerner says. "The shapes can be used independently, as a supporting system. When we presented the program to WRQ, we also presented how the design language could evolve over the next ten years without altering or adding to the core palette of colors or design language. It is simply a matter of dialing up the use of certain elements and dialing down others to place the emphasis on pertinent parts of the WRQ story."

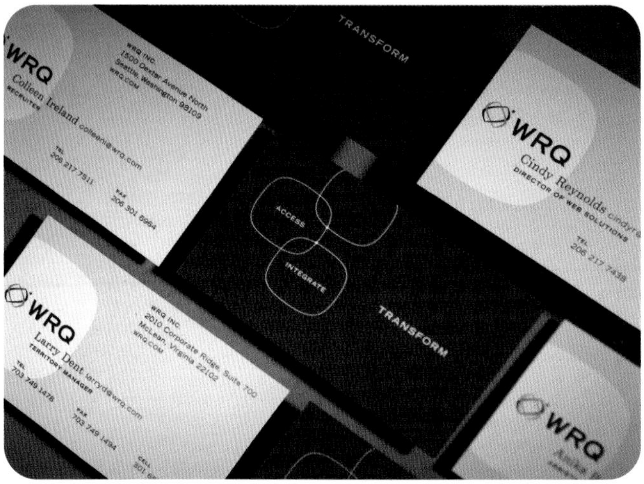

A B C D

LOGO SEARCH

Keywords: Shapes

Type: ◯ Symbol ◯ Typographic ◯ Combo ◉ All

1

2

EARTH AFRICA™
A Fingerprint of Africa
made on earth

flat earth

HUFFY

3

ASTRA

TIME
100

AMERICA AND THE WORLD

4

CABLE & WIRELESS

metaDOT

5

TIMES SQUARE 2000

METAFORE™

GROUP | ONE

Ⓓ = Design Firm Ⓒ = Client

1C Ⓓ thomasvasquez.com Ⓒ US State Department 1D Ⓓ Sabingrafik, Inc. Ⓒ Institute for Continued Learning 2A Ⓓ Enterprise IG Ⓒ Earth Africa 2B Ⓓ Newbomb Design Ⓒ Flat Earth 2C Ⓓ Duffy & Partners Ⓒ The Coca-Cola Company 2D Ⓓ VMA Ⓒ Huffy Bicycles 3A Ⓓ Landor and Associates Ⓒ Astra International 3B Ⓓ Dotzero Design Ⓒ GlobalEye 3C Ⓓ Duffy & Partners Ⓒ *TIME* Magazine 3D Ⓓ Convexus Consulting, Inc. Ⓒ America and the World 4A Ⓓ Landor and Associates Ⓒ Cable Wireless 4B Ⓓ Brandon Tabiolo Ⓒ Altaway Technologies, Inc. 4C Ⓓ Giraffe, Inc. Ⓒ Riverside Park 4D Ⓓ Fernandez Design Ⓒ MetaDot 5A Ⓓ the atmosfear Ⓒ Lenni 5B Ⓓ Landor and Associates Ⓒ Times Square 5C Ⓓ Scribblers' Club Ⓒ Metafore 5D Ⓓ Group One Ⓒ Group One

	A	B	C	D
1	Carrix Global Gateway Solutions	Constellation Holdings	TOUCHSTONE	Hongkong Telecom 香港電訊
2		REVATI	CHEROKEE HERITAGE TRAILS	thoughts
3	sicom servicios integrados de compra	SUNTECH	MARRIAGENCOUNTER	VIAYOGA
4	Downtown Phoenix Gallery Association	radii	Bellevue Art Museum INQUIRE WITHIN	Lucent Technologies Bell Labs Innovations
5				

Ⓓ = Design Firm Ⓒ = Client

1A Ⓓ Methodologie Ⓒ Carrix 1B Ⓓ Landor and Associates Ⓒ Constellation Holdings 1C Ⓓ Landor and Associates Ⓒ Touchstone 1D Ⓓ Landor and Associates Ⓒ Hong Kong Telecom 2A Ⓓ On Duty Design Ⓒ Cleary Gottlieb 2B Ⓓ Art Chantry Ⓒ Revati 2C Ⓓ Design One Ⓒ North Carolina Arts Council 2D Ⓓ Jeff Kern Design Ⓒ Jeff Kern Design 3A Ⓓ cincodemayo Ⓒ micomprador.com 3B Ⓓ Williams Collins Design & Development Ⓒ Suntech 3C Ⓓ dmaynedesign Ⓒ Marriage Encounter 3D Ⓓ Chuck Pennington Ⓒ Via Yoga 4A Ⓓ the atmosfear Ⓒ Downtown Phoenix Gallery Association 4B Ⓓ FutureBrand Ⓒ Park Hyatt 4C Ⓓ Landor and Associates Ⓒ Bellevue Art Museum 4D Ⓓ Landor and Associates Ⓒ Lucent Technologies 5A Ⓓ Richards Brock Miller Mitchell & Associates Ⓒ Dallas Museum of Nature and Science 5B Ⓓ Spin Design Ⓒ Financial Consulting & Solutions 5C Ⓓ Essex Two Incorporated Ⓒ Strategic Alliance International 5D Ⓓ Mike Quon/Designation Ⓒ None-Available

	A	B	C	D
1				
2				
3				
4				
5				

Ⓓ = Design Firm Ⓒ = Client

1A Ⓓ Rickabaugh Graphics Ⓒ Seton Hall University 1B Ⓓ Landor and Associates Ⓒ Tokyu Hotels 1C Ⓓ Design Continuum Inc Ⓒ Vivatone Hearing Systems LLC 1D Ⓓ Peter Montoya Inc. Ⓒ David Kern Asset Management 2A Ⓓ VINE360 Ⓒ VINE360 2B Ⓓ Gardner Design Ⓒ Kroger Convenience Stores 2C Ⓓ Duffy & Partners Ⓒ RED 2D Ⓓ Proart Graphics/Gabriel Kalach Ⓒ OMC/Original Media Concepts 3A Ⓓ Landor and Associates Ⓒ Visteon 3B Ⓓ Brandbeat Ⓒ IMF WORLD BANK & DUBAI GOVERNMENT 3C Ⓓ Essex Two Incorporated Ⓒ Pilsbury 3D Ⓓ Hausch Design Agency LLC Ⓒ Octodea: A multi-armed marketing cooperative 4A Ⓓ octane inc. Ⓒ Patrick Choate 4B Ⓓ FutureBrand Ⓒ OPSM eye care 4C Ⓓ Landor and Associates Ⓒ Agilent 4D Ⓓ switchfoot creative Ⓒ Interact Power 5A Ⓓ Mortensen Design Ⓒ CPP, Inc. 5B Ⓓ Dan Rood Design Ⓒ Raviant Technologies 5C Ⓓ Landor and Associates Ⓒ Astrium 5D Ⓓ Kraftaverk - Design Studio Ⓒ Throun

	A	B	C	D	
	GLIDES INTERNATIONAL	afi	FORTIS	THE ISLANDS OF THE bahamas	1
	north island SEYCHELLES	scient	MTV MUSIC TELEVISION	standard™ lifestyl.	2
	polpharma	resource	cilys	red cell	3
	andisa	alego		wolken communica	4
					5

Ⓓ = Design Firm Ⓒ = Client

1A Ⓓ Methodologie Ⓒ Glides International 1B Ⓓ FutureBrand Ⓒ Australian Film Institute 1C Ⓓ Landor and Associates Ⓒ Fortis 1D Ⓓ Duffy & Partners Ⓒ The Bahamas Ministry of Tourism 2A Ⓓ Enterprise IG Ⓒ North Island 2B Ⓓ Design Continuum Inc Ⓒ Scient 2C Ⓓ Ames Design Ⓒ MTV 2D Ⓓ Gardner Design Ⓒ The Standard 3A Ⓓ Delikatessen Ⓒ Polpharma 3B Ⓓ Pressley Jacobs: a design partnership Ⓒ Resource Graphic 3C Ⓓ cesart.com Ⓒ Cilys 3D Ⓓ Landor and Associates Ⓒ Red Cell 4A Ⓓ Enterprise IG Ⓒ Andisa 4B Ⓓ Q Ⓒ alego 4C Ⓓ Gardner Design Ⓒ Refined Technologies Inc. 4D Ⓓ Wolken communica Ⓒ self 5A Ⓓ Landor and Associates Ⓒ Thai Airways 5B Ⓓ Gardner Design Ⓒ Kroger Convenience Stores 5C Ⓓ Peter Montoya Inc. Ⓒ Denise A. Izatt 5D Ⓓ Crosby Associates Ⓒ Old St. Patrick's Cathedral

Ⓓ = Design Firm Ⓒ = Client

1A Ⓓ Alesce Ⓒ Network Photonics 1B Ⓓ Dotzero Design Ⓒ INI 1C Ⓓ Scott Lewis Design Ⓒ DeepWeave Technology Consulting 1D Ⓓ Crosby Associates Ⓒ Lutheran General HealthSystem
2A Ⓓ Nonni & Manni/Ydda Ⓒ Siminn 2B Ⓓ Dan Rood Design Ⓒ Signature Flight Support 2C Ⓓ The Bradford Lawton Design Group Ⓒ Air Force Credit Union 2D Ⓓ Crosby Associates Ⓒ MeriStar
3A Ⓓ Landor and Associates Ⓒ H&R Block 3B Ⓓ helium.design Ⓒ G2 Innenarchitektur 3C Ⓓ Landor and Associates Ⓒ B Business Partners 3D Ⓓ Landor and Associates Ⓒ Altria
4A Ⓓ Landor and Associates Ⓒ Microsoft 4B Ⓓ Enterprise IG Ⓒ SYSPRO 4C Ⓓ Landor and Associates Ⓒ Messe Frankfurt 4D Ⓓ CDI Studios Ⓒ Ambiance Design Group
5A Ⓓ Landor and Associates Ⓒ Singapore Telecom 5B Ⓓ Methodologie Ⓒ Methodologie 5C Ⓓ Brandon Tabiolo Ⓒ Account Management Associates 5D Ⓓ Z-Design Ⓒ Hachen

A B C D

1

2

3

4

5

Ⓓ = Design Firm Ⓒ = Client

1A Ⓓ Duffy & Partners Ⓒ International Truck and Engine Corporation 1B Ⓓ What Design, Inc. Ⓒ Torque Consulting 1C Ⓓ Segura Inc. Ⓒ Lightflow.com 1D Ⓓ Landor and Associates Ⓒ Black and Decker
2A Ⓓ design bridge incorporated Ⓒ Design Bridge Incorporated 2B Ⓓ Gardner Design Ⓒ Refined Technologies Inc. 2C Ⓓ Dept 3 Ⓒ ToolSyndicate 2D Ⓓ Landor and Associates Ⓒ Colmena
3A Ⓓ Gardner Design Ⓒ VizWorx Photolab 3B Ⓓ Segura Inc. Ⓒ XXX Snowboards 3C Ⓓ Landor and Associates Ⓒ Paxonix 3D Ⓓ Landor and Associates Ⓒ Bank Danamon
4A Ⓓ Essex Two Incorporated Ⓒ Paslode Corporation 4B Ⓓ Bonfilio Design Ⓒ Joseph Pallante 4C Ⓓ Landor and Associates Ⓒ Acterna 4D Ⓓ Tom Fowler, Inc. Ⓒ TIAA/CREF
5A Ⓓ Landor and Associates Ⓒ Mercedes 5B Ⓓ Logoboom Ⓒ Deforum.ru 5C Ⓓ Dept 3 Ⓒ Freebord 5D Ⓓ VINE360 Ⓒ Raccoon Interactive

	A	B	C	D
1		LOHRMANN INTERNATIONAL	studiobox	New Destiny
2		Atorvastatin Landmark Program™ Building Insight Through Investigation™		مدينة دبي للإغاثة DUBAI AID CITY
3			TECHNOLOGY SOLUTIONS GROUP for your success	WESTERN ATLAS
4	SATURN™	RED WINGS	TIPTAPE INFORMATION FÜR IHREN KÖRPER	STARFSMENNT
5	AEIVEOS SCIENCES GROUP	song™		VENDARIA moving pictures. moving products.

Ⓓ = Design Firm Ⓒ = Client

1A Ⓓ Crosby Associates Ⓒ Illinios Savings and Loan 1B Ⓓ Q Ⓒ Lohrmann International 1C Ⓓ Chemi Montes Design Ⓒ studio 1D Ⓓ Pump Graphic Ⓒ Unpublished
2A Ⓓ O'Connor Identity Development Ⓒ National Commercial Bank of Jamaica 2B Ⓓ Landor and Associates Ⓒ Lipitor 2C Ⓓ Gardner Design Ⓒ Ensignal Cellular Service 2D Ⓓ Brandbeat Ⓒ Dubai Aid City
3A Ⓓ Essex Two Incorporated Ⓒ Pediatric Palliative Care Institute 3B Ⓓ Betactive Ⓒ Pop-Akademie 3C Ⓓ Methodologie Ⓒ Washington Mutual 3D Ⓓ Monigle Associates Inc. Ⓒ Western Atlas
4A Ⓓ Landor and Associates Ⓒ Saturn 4B Ⓓ CAPSULE Ⓒ Red Wing Shoes 4C Ⓓ helium.design Ⓒ TipTape 4D Ⓓ Kraftaverk - Design Studio Ⓒ BSRB
5A Ⓓ Platform Creative Group Ⓒ Aeiveos Science Group 5B Ⓓ Landor and Associates Ⓒ Song 5C Ⓓ Critheorian Ⓒ Boomori 5D Ⓓ Methodologie Ⓒ Vendaria

Kroger
Identity Design

Gardner Design, Wichita, Kansas

Quik Stop. Loaf 'n Jug. Mini-Mart. Turkey Hill. Tom Thumb. Kwik Shop.

Chances are you already recognize that these are names of conveniences stores. What most people do not know is all these chains are owned by Kroger, Inc., and there are about 900 individual stores located across the United States, as well as about 500 gas outlets at Kroger-owned supermarkets.

Management have been working hard to take advantage of its economy of scale in the purchase of supplies used in and products purchased at the stores. Having enjoyed significant savings in this way, managers also began considering how to achieve this same success in other areas.

"It became more and more evident that handling all the diverse identities was costing Kroger in a number of ways. It did not give them clout through numbers: They had to buy signage and all other identifiers by chain. They asked us to find the best way to develop unity among all the convenience stores," explains Bill Gardner, principal of Gardner Design, Wichita, Kansas, whose team was selected by Kroger to consider the design problems this enormous coordination effort presented.

Gardner Design had several options. The designers could suggest that all the names be abandoned in lieu of a completely new brand name. They might also select one of the chain names and apply it to all the others. But consumer research had revealed that each of the regional divisions enjoyed real brand loyalty in their areas.

Gardner suggested a third and more unexpected solution: Let all the chains keep their respective names, but develop a single logo and visual treatment that would unify the group.

"Kroger's convenience stores cover the country, and when you start to spot all their larger grocery stores in their many locations—Kroger also owns Ralph's, King Super, and Dillon's stores, among many others—this really is a national brand that goes from coast to coast. Travelers will recognize the graphics of the rebranded convenience stores, no matter which store they visit and no matter what name is on the store," explains Gardner.

The designer considered many conceptual aspects of convenience stores—that they are not a destination but are more of a stop along a journey; that they are inexorably linked to travel and vehicles; that customers are usually in a hurry; and that they are open day and night.

A logo exploration that tied some of these concepts together was a diamond-shaped mark that contained what at first looks like a collection of colored, organic shapes, but on closer inspection is clearly a liberal interpretation of the shape of the United States.

Each of the various store names will be shown in red, handled in the same typographic style, and shown with the new logo. In-store signage and other graphics will contain the diamond-shaped logo. It is used as a background pattern, sometimes subtly, in a manner that ties together all the designs, whether they appear in California or Florida.

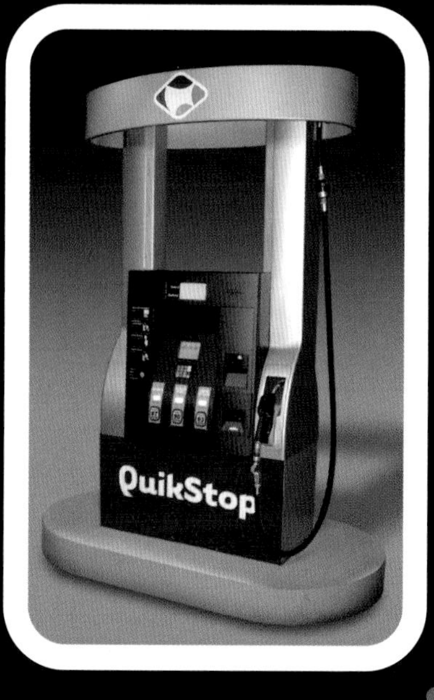

Gardner believes the final design invites the customer to become invested in the mark. "Sometimes a very literal mark gives the viewer too much information," he says. "When a customer discovers something in a design, it not only is an 'a-ha!' moment, but that person also takes ownership in the mark."

	A	B	C	D
1	LOGO SEARCH Keywords: Symbols Type: ◯ Symbol ◯ Typographic ◯ Combo ◉ All			MIGHTY LOVE
2				
3	Second Start A Welfare to Work Program	One Good Turn		
4				
5	milagros		pcc	GLOBAL Chaos

Ⓓ = Design Firm Ⓒ = Client

1C Ⓓ greteman group Ⓒ Heart Hospital 1D Ⓓ Device Ⓒ Mighty Love 2A Ⓓ Blattner Brunner Ⓒ Johnson & Johnson 2B Ⓓ Allen Creative Ⓒ Grace Fellowship Church
2C Ⓓ The Bradford Lawton Design Group Ⓒ marriage and family counseling 2D Ⓓ The Bradford Lawton Design Group Ⓒ Save-A-Baby 3A Ⓓ Evolve Visual Ⓒ World Vision 3B Ⓓ Howling Good Designs Ⓒ One Good Turn
3C Ⓓ Howalt Design Studio, Inc. Ⓒ VitaCandy 3D Ⓓ Eagle Imagery (PhotoGraphics) Ⓒ Organbroker 4A Ⓓ Cheri Gearhart, graphic design Ⓒ Cheri Gearhart 4B Ⓓ Creative Madhouse Ⓒ Two Topia
4C Ⓓ Simon & Goetz Design Ⓒ vireal/global sports village 4D Ⓓ the atmosfear Ⓒ theatmosfear 5A Ⓓ logobyte Ⓒ Milagros 5B Ⓓ Glitschka Studios Ⓒ Sports NW 5C Ⓓ Octane Ⓒ Paramount Custom Cycles
5D Ⓓ Fernandez Design Ⓒ Global Chaos

A B C D

1

2

3

4

5

Ⓓ = Design Firm Ⓒ = Client

1A Ⓓ Gardner Design Ⓒ BigDog Motorcycles 1B Ⓓ Gardner Design Ⓒ Big Dog Motorcycles 1C Ⓓ Howalt Design Studio, Inc. Ⓒ *MacWorld* Magazine 1D Ⓓ Glitschka Studios Ⓒ Upper Deck Company
2A Ⓓ Davidson Design Ⓒ Target 2B Ⓓ Glitschka Studios Ⓒ Now defunct Band 2C Ⓓ Hinge Ⓒ Geoff Camphire 2D Ⓓ Landor and Associates Ⓒ Camp Fire USA
3A Ⓓ Landor and Associates Ⓒ Corning 3B Ⓓ Soloflight Design Studio Ⓒ Lightertime 3C Ⓓ Alesce Ⓒ Human Rights Watch 3D Ⓓ greteman group Ⓒ Inspiring Leadership
4A Ⓓ Gardner Design Ⓒ rti 4B Ⓓ McAndrew Kaps Ⓒ Athletica Inc. 4C Ⓓ Critheorian Ⓒ Incendo Marketing 4D Ⓓ Design Continuum Inc Ⓒ MusicFans.com
5A Ⓓ STUART ROWLEY DESIGN Ⓒ Stuart Rowley Design 5B Ⓓ Glitschka Studios Ⓒ Volcanic Roasters 5C Ⓓ Sheehan Design Ⓒ Heatwerks 5D Ⓓ Houston Design Ⓒ Fan Brands

	A	B	C	D
1	LIBERTY IRRIGATION	HUMAN RIGHTS WATCH		
2			send	VISION2HIRE
3		Family tree PRODUCTIONS		
4		Independent Colleges of Indiana	M13 MECCA	
5			Hiatus 100	Destina.ca

Ⓓ = Design Firm Ⓒ = Client

1A Ⓓ Kendall Creative Shop, Inc. Ⓒ Liberty Irrigation 1B Ⓓ Alesce Ⓒ Human Rights Watch 1C Ⓓ Eskil Ohlsson Assoc. Inc. Ⓒ Norris Industries 1D Ⓓ Gardner Design Ⓒ Reno Cooking Conveyors
2A Ⓓ Richards Brock Miller Mitchell & Associates Ⓒ Cross Cloud 2B Ⓓ Gardner Design Ⓒ CRC Environmental Construction 2C Ⓓ Kristian Andersen, Inc. Ⓒ Southeast Neighborhood Development
2D Ⓓ karacters design group Ⓒ Vision 2 Hire 3A Ⓓ Critheorian Ⓒ Water.com 3B Ⓓ Design Continuum Inc Ⓒ Family Tree 3C Ⓓ Critheorian Ⓒ Starpointe Properties 3D Ⓓ Diana Graham Ⓒ Clean Air Community
4A Ⓓ Square One Ⓒ Dallas Cowboys 4B Ⓓ Essex Two Incorporated Ⓒ Independent Colleges of Indiana 4C Ⓓ BC Design Ⓒ Mecca 4D Ⓓ Jonathan Rice & Company Ⓒ MusicFans.com
5A Ⓓ Deep Design Ⓒ Georgia Music Hall of Fame 5B Ⓓ thomasvasquez.com Ⓒ Texas Tile Co. 5C Ⓓ Union Design & Photo Ⓒ Hiatus 5D Ⓓ karacters design group Ⓒ Air Canada

	A	B	C	D	
	gifts.com	dreamlab	APRIA HEALTHCARE A New Dimension in Homecare		1
		Humility		CALTEX	2
	SWEEDISH Council of America		U.S. Canoe and Kayak Team	Chicago2001 For the time of your life.	3
		The Learning Congregation			4
	Nemzoff Roth		Creative Learning	Technology	5

Ⓓ = Design Firm Ⓒ = Client

1A Ⓓ Landor and Associates Ⓒ gifts.com 1B Ⓓ Evenson Design Group Ⓒ Rubin Postaer 1C Ⓓ Landor and Associates Ⓒ Apria Heathcare 1D Ⓓ Landor and Associates Ⓒ La Caixa
2A Ⓓ Kircher, Inc. Ⓒ National Association of Home Builders 2B Ⓓ greteman group Ⓒ Humility 2C Ⓓ Brian Blankenship Ⓒ Fort Worth Public Library Foundation 2D Ⓓ Landor and Associates Ⓒ Caltex
3A Ⓓ Gardner Design Ⓒ Swedish Council of America 3B Ⓓ SUMO Ⓒ UnionFonts.com 3C Ⓓ Crosby Associates Ⓒ U.S. Canoe and Kayak Team 3D Ⓓ Crosby Associates Ⓒ City of Chicago Millennium Celebration
4A Ⓓ Beth Singer Design Ⓒ International Committee on Holocaust Era Insurance Claims 4B Ⓓ Garfinkel Design Ⓒ Rodef Shalom Temple 4C Ⓓ Lomangino Studio Inc. Ⓒ Potomac Floor Covering, Inc. 4D Ⓓ Fernandez Design Ⓒ Wallsource
5A Ⓓ Art Chantry Ⓒ Nemzoff Roff 5B Ⓓ And Partners Ⓒ National Council of Jewish Women 5C Ⓓ Sabingrafik, Inc. Ⓒ Creative Learning Systems 5D Ⓓ Sabingrafik, Inc. Ⓒ McGraw Hill Home Interactive

	A	B	C	D
1	**LOGO SEARCH** Keywords: Arts. Type: Symbol, Typographic, Combo, All		FOTOMOTEL rental studio	PHOTOSTORIES
2				
3				FILM CADDY
4			moviepix	
5	C SPOT RUN PRODUCTIONS	GHET-O-VISION ENTERTAINMENT	VISIONWORKS	

Ⓓ = Design Firm Ⓒ = Client

1C Ⓓ Delikatessen Ⓒ Fotomotel Hamburg 1D Ⓓ Jon Flaming Design Ⓒ Stephanie Jamail 2A Ⓓ Gardner Design Ⓒ VizWorx Photolab 2B Ⓓ Square One Ⓒ Cinema Fighting Cancer 2C Ⓓ Sabingrafik, Inc. Ⓒ Sin Film 2D Ⓓ judson design associates Ⓒ Mark Green 3A Ⓓ Rick Johnson & Company Ⓒ Eaves Movie Ranch 3B Ⓓ Eskil Ohlsson Assoc. Inc. Ⓒ Cline Davis & Mann.Inc. 3C Ⓓ Critheorian Ⓒ Public Executions 3D Ⓓ Jon Flaming Design Ⓒ Film Caddy 4A Ⓓ Kraftaverk - Design Studio Ⓒ Cinema Sound 4B Ⓓ Design Army Ⓒ The Embassy of Norway 4C Ⓓ Aahbullay Ⓒ Astral Media 4D Ⓓ Squires & Company Ⓒ Motion Projects 5A Ⓓ Dennis Purcell Design Ⓒ C Spot Run Productions 5B Ⓓ GOLDFINGER c.s. Ⓒ Ghetovision Entertainment 5C Ⓓ James Stevens Ⓒ Vision Works 5D Ⓓ Diana Graham Ⓒ National Captioning Institut

	A	B	C	D
1	V C R	Happy Computer℠		
2	Connecting Point	NATIONAL DO NOT CALL REGISTRY		co:mission
3	LUNCH RECORDS		PÓSTURINN	a whisper of jazz
4	TACO BELL®	the Blues TUNE SOUL		
5				

Ⓓ = Design Firm Ⓒ = Client

1A Ⓓ Hubbell Design Works Ⓒ Blockbuster Video 1B Ⓓ Union Design & Photo Ⓒ Happy Computer 1C Ⓓ Gardner Design Ⓒ AIGA Wichita 1D Ⓓ Felixsockwell.com Ⓒ epson 2A Ⓓ Gardner Design Ⓒ Connecting Point 2B Ⓓ Mike Quon/Designation Ⓒ JDG Communications 2C Ⓓ Insight Design Ⓒ Excel 2D Ⓓ On Duty Design Ⓒ Gigabeats 3A Ⓓ Alphabet Arm Design Ⓒ Paul Buckley/Lunch Records 3B Ⓓ Rickabaugh Graphics Ⓒ City of Dublin, Ohio 3C Ⓓ Nonni & Manni/Ydda Ⓒ Islandspostur 3D Ⓓ Lisa Wood Design Ⓒ national ovarian cancer coalition 4A Ⓓ Landor and Associates Ⓒ Taco Bell 4B Ⓓ Integer Group - Midwest Ⓒ River Music Experience 4C Ⓓ Jonathan Rice & Company Ⓒ Greater Fort Worth Youth Orchestra 4D Ⓓ Hotdog Creative Ⓒ Dallas Symphony 5A Ⓓ REINES DESIGN INC. Ⓒ FUNDACION BERACASA 5B Ⓓ Jon Flaming Design Ⓒ Jake Flaming 5C Ⓓ Hubbell Design Works Ⓒ the Coast Connection 5D Ⓓ Hubbell Design Works Ⓒ the Coast Connection

	A	B	C	D
1	H E f	ESTB 1985 PRINTMASTER	THE ARTS COUNCIL	CATAPULT
2				CHRISTA VELBEL DOING THE WRITE THING
3	Post Office	gift box	کتاب مهر	
4		couponquarters	SOFA KING RUDE	the Stone Chair
5	SitOnIt Seating	Quality of Life Council A meeting of minds	JUNE DAY	thelounge

Ⓓ = Design Firm Ⓒ = Client

1A Ⓓ Gardner Design Ⓒ Hastings Oil Filter's 1B Ⓓ Gardner Design Ⓒ Printmaster 1C Ⓓ Insight Design Ⓒ The Art Council 1D Ⓓ Chaney, Nieman, Munson & Son Ⓒ Catapult Strategic Design
2A Ⓓ Richards Brock Miller Mitchell & Associates Ⓒ Galahad Books 2B Ⓓ Gardner Design Ⓒ Cramer Calligraphy 2C Ⓓ greteman group Ⓒ Costa Rica Natural Paper 2D Ⓓ Miaso Design Ⓒ Christa Velbel
3A Ⓓ Enterprise IG Ⓒ SA Post Office 3B Ⓓ Atlanta College of Art Ⓒ Gift Box 3C Ⓓ Did Graphics Ⓒ Mehr Publications, Tehran 3D Ⓓ Essex Two Incorporated Ⓒ Unisource Paper Fair
4A Ⓓ Hubbell Design Works Ⓒ Jobdoctor.com 4B Ⓓ Union Design & Photo Ⓒ Coupon Quarters 4C Ⓓ Chaney, Nieman, Munson & Son Ⓒ Sofa King Rude 4D Ⓓ Dotzero Design Ⓒ The Stone Chair
5A Ⓓ BBK Studio Ⓒ SitOnIt Seating 5B Ⓓ Keyword Design Ⓒ Quality of Life Council 5C Ⓓ mitchel design inc. Ⓒ June Day Productions 5D Ⓓ Frontmedia Ⓒ Flamingo International

Lot 44
Identity Design

Howalt Design, Gilbert, Arizona

When the Richmond, Virginia–based digital imaging and photo manipulation studio, Liquid Pictures, was bought out by Vertis, a much larger company, in 2002, its owners chafed at the thought of applying the parent company's corporate branding to its office. Known for its technically proficient and individually crafted visual solutions, Liquid Pictures wanted to maintain its distinct identity.

The new relationship with Vertis required a move to a historic warehouse district of Richmond. A packing crate used in the move was stamped with the cryptic words, Lot 44. The firm's creatives liked the industrial tone of the message and decided to adopt it as the business's name.

"'Lot 44' has a no-frills feel about it, like their new space," explains Paul Howalt of Howalt Design, the designer hired to create the new logo.

When Howalt heard the story of the moving crate and understood the need for this new company to carve out a distinct identity, he began to look for visual cues in other unfinished spaces: the insides of fuse boxes and toilet tanks, on old cardboard boxes and air-conditioning vents.

"These spaces always have ambiguous markings on them, and no one really understands what they mean. But there can be really interesting things happening in the typography that a designer can pick up and add his own slant to," the designer says.

Howalt photographed, sketched, and scanned dozens of these mysterious little markings. His options were many at this point, especially due to the fact that the client did not want just one logo but several—all with the same flavor, but each decidedly different.

Lot 44 wanted to remain consistently fresh in their customers' eyes. Above all, they wanted to avoid a staid, corporate look, despite their new affiliation.

The multiple-logo concept takes the pressure off the idea that a single logo must carry the entire visual personality and professional weight of a company, Howalt says.

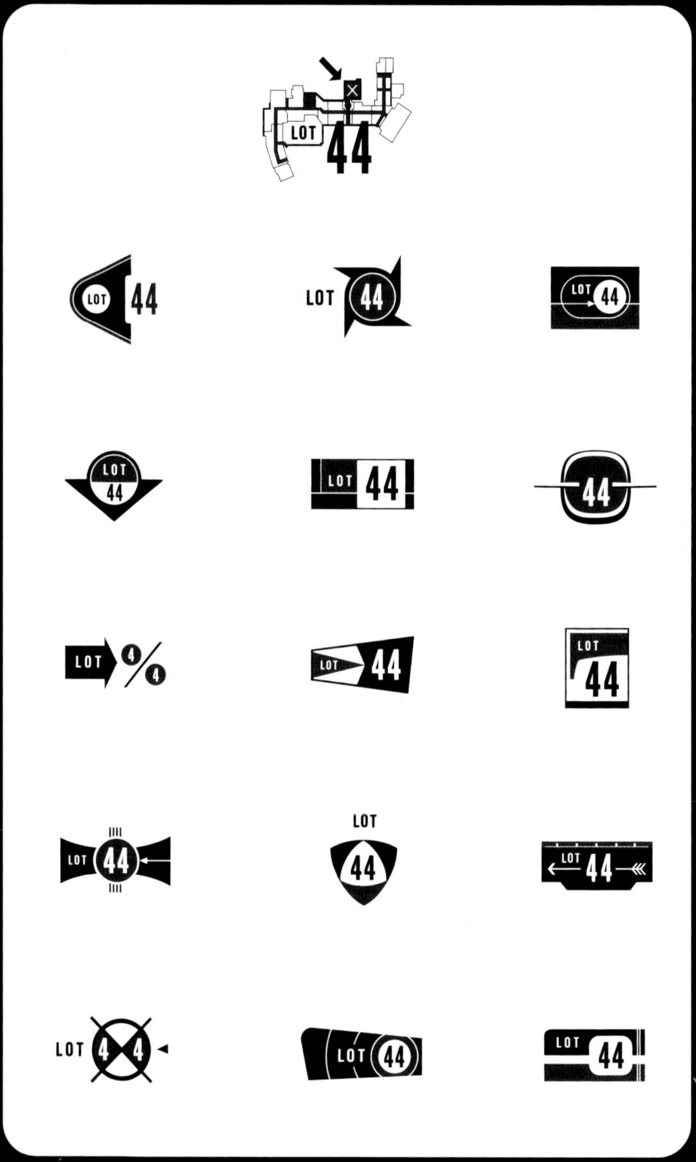

By extensively experimenting with positive and negative space and combining and recombining found elements and shapes with the words Lot 44—the typography of which always stays the same—Howalt eventually came up with a set of twenty marks that the presented to the client. They loved the effect.

Today, the studio uses the logos on its website, on service tags, in business collateral, and on signage, stickers, and rubber stamps. Lot 44 in-house creatives have begun to work with the marks to discover even more iterations.

A B C D

LOGO SEARCH

Keywords: Miscellaneous

Type: Symbol Typographic Combo All

1

2

3

4

5

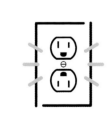

D = Design Firm C = Client

1C D Critheorian C PTI 1D D Landor and Associates C Key Corp 2A D Gardner Design C Scripmaster 2B D Pixelube C Elixir Studios 2C D the atmosfear C NNM Addys 2D D Squires & Company C Procloning
3A D Howalt Design Studio, Inc. C Nucleus Solutions 3B D greteman group C O2 Design 3C D Felixsockwell.com C tnn 3D D Squires & Company C Comfort Air
4A D switchfoot creative C The Gavel Group 4B D Newbomb Design C TMP Construction 4C D Squires & Company C Cornwell Tools 4D D Creative Devil Design C Button Construction
5A D Hubbell Design Works C Samsung 5B D BLANK, Inc. C AnswerLogic 5C D CrossGrain Creative Studios C intellinote 5D D Felixsockwell.com C bloomberg

A B C D

1

2

3

4

5

Ⓓ = Design Firm Ⓒ = Client

1A Ⓓ Critheorian Ⓒ Vivid Gray 1B Ⓓ Gardner Design Ⓒ Blue Hat Media 1C Ⓓ Born to Design Ⓒ Premiere Credit of North America, LLC 1D Ⓓ Hubbell Design Works Ⓒ Hanes/USA 2A Ⓓ the fovea project Ⓒ Clothes Out 2B Ⓓ Insight Design Ⓒ Richard Lynn's Shoe Market 2C Ⓓ Crosby Associates Ⓒ Zell Aneshe 2D Ⓓ BC Design Ⓒ Gift 3A Ⓓ BC Design Ⓒ Gift 3B Ⓓ BC Design Ⓒ Gift 3C Ⓓ John Langdon Design Ⓒ Rehabilitation Hospitals of America 3D Ⓓ Gardner Design Ⓒ IntraCare 4A Ⓓ Church Logo Gallery Ⓒ Church Logo Gallery 4B Ⓓ Squires & Company Ⓒ Cowboy Church 4C Ⓓ Jon Flaming Design Ⓒ Objex, Inc 4D Ⓓ Art Chantry Ⓒ Estrus 5A Ⓓ Matsumoto Design Ⓒ Microworkz.com 5B Ⓓ Gardner Design Ⓒ Hite Fanning Honeyman 5C Ⓓ Virtual Cubed Inc. Ⓒ MatchStorm Studios 5D Ⓓ The Office of Bill Chiaravalle Ⓒ The Hangar

A B C D

1

LOGO SEARCH

Keywords: Food

Type: Symbol Typographic Combo All

2

3

4

5

Ⓓ = Design Firm Ⓒ = Client

1C Ⓓ Delikatessen Ⓒ Katelbach Coffee 1D Ⓓ Glitschka Studios Ⓒ Bakewoods Coffee 2A Ⓓ Gardner Design Ⓒ The Coffee Millers 2B Ⓓ Moonlit Creative Group Ⓒ The Grounds 2C Ⓓ greteman group Ⓒ greteman group 2D Ⓓ Creative Madhouse Ⓒ Picasso Cafe 3A Ⓓ Bonfilio Design Ⓒ Dockside Cafe 3B Ⓓ Mitchell Design Ⓒ Sun Microsystems 3C Ⓓ Richards Brock Miller Mitchell & Associates Ⓒ Confession Café 3D Ⓓ Duffy & Partners Ⓒ Bill Westbrook/RoundTable Cafe 4A Ⓓ Simon & Goetz Design Ⓒ gmund 4B Ⓓ Boelts/Stratford Associates Ⓒ Epic Cafe 4C Ⓓ Blacktop Creative Ⓒ Diminished Fifth Band 4D Ⓓ Integer Group - Midwest Ⓒ WineFest Des Moines 5A Ⓓ Landor and Associates Ⓒ Digeno 5B Ⓓ Creative Madhouse Ⓒ Avenue Bistro 5C Ⓓ G&G Advertising Ⓒ Santa Fe Opera 5D Ⓓ Sayles Graphic Design, Inc. Ⓒ 308 Martini Bar

	A	B	C	D
1	perrier FRANCE	2	THE DAIRY® CENTER FOR THE ARTS	NORTH SHORE DAIRY DELIVERY
2	CITRUS CHEMICAL INC	NEW YORK CITY UNIVERSITY	KINETICHEALTH	
3	tré limone™	S™	string beans	mesazón
4	LUIGI'S RISTORANTE ITALIANO	MUSCO FAMILY OLIVE CO. MUSCO		iScream for SUMMER™
5	the noodle house			

Ⓓ = Design Firm Ⓒ = Client

1A Ⓓ Scribblers' Club Ⓒ Perrier France 1B Ⓓ greteman group Ⓒ O2 Glass Mark 1C Ⓓ Alesce Ⓒ The Dairy Center for the Arts 1D Ⓓ Kern Design Group Ⓒ North Shore Dairy 2A Ⓓ LeVesque Design Ⓒ Citrus Chemical, Inc. 2B Ⓓ LeVesque Design Ⓒ New York City University 2C Ⓓ Enterprise IG Ⓒ Kinetic Health 2D Ⓓ Sabingrafik, Inc. Ⓒ Creative Learning Systems 3A Ⓓ karacters design group Ⓒ Clearly Canadian Beverage Corporation 3B Ⓓ Sibley/Peteet Design, Inc. Ⓒ Chili's Grill 3C Ⓓ Sabingrafik, Inc. Ⓒ String Beans 3D Ⓓ TD2, S.C. Ⓒ MESAZON 4A Ⓓ judson design associates Ⓒ Luigi Ferrer 4B Ⓓ tesser Ⓒ Musco Family Olive Co. 4C Ⓓ helium.design Ⓒ Österreich Werbung 4D Ⓓ Duffy & Partners Ⓒ Target Stores 5A Ⓓ Brandbeat Ⓒ JUMEIRAH INTERNATIONAL 5B Ⓓ Gardner Design Ⓒ Cargill 5C Ⓓ Gardner Design Ⓒ Cargill 5D Ⓓ Gardner Design Ⓒ Excel

Ⓓ = Design Firm Ⓒ = Client

1A Ⓓ Maria Lee Design Ⓒ n/a 1B Ⓓ Compass Design Ⓒ Sunrise Gourmet 1C Ⓓ Hornall Anderson Ⓒ Dayberries Bakery & Café 1D Ⓓ Enterprise IG Ⓒ Fattis & Monis 2A Ⓓ Gardner Design Ⓒ Scone On the Range 2B Ⓓ Born to Design Ⓒ FontMart.com 2C Ⓓ helium.design Ⓒ Cake 2D Ⓓ R&R Partners (Randy Heil) Ⓒ Nevada Power 3A Ⓓ Wolken communica Ⓒ Grace's Kitchen 3B Ⓓ Hubbell Design Works Ⓒ The Hurried Chef 3C Ⓓ BC Design Ⓒ Dankens 3D Ⓓ Creative Madhouse Ⓒ Hausware Designs 4A Ⓓ Redbeard Communications Inc. Ⓒ Creme De La Creme Catering 4B Ⓓ Gardner Design Ⓒ The Lord's Diner 4C Ⓓ Oxide Design Co. Ⓒ Campus Kitchens Project 4D Ⓓ Sayles Graphic Design, Inc. Ⓒ B Brurner Grille 5A Ⓓ Synergy Graphix Ⓒ Dining Experience 5B Ⓓ Creative Madhouse Ⓒ Private Fundraiser 5C Ⓓ Ventress Design Group, Inc Ⓒ Walker Foods 5D Ⓓ Richards Brock Miller Mitchell & Associates Ⓒ Button's Café

Umogul
Identity Design

Michael Doret, Hollywood, California

Umogul was an online company that allowed the average Joe or Jane to invest money in a fund for specific Hollywood productions. If the investor's instincts were correct, he or she could make a profit.

It was a concept that evoked the glamour of the 1920s and '30s—an era that still has appeal today, says designer and artist Michael Doret. "The idea of being a mogul, of being someone who could invest money and withstand the risk, is glamorous," he adds.

Doret's first direction for the client had the feeling of a movie marquee. The artist's sketch also contained the skyline of a big city to suggest the big-business nature of the venture.

"As I work, I see the sequence of the letterforms and how they relate to each other. I see what I can create from those forms," he says.

A second concept suggested a city of the future as envisioned in the past, with a raceway in the sky and beams of light presiding over all. The client liked this approach, because it had a desirable "big movie house" feel, but Doret felt that the ".com" portion of the design was distracting.

Another design explored even further how the letterforms could work together—specifically, how to lessen the impact of the dot. A more Art Deco–styled sketch deemphasized the dot even more, making part of a leg on the letter *M.*

"This type of design is from the 1930s, where the letters all run together inside a shape, jumbled up in different sizes. It really proved to be too complex for the project, Doret says.

So the designer sought a simpler solution. He discovered that, with a rounded type form, he could turn the *U* portion of the name into a little character and almost hide the dot by giving the now top-hatted *U* a monocle and using the counters of the letters *o* and *g* to form additional dots.

"I want to not only set some type but also create things that don't exist in a font," he says.

The design that was ultimately chosen combines several of these "found" factors. There is a reference to the pyramid element on the back of a dollar bill, but an Art Deco twist creates another little character—legs spread and arms held up, or a winking, twinkling eye with eyelashes.

The final design contains more squared-off, copperplate-like letterforms and refers to money through its gold and cream coloration. More important, says Doret, is that the client agreed to drop the ".com" portion of the name in the design. Dealing with this onerous suffix is a problem many designers face, he notes. Encourage the client to refer to the product or service in the same way as customers do—"eBay," to cite a common example, not "eBay.com."

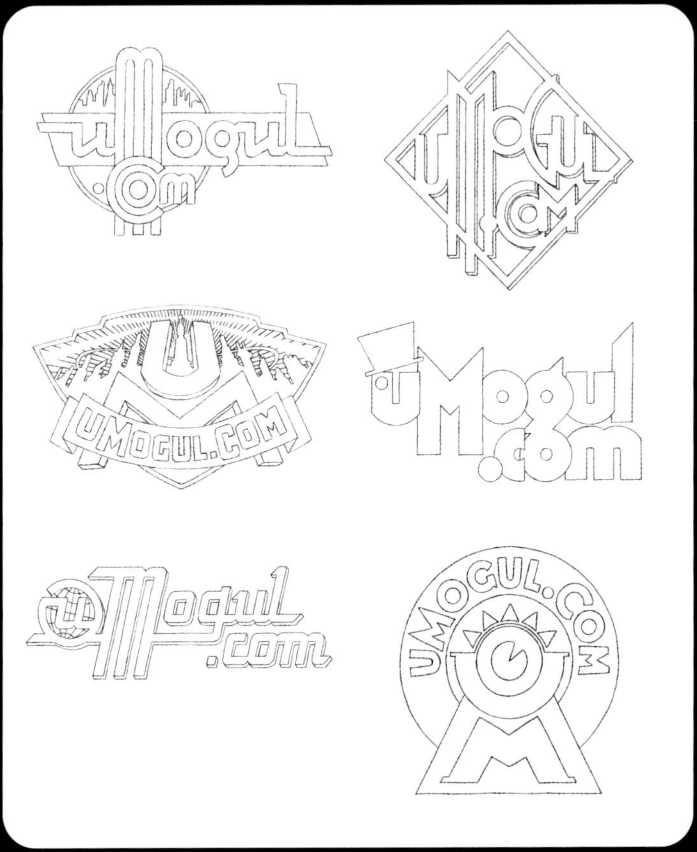

	A	B	C	D
1	LOGO SEARCH Keywords: Structures Type: ◯ Symbol ◯ Typographic ◯ Combo ◉ All			the neighborhood early childhood center
2	MODULAR	the journey home	INDEPENDENT COLLEGES OF INDIANA	Corrie's House A Home of Hope.
3	CORNERSTONE MORTGAGE OF IOWA		north coast Community Homes	selecthome
4	ARC	Bundesen REAL ESTATE	MAIN GATE	
5		PROJECT FILM & TV		CRC

Ⓓ = Design Firm Ⓒ = Client

1C Ⓓ Brad Norr Design Ⓒ Augsburg Fortress Publishers 1D Ⓓ Dotzero Design Ⓒ The Neighborhood Daycare 2A Ⓓ Design Continuum Inc Ⓒ id8 Group 2B Ⓓ SPUR Ⓒ Community Partnership for the Homeless 2C Ⓓ Jeff Kern Design Ⓒ Indiana Colleges of Indiana - Hirons and Company 2D Ⓓ Glitschka Studios Ⓒ Corries House 3A Ⓓ Burd & Patterson Ⓒ Cornerstone Mortgage of Iowa 3B Ⓓ Dotzero Design Ⓒ The Neighborhood Daycare 3C Ⓓ Newbomb Design Ⓒ North Coast Community Homes 3D Ⓓ Hubbell Design Works Ⓒ Select Home.com 4A Ⓓ Monigle Associates Inc. Ⓒ Affordable Residential Communities 4B Ⓓ octane inc. Ⓒ Bundesen Real Estate 4C Ⓓ Boelts/Stratford Associates Ⓒ of Tucson 4D Ⓓ Fernandez Design Ⓒ Willis Homes 5A Ⓓ Duffy & Partners Ⓒ Mess Hall Music 5B Ⓓ Design Continuum Inc Ⓒ Project Film & TV 5C Ⓓ Gardner Design Ⓒ Refined Technologies Inc. 5D Ⓓ Gardner Design Ⓒ CRC Environmental Construction

A B C D

1

2

3

4

5

Ⓓ = Design Firm Ⓒ = Client

1A Ⓓ Essex Two Incorporated Ⓒ Urban Shopping Centers, Inc. 1B Ⓓ judson design associates Ⓒ Metro National 1C Ⓓ SPUR Ⓒ Mason Retail Group 1D Ⓓ Gardner Design Ⓒ A Little Biz
2A Ⓓ Bonfilio Design Ⓒ Buchbinder & Warren 2B Ⓓ DDB Ⓒ Lake Forest Independence Party 2C Ⓓ judson design associates Ⓒ T. Cay Rowe 2D Ⓓ Frederick & Froberg Design Office Ⓒ NBA
3A Ⓓ Go Welsh! Ⓒ Appalachian Brewing Company 3B Ⓓ greteman group Ⓒ Hotel at Oldtown 3C Ⓓ Sabingrafik, Inc. Ⓒ Yamaha Watercraft 3D Ⓓ Rickabaugh Graphics Ⓒ Morgan State University
4A Ⓓ Insight Design Ⓒ Spangenberg Phillips 4B Ⓓ S Design, Inc. Ⓒ Center For Economic Development Law 4C Ⓓ Blacktop Creative Ⓒ Kansas City—City Market 4D Ⓓ HardBall Sports Ⓒ Gotham City Limits
5A Ⓓ Smith-Boake Designwerke Inc. Ⓒ Mackenzie Financial Corporation 5B Ⓓ logobyte Ⓒ Citadel Consulting 5C Ⓓ 2B1A Ⓒ wolf tax accountancy 5C Ⓓ SUMO Ⓒ Newcastle upon Tyne 5D Ⓓ SUMO Ⓒ Newcastle upon Tyne

	A	B	C	D
1				
2				
3				
4				
5				

Ⓓ = Design Firm Ⓒ = Client

1A Ⓓ Sayles Graphic Design, Inc. Ⓒ Meredith Corporation 1B Ⓓ CAPSULE Ⓒ Byerlys/Lund foods 1C Ⓓ Sayles Graphic Design, Inc. Barn Bash 1D Ⓓ Gardner Design Ⓒ Pride of the Farm 2A Ⓓ Duffy & Partners Ⓒ Gibbs Farm 2B Ⓓ Watts Design Ⓒ darriwill farm 2C Ⓓ Cloudjammer Studio Ⓒ Kennesaw State University 2D Ⓓ Deep Design Ⓒ Pinnacle South 3A Ⓓ BDG Studio Ronin Ⓒ Consortium Healthcare (proposed) 3B Ⓓ Davidson Design Ⓒ Sydney Tower 3C Ⓓ Soloflight Design Studio Ⓒ Southeast Gulfcoast Sales 3D Ⓓ Mike Quon/Designation Ⓒ British Airways 4A Ⓓ Gardner Design Ⓒ Buena Vista University 4B Ⓓ Gardner Design Ⓒ Buena Vista University 4C Ⓓ Evenson Design Group Ⓒ Vistamar School 4D Ⓓ Morello+Company Ⓒ Damelio Construction Comany 5A Ⓓ greteman group Ⓒ Bank of Kansas 5B Ⓓ Prejean LoBue Ⓒ Teche Holding Company 5C Ⓓ Synergy Graphix Ⓒ Technimentals Research Group 5D Ⓓ BT Graphics Ⓒ Tuscany Spa.Salon

A B C D

(D) = Design Firm
(C) = Client

LOGO SEARCH

Keywords: Transportation

Type: ◯ Symbol ◯ Typographic ◯ Combo ◉ All

1

2

3

4

5

(D) = Design Firm (C) = Client

1C (D) R&R Partners (Randy Heil) (C) Airwave 1D (D) R&R Partners (Randy Heil) (C) Primp 2A (D) bob neace graphic design, inc (C) Aircraft Travel Solutions 2B (D) Flynn Design (C) Eaton Aerospace 2C (D) Pennebaker (C) Chelsea Catering 2D (D) greteman group (C) Flight Tek 3A (D) Creative Development Associates, Inc. (C) Integrated Aerospace 3B (D) Gardner Design (C) SafeTemp 3C (D) bob neace graphic design, inc (C) MidWest Corporate Aviation 3D (D) Howling Good Designs (C) Scott Cooper Associates 4A (D) (twentystar) (C) Jeppesen 4B (D) Gardner Design (C) VizWorx Photolab 4C (D) stay gold creative (C) Stay Gold Art 4D (D) Device (C) Great Escapes 5A (D) Felixsockwell.com (C) tnn 5B (D) KENNETH DISENO (C) Gudino Brothers Trucking 5C (D) Element (C) Flatlanders 5D (D) elf design (C) iHaul

	A	B	C	D
1	networkfleet™	e-GO		
2	CHRYSLER'S CHICAGO VINTAGE GRAND PRIX & Concours d'Elegance	Lobello Racing	Motor SKILLS	1 DRIVEN DESIGN PERFORMANCE
3	PG d		LAND STABILIZERS	UNDER THE SON EXCAVATING, INC.
4	THE HAMMER HEADS		DAYTON MUSEUM OF BICYCLES	
5	SKOLADU HEIMINN			MTV MUSIC TELEVISION

Ⓓ = Design Firm Ⓒ = Client

1A Ⓓ switchfoot creative Ⓒ Networkcar, Inc. 1B Ⓓ Hoyne Design Ⓒ Carlins 1C Ⓓ Felixsockwell.com Ⓒ wsj 1D Ⓓ bob neace graphic design, inc Ⓒ MetroCourier 2A Ⓓ VMA Ⓒ Chrysler 2B Ⓓ Mires>Design for Brands Ⓒ Eric Lobello 2C Ⓓ Tim Frame Design Ⓒ Graphic Design Society 2D Ⓓ Tim Frame Design Ⓒ Tim Frame Design 3A Ⓓ Popgun Ⓒ Popgun Design 3B Ⓓ Gardner Design Ⓒ US Agbank 3C Ⓓ Jon Flaming Design Ⓒ Land Stabilizers 3D Ⓓ CDI Studios Ⓒ Under the Son Excavating 4A Ⓓ Squires & Company Ⓒ The Hammerheads 4B Ⓓ Jon Flaming Design Ⓒ Share the Road Texas 4C Ⓓ VMA Ⓒ Dayton Museum of Bicycles 4D Ⓓ Felixsockwell.com Ⓒ citystreets.org 5A Ⓓ Kraftaverk - Design Studio Ⓒ Student Travel 5B Ⓓ Gardner Design Ⓒ BigDog Motorcycles 5C Ⓓ elevation Ⓒ cosmic catering 5D Ⓓ Segura Inc. Ⓒ MTV

A B C D

1

2

3

4

5

D = Design Firm C = Client

1A D Sabingrafik, Inc. C The Buie Family 1B D Bruce E. Morgan Graphic Design C Potomac Boardsailing 1C D BrandLogic C Navistream 1D D Landor and Associates C Fleet Financial Goup
2A D greteman group C Starboard Academy 2B D Sabingrafik, Inc. C Crazy Shirts 2C D Cloudjammer Studio C Cloudjammer Studio 2D D Gabriela Gasparini Design C Harper Collins Publishers
3A D Sabingrafik, Inc. C Harcourt & Co. 3B D Gardner Design C Swedish Council of America 3C D Sabingrafik, Inc. C Harcourt & Co. 3D D Sabingrafik, Inc. C Pacific Marine Credit Union 4A D Art Chantry C Seaventure Bermuda
4B D Sabingrafik, Inc. C Yamaha Watercraft 4C D Simon & Goetz Design C breakwaters gmbh 4D D Williams Collins Design & Development C Impact Streetwear 5A D Boelts/Stratford Associates C City of Tucson
5B D Sabingrafik, Inc. C The Express Group 5C D Sabingrafik, Inc. C The Express Group 5D D Sayles Graphic Design, Inc. C John Sayles

index

LogoLounge is too big for our two books, so we've created a website, too. Log onto www.logolounge.com/book2 for electronic access to the logos in this book. Search for logos by keywords, client or design firm name, client industry, or type of mark, and get designer credits and contact information along with the logos.

And while you're at the site, take a few minutes to catch up on identity-industry news and and trends, check out our monthly picks of great logos, and look inside the studio of our featured designer. With all that inspiration, you're sure to come up with great logo designs of your own.

---

directory

@radical.media
United States
212.462.1569

2b1a
Germany
49.175.1968379
www.2b1a.de

A & Company
France
33.56.53.56.00
www.a-co.fr

Aahbullay
United States
818.551.9875

ADD [art direction + design]
United States
847.733.1138

Addis
United States
510.704.7500
www.addis.com

Alesce
United States
303.229.8100
www.alesce.com

Alexander Isley Inc.
United States
203.544.9692
www.alexanderisley.com

Allen Creative
United States
770.972.8862
www.allencreative.com

Alphabet Arm Design
United States
617.451.9990
www.alphabetarmdesign.com

Ames
United States
206.516.3020
www.amesbros.com

And Partners
United States
212.414.4700

angela tu
United States
949.854.3710

antoa
United States
415.272.3695

Art Chantry
United States
314.773.9421

Artomat Design
United States
206.623.9294
www.artomatdesign.com

Associated Advertising Agency, Inc.
United States
316.683.4691
www.associatedadv.com

Atha Design
United States
641.673.2820

Atlanta College of Art
United States
770.409.1531

b5 Marketing & Kommunikation GmbH
Germany
49.06201.8790730
www.b5-media.de

Basic Function
United States
732.777.0073
www.basicfunction.com

BBDO Detroit Design Group
United States
www.bbdo.com

BBK Studio
United States
616.459.4444
www.bbkstudio.com

BC Design
United States
206.652.2494
www.bcdesign.com

BDG Studio Ronin
United States
240.505.4774

Be Design
United States
415.451.3530
www.beplanet.com

Ben Schwabauer
United States
919.444.6013
www.whoisben.com

Bernhardt Fudyma Design Group
United States
212.889.9337
www.bfdg.com

Betactive
Germany
49.6201.259010
www.betactive.de

Beth Singer Design
United States
703.469.1900
www.bethsingerdesign.com

Blacktop Creative
United States
816.221.1585
www.blacktopcreative.com

BLANK, Inc.
United States
202.319.3120

Blattner Brunner
United States
202.741.8091
www.blattnerbrunner.com

BlueSpark Studios
United States
310.394.9080

bob neace graphic design, inc
United States
316.264.4952

Boelts/Stratford Associates
United States
520.792.1026
www.boelts-stratford.com

Bonfilio Design
United States
212.532.4801
www.bonfiliodesign.com

Born to Design
United States
317.838.9404

bp360
United States
650.678.0924
www.bp360.com

Brad Norr Design
United States
612.339.2104

Brandbeat
United Arab Emirates
97.31432.10007

BrandLogic
United States
203.834.0087
www.brandlogic.com

Brandon Tabiolo
United States
808.295.7066
www.bluekahuna.com

Braue; Branding & Corporate Design
Germany
49.471.983820
www.braue.info

Brian Blankenship
United States
817.917.8379
www.brianblankenship.com

Bruce E. Morgan Graphic Design
United States
301.231.5467

BT Graphics
United States
513.777.8816

Burd & Patterson
United States
515.222.3162
www.burdandpatterson.com

Cam Stewart Graphic Design
United States
480.835.0003

Capital Associated Industries
United States
919.878.9222

CAPSULE
United States
612.341.4525
www.capsule.us

Carousel30
United States
301.996.4514
www.carousel30.com

Catalyst Creative, Inc.
United States
303.380.9100
www.catalystcreativeinc.com

Catapult Strategic Design
United States
602.381.0304

Cave
United States
561.417.0780

CDI Studios
United States
702.876.3316

cesart.com
Canada
514.909.3122

Chaney, Neiman, Munson & Son
United States
702.564.4301
www.rrpartners.com

Chemi Montes Design
United States
703.893.9272

Cheri Gearhart, graphic design
United States
708.366.4855
www.gearhartdesign.com

Chuck Pennington
United States
206.300.5007

Church Logo Gallery
United States
760.231.9368

Chute Gerdeman Retail
United States
614.469.1002

cincodemayo
Mexico
52.818.342.5242
www.cincodemayo.com.mx

Cirque de Darmon
United States
402.202.9119
www.cirquededarmon.com

Clive Jacobson Design
United States
212.912.9139
clivejacobson.com

Cloudjammer Studio
United States
678.795.1444
www.cloudjammer.com

Cognition Design
United States
949.425.0264
www.cognitiondesign.com

Colin Gearing / Design
United States
419.832.0526

Communications Nemesis Inc.
Canada
450.969.3732
www3.sympatico.ca/desaulniers.luc

Communique
United States
303.220.5080

Compass Design
United States
612.339.1595

CONCEPTiCONS
United States
818.269.2725
www.concepticons.net

Context
United States
714.288.0228

ContrerasDesign
United States
415.824.5538

Convexus Consulting, Inc
United States
303.297.0097
www.convexus.com

Courtney & Co. design
United States
315.622.0085

CRE8 communications, inc.
United States
612.227.0908
e-cre8.com

Creative Development Associates, Inc.
United States
626.685.8977
www.creadev.com

Creative Devil Design
United States
509.633.3612
www.creativedevil.com

Creative FX Communications
United States
954.965.0707
www.creativefx.cc

Creative Madhouse
United States
817.531.7493
www.creativemadhouse.com

Critheorian
United States
480.221.5817
www.critheorian.com

Crosby Associates
United States
312.346.2900
www.crosbyassociates.com

CrossGrain Creative Studios
United States
714.628.9586

Custom Art Company
United States
740.420.9151
www.customartco.com

cYclops
United States
212.633.2825
www.cyclopspictures.com

d4 creative group
United States
215.483.4555

Dan Rood Design
United States
785.842.4870
www.danrooddesign.com

Davidson Design
Australia
03.9429.1288
www.davidsondesign.com.au

DDB
United States
312.552.6124

Deep Design
United States
678.443.7270
deepdesign.com

Delikatessen
Germany
49.40.3508060
www.delikatessen-hamburg.com

Dennis Purcell Design
United States
310.328.2350
www.dpdstudio.com

Dept 3
United States
415.999.0690
www.dept3.com

DeShetler Design
United States
614.272.6624
deshetlerdesign.com

Design and Image
United States
303.292.3455
www.d-and-i.com

Design Army
United States
202.797.1018
www.designarmy.com

design bridge incorporated
United States
406.253.5844

Design Continuum Inc
United States
617.928.9598
www.dcontinuum.com

Design Guys
United States
612.338.4462
www.designguys.com

Design MG
Panama Republic of Panama
507.214.1781

Design Nut
United States
202.237.1538
www.design-nut.com

Design One
United States
828.254.7898
www.d1inc.com

Device
United Kingdom
44.7979.60.22.72
www.devicefonts.co.uk

dialogbox
United States
917.721.8382
dialogbox.com

Diana Graham
Germany
49.8143.94139

Did Graphics
Iran
98.21.875.0217
www.didgraphics.com

Digital Soup
United States
310.202.7687
www.digitalsoup.com

dmaynedesign
United States
417.823.8058
www.dmaynedesign.com

Dogtrick Creative
United States
619.813.8051

Dotzero Design
United States
503.892.9262
www.dotzerodesign.com

Doug Beatty
Canada
416.826.3684
www.taxizone.com

Doug Chatham Design
United States
770.943.1886
www.dougchatham.com

DRAFT INDONESIA
Indonesia
62.21.725.4849
www.loweworldwide.com

Dreigestalt
Germany
49.07000.0033033
www.dreigestalt.com

Duffy & Partners
United States
www.duffy.com

Eagle Imagery (PhotoGraphics)
United Kingdom
44.07787.182049
www.eagleimagery.co.uk

E-Dcube
United States
917.770.8565

Element
United States
614.447.0906
www.elementdesigngroup.com

elevation
United States
618.655.0235

elf design
United States
650.358.9973

EM Design
United States
770.321.4544
www.emvance.com

Emery Vincent Design
Australia
61.2.9280.4233
www.emeryvincentdesign.com.au

Enterprise IG
United States
212.755.4200
www.enterpriseig.com

ErikArt Design
United States
615.496.6703
www.erikart.com

Eskil Ohlsson Assoc. Inc.
United States
212.907.4303

Essex Two Incorporated
United States
773.489.1400
www.sx2.com

Estudio Ray
United States
602.840.1580
www.estudioray.com

Evenson Design Group
United States
310.204.1995

Evolve Visual
United States
310.327.7682

Factor Design
United States
415.896.6051
www.factorydesign.com

faux koi
United States
612.251.4277
www.fauxkoi.com

Felixsockwell.com
United States
917.657.8880
www.felixsockwell.com

Fernandez Design
United States
713.747.9403
www.fernandezdesign.com

Firewheel Design
United States
817.741.2980
www.firewheeldesign.com

five D
Australia
61.405.53.56.53
www.fivedee.com

Flynn Design
United States
601.969.6448

Frederick & Froberg Design Office
United States
973.509.0202

Freemind Studio
United States
916.448.8840
freemindstudio.com

Frontmedia
United Kingdom
44.0137.65.00877
www.frontmedia.co.uk

FutureBrand
Australia
61.3.9254.0254
www.futurebrand.com

G&G Advertising
United States
505.843.8113

Gabriela Gasparini Design
United States
718.417.1064
www.gabrielagasparini.com

Gardner Design
United States
316.691.8808
www.gardnerdesign.com

Garfinkel Design
United States
706.369.6831
www.garfinkeldesign.com

Giraffe, Inc.
United States
330.425.7601
www.giraffesite.com

Glenn Sakamoto Design
United States
310.971.7449
www.glennsakamoto.com

Glitschka Studios
United States
503.581.5340
www.vonglitschka.com

Go Welsh!
United States
717.569.4040

GOLDFINGER c.s.
United States
404.352.1952
www.goldfingercreative.com

Graham Hanson Design
United States
212.481.2858
www.grahamhanson.com

Grassroots Studios
United States
713.586.0560

Great Scott Design
United States
423.477.5733
greatscottdesign.com

greteman group
United States
316.263.1004
www.gretemangroup.com

Group One
United States
612.334.8100
www.group-1.com

hand made group
Italy
39.0575.582083
www.hmg.it

HardBall Sports
United States
904.399.2623
www.hardballsports.com

Hausch Design Agency LLC
United States
414.628.3976
www.hauschdesign.com

helium.design
Germany
0611.900686.0
www.heliumdesign.de

hendler-johnston
United States
952.346.9258

Hinge
United States
703.378.9655

Honey Design
Canada
519.679.0786
www.beebrand.com

Hornall Anderson
United States
206.467.5800
www.hadw.com

Hot Chilli
Australia
61.2.9565.2400
www.hotchilli.com.au

Hotdog Creative
United States
www.hotdogcreative.com

Houston Design
United States
678.990.0260
www.houstondesign.net

Howalt Design Studio, Inc.
United States
480.558.0390
www.howaltdesign.com

Howerton+White Interactive
United States
316.262.6644
www.hwinteractive.com

Howling Good Designs
United States
631.427.4769
howlinggooddesigns.com

Hoyne Design
Australia
61.3.9537.1822
www.hoyne.com.au

Hubbell Design Works
United States
714.227.3457

Huber Design Office
United States
614.291.3436

Hutchinson Associates, Inc.
United States
312.455.9191
www.hutchinson.com

I Design Creative Group
United States
316.264.8499
www.idcreativegroup.com

Idea Bank Marketing
United States
402.463.0588

Imatrix
United States
214.764.7939

INA SHOKAI
Japan
03.3486.3686
www33.ocn.ne.jp/~inainc

Indicia Design
United States
816.471.6200
www.indiciadesign.com

Insight Design
United States
316.262.0085

Integer Group - Midwest
United States
515.247.2603

Intrinsic Design
United States
770.410.1626
www.intrinsic-design.biz

James Ross Advertising
United States
954.974.6640

James Stevens
United States
615.414.3885

Jane Cameron Design
Australia
61.8.8227.2078

JCharlier Communication Design
United States
716.884.3274

Jeff Fisher LogoMotives
United States
503.283.8673
www.jfisherlogomotives.com

Jeff Kern Design
United States
417.890.8199
www.jeffkerndesign.com

John Langdon Design
United States
215.523.9469
www.johnlangdon.net

John VanCleaf, Rutgers University
United States
732.545.8038

Jon Flaming Design
United States
214.922.9757

Jonathan Rice & Company
United States
817.886.6640
www.jriceco.com

judson design associates
United States
713.520.1096

karacters design group
Canada
604.640.4399
www.karacters.com

Kendall Creative Shop, Inc.
United States
214.827.6680

KENNETH DISENO
Mexico
52.452.5.23.17.38

Kern Design Group
United States
203.329.7070

Keyword Design
United States
219.923.5279
www.keyworddesign.com

KFDunn
United States
302.328.3347

Kiku Obata & Company
United States
314.361.3110
www.kikuobata.com

Kircher, Inc.
United States
202.371.0700
www.kircherinc.com

Koch Business Solutions
United States
316.828.2208

Kraftaverk - Design Studio
Iceland
354.561.9261
www.kraftaverk.is

Kristian Andersen, Inc.
United States
317.251.4985
www.kristianandersen.com

Landor and Associates
United States
415.365.3829
www.sfo.landor.com

Lapada Visual
United States
619.708.8931
www.lapadavisual.com

LeVesque Design
United States
845.348.3278
www.levesquedesign.com

Lewis & Son Creative
United States
404.261.8836
lewisandson.com

LIFT HERE, Inc.
United States
786.252.9277
www.lifthere.com

Lipson Alport Glass & Associates
United States
847.291.0500

Lisa Wood Design
United States
916.961.8744

Liska & Associates
United States
212.627.3200
www.liska.com

Logoboom
United States
323.650.6513
www.logoboom.com

logobyte
Turkey
90.535.666.6292
www.logobyte.com

Lomangino Studio Inc.
United States
202.338.4110
www.lomangino.com

m+
United States
914.941.9271

Mad Dog Graphx
United States
907.276.5062

Maria Lee Design
United States
408.544.7135

Marius Fahrner Design
Germany
49.040.43.27.1234

MarketSource
United States
609.655.8990

Martini Time Design
United States
847.604.3383

Massive Studio
United States
718.438.2563

Matsumoto Design
United States
206.270.6686
matsumotodesign.com

McAndrew Kaps
United States
480.580.5113
www.mcandrewkaps.com

McArtor Design
United States
515.274.9500
www.mcartordesign.com

McMillian Design
United States
718.636.2097
www.mcmilliandesign.com

MEDICIbrands
United States
310.936.0136
www.medicibrands.com

Methodologie
United States
206.623.1044
www.methodologie.com

Metroparks of the Toledo Area
United States
419.535.3050

Miaso Design
United States
773.525.6148
www.miasodesign.com

Michael Doret Graphic Design
United States
323.467.1900
www.michaeldoret.com

Michael Powell Design
United States
901.578.7898

Mike Quon/Designation
United States
212.226.6024
www.mikequondesign.com

Milton Glaser, Inc.
United States
212.889.3161
www.miltonglaser.com

MINE
United States
415.647.6364
www.alterpop.com

Mires>Design for Brands
United States
619.234.6631

Miriello Grafico, Inc.
United States
619.234.1124
www.miriellografico.com

mitchel design inc.
United States
213.380.4167
www.mitcheldesign.com

Mitchell Design
United States
650.463.1935
www.mitchdesign.com

Mitre Design
United States
336.722.3635
www.mitredesign.com

Mitten Design
United States
415.821.0144

MLS Creative Services
United States
212.450.1258
www.mlsnet.com

MocaLoca Inc.
United States
305.756.6368
www.mocaloca.com

Modern Dog Design Co.
United States
206.789.7667
www.moderndog.com

Molly Z. Illustration
United States
513.651.0007
www.mollyz.biz

Mona MacDonald Design
United States
412.521.0555

Monigle Associates Inc.
United States
303.388.9358
www.monigle.com

Moonlit Creative Group
United States
770.978.0116

Morello+Company
United States
973.283.0006

Mortensen Design
United States
650.988.0946

Nancy Wu
Canada
604.640.4399
www.nancywudesign.com

Neoalchemia Design Lab
United States
510.304.0450

Nestor Stermole VCG
United States
212.229.9377

Newbomb Design
United States
216.431.1730

Nicole Imbert Design
Dominican Republic
809.540.7773

Nonni & Manni / Ydda
Iceland
354.570.8700
www.nm.is

oakley design studios
United States
503.241.3705
oakleydesign.com

O'Connor Identity Development
United States
323.779.5600
www.petermontoya.com.

Octane
United States
775.323.7887
www.octanestudios.com

octane inc.
United States
828.693.6699
hi-testdesign.com

Offbeat Design
United States
734.214.1996

On Duty Design
United States
718.499.5521
www.ondutydesign.com

OPEN
Israel
972.3.6209947
www.open.co.il

Oxide Design Co.
United States
402.344.0168
www.oxidedesignco.com

Pageworks Communication Design, Inc.
United States
303.337.7907

Paragon Design International
United States
312.832.1030
www.paragondesigninternational.com

Paul Black Design
United States
214.537.9780

Pennebaker
United States
713.963.8607
www.pennebaker.com

Perks Design Partners
Australia
61.3.9620.5911

Peter Montoya Inc.
United States
323.779.5600
www.petermontoya.com

Pickard Advertising & Design
United States
301.538.0998
www.pickardadvertising.com

Pixelube
United States
206.216.0278
www.pixelube.com

Planet Propaganda
United States
608.256.0000
www.planetpropaganda.com

Platform Creative Group
United States
206.621.1855

PM & Co
United States
212.714.1700
www.designpm.com

Popgun
United States
415.402.0080

Prejean LoBue
United States
337.593.9051
www.prejeanlobue.com

Pressley Jacobs: a design partnership
United States
312.263.7485

Proart Graphics/Gabriel Kalach
United States
305.532.2336

Pump Graphic
United States
858.274.2956

Pure Fusion Media
United States
615.207.6420
www.purefusionmedia.com

Q
Germany
49.611.181310
www.q-home.de

R&R Partners (Randy Heil)
United States
702.564.4301
www.rrpartners.com

Redbeard Communications Inc.
United States
831.634.4633
www.redbeard.com

redinwyden
United States
818.648.6870
www.tatico.com

REINES DESIGN INC.
United States
305.467.4182
www.reinesdesign.com

Renata Graw
United States
847.313.6365

Richards Brock Miller Mitchell & Associates
United States

Rick Johnson & Company
United States
505.266.1100
www.rjc.com

Rickabaugh Graphics
United States
614.337.2229
rickabaughgraphics.com

Riordon Design
Canada
905.339.0750
www.riordondesign.com

Ross Creative + Strategy
United States
309.680.4143

Rottman Creative Group, LLC
United States
301.753.4226

Russell Design Co.
United States
360.850.1043

S Design, Inc.
United States
405.608.0556
www.sdesigninc.com

Sabingrafik, Inc.
United States
760.431.0439
tracy.sabin.com

Sackett Design
United States
415.929.4800
www.sackettdesign.com

Sanna Design Group, Inc.
United States
516.719.6235
www.4sdg.com

Sayles Graphic Design, Inc.
United States
515.279.2922
www.saylesdesign.com

Scott Lewis Design
United States
804.353.6485
www.lewisdesign.net

Scribblers' Club
Canada
519.570.9402
www.scribblersclub.com

SD Graphic Design
United States
617.523.5144
www.delaneygroup.com

Segura Inc.
United States
773.862.5667
www.segura-inc.com

Sheehan Design
United States
619.328.6990

Sibley/Peteet Design, Inc.
United States
512.473.2333
www.spdaustin.com

Simon & Goetz Design
Germany
49.69.96.88.55.0
www.simongoetz.de

Smith Design
United States
973.429.2177

Smith-Boake Designwerke Inc.
Canada
416.362.6000
www.designwerke.com

SO / Sullivan Office
United States
801.422.5062

Soloflight Design Studio
United States
770.792.8645
www.soloflightdesign.com

Spin Design
United States
314.752.4050

SPUR
United States
410.235.7803
www.spurdesign.com

Square One
United States
214.749.1111

Squires & Company
United States
214.939.9194
www.squirescompany.com

Stacy Bormett Design, LLC
United States
651.748.0872

stay gold creative
United States
415.385.4691
www.staygoldcreative.com

Stephen Averitt
United States
702.452.2951

Stiles+co
United States
510.486.1900
www.danstiles.com

StrategyBase
United States
678.613.5116
www.strategybase.com

STUART ROWLEY DESIGN
United States
518.483.9749
www.stuartrowleydesign.com

Stuph Clothing
United States
800.242.9166
www.stuphclothing.com

substance151
United States
410.732.8379
www.substance151.com

SUMO
England
0191.261.9894
www.sumodesign.co.uk

switchfoot creative
United States
760.720.4255
www.switchfootcreative.com

Synergy Graphix
United States
212.968.7568
www.synergygraphix.com

Tallgrass Studios
United States
785.887.6049

Taylor George
Canada
204.988.5023
www.taylorgeorge.com

TD2, S.C.
Mexico
55.52816999
www.td2.com.mx

Tenacious Design
United States
301.519.2422
www.tenaciousdesign.com

tesser
United States
415.541.9999

Tharp Did It
United States
408.354.6726
www.tharpdidit.com

the atmosfear
United States
702.804.4117
theatmosfear.com

The Bradford Lawton Design Group
United States
210.832.0555
www.bradfordlawton.com

The David Group
United States
216.685.4465

the fovea project
United States
405.748.7078
www.thefoveaproject.com

The Mixx
United States
212.695.6663

The Office of Bill Chiaravalle
United States
541.549.4425
www.officeofbc.com

Thielen Designs
United States
505.396.3900

THINKMULE.com
United States
402.438.4280
www.thinkmule.com

Thomas Manss Design
United Kingdom
44.20.72.51.77.77
www.manss.com

thomasvasquez.com
United States
718.422.1948

Tim Frame Design
United States
937.766.3749
www.timframe.com

TMCA, Inc.
United States
803.256.3010

Tom Fowler, Inc.
United States
203.845.0700

Townsend
United States
612.821.0432

Tribe Design Houston
United States
713.523.5119
www.tribedesign.com

(twentystar)
United States
303.455.7144
www.twentystar.com

Ty Wilkins
United States
478.390.3759

Typonic
United Kingdom
44.07710.866649
www.typonic.com

Union Design & Photo
United States
352.472.4847
union.sepiamoons.com

Ventress Design Group, Inc
United States
615.727.0155
www.ventress.com

VINE360
United States
952.893.0504
www.vine360.com

Virtual Cubed Inc.
United States
559.441.7722
www.virtualcubed.com

VMA
United States
937.223.7500
www.vmai.com

VSA Partners
United States
212.869.1188
www.vsapartners.com

Wages Design
United States
404.876.0874
www.wagesdesign.com

Wallace Church Design
United States
212.755.2903
www.wallacechurch.com

Watts Design
Australia
61.3.9696.4116
www.wattsdesign.com.au

Webb Scarlett
United States
312.575.0700
www.webbscarlett.com

wedge.a&d
Canada
403.215.4030

What Design, Inc.
United States
617.789.4736
www.whatweb.com

Whitney Edwards LLC
United States
410.822.8335

wilhelmedwardopatz
Germany
49.69.95403533
www.opatz.de

William Herod Design
United States
360.297.1288

Williams Collins Design & Development
United States
661.322.2650
www.williamscollins.com

Wolken communica
United States
206.545.1696
www.wolkencommunica.com

yellow dog design
United States
301.834.6577

Z-Design
Italy
39.349.7511471

Zenarts Design Studio
United States
703.757.9551
www.tangled-web.com

about the authors

Bill Gardner is president of Gardner Design and has produced work for Learjet, Thermos, Nissan, Pepsi, Pizza Hut, Kroger, Hallmark, Cargill Corporation, and the 2004 Athens Olympics. His work has been featured in *Communication Arts, Print, Graphis, New York Art Directors, Step By Step,* Mead Top 60, the Museum of Modern Art, and many other national and international design exhibitions. He lives in Wichita, Kansas.

Catharine Fishel runs Catharine & Sons, an editorial company that specializes in working with and writing about designers and related industries. She frequently writes for *Step Inside Design, PRINT, U&lc Online, ID,* and other trade publications, and provides editorial support for LogoLounge.com. She is the author of *Paper Graphics, Minimal Graphics, Redesigning Identity, The Perfect Package, Designing for Children, The Power of Paper in Graphic Design,* and *Inside the Business of Graphic Design.*